Praise for *In All Fairness*:

"How, between the covers of a single volume, could one hope to illuminate the vast sea of moral, intellectual, and political failures that add up to modern egalitarianism? Only by combining the expertise and insights of historians, economists, political scientists, philosophers, legal scholars and more. With the book *In All Fairness*, the Independent Institute has done so brilliantly. Each author's contribution stands on its own and can be read with profit. Taken together, they complement each other to create a whole that far exceeds the sum of its parts."

—**Steven E. Landsburg**, Professor of Economics, University of Rochester

"Fairness counts among humankind's most fundamental social desiderata—demanded even by small children on the playing field. The difficulty is that it is easier to say what fairness is than to determine what is fair. The many faceted book *In All Fairness*, edited by Robert M. Whaples, Michael C. Munger, and Christopher J. Coyne, does justice to the complexity of the topic in its historical, philosophical, and economic dimensions. Anyone who has ever been inclined to say 'but that's just not fair'—which includes just about all of us—will find enlightenment and information in this thoughtfully compiled, instructive, and constructive book."

—**Nicholas Rescher**, Distinguished University Professor of Philosophy, University of Pittsburgh; Founding Editor, *American Philosophical Quarterly*; author, *Fairness: Theory and Practice of Distributive Justice*

"The authors of the timely book, *In All Fairness: Equality, Liberty, and the Quest for Human Dignity*, edited by Robert M. Whaples, Michael C. Munger, and Christopher J. Coyne, dig creatively into the roots of inequality, drawing from philosophy, economics, and religion going way back in human history. This fascinating book shows that realizing proposed egalitarian wealth or income distributions requires a great deal of coercive power, unfairly affects 'The Forgotten Man,' and breeds unintended consequences. The book rightly stresses equality of opportunity achieved through economic freedom over equality of outcomes."

—**John B. Taylor**, Mary and Robert Raymond Professor of Economics, Stanford University; George P. Shultz Senior Fellow in Economics, Hoover Institution

"The beautiful book *In All Fairness* describes how rapidly growing efforts to impose equality of outcomes *necessarily* damages everyone's personal and economic freedom, creates harmful social and cultural divisions, and depresses economic growth that could give millions of people a better life. You will benefit enormously from reading this book, irrespective of where you stand on the debate about inequality."

—**Lee E. Ohanian**, Professor of Economics and Director of the Ettinger Family Program in Macroeconomic Research, UCLA; Senior Fellow, Hoover Institution

"*In All Fairness* is a masterful and insightful book devoted to exposing the shaky foundations and the likely moral, social, and political costs of the campaign for state-enforced equal outcomes for all. This campaign jettisons liberal concern for equal liberty and equality before the law for the elusive and yet destructive end of equal wellbeing or at least equal income. The goal of equality is elusive because of the deep difficulties of determining when equal wellbeing or income has been achieved and whose ox will be gored and which liberties must be denied to achieve it. The focus on equal outcomes shifts attention from growth-friendly policies that have raised many hundreds of millions up from poverty to redistributive policies that undermine growth. In many distinct but converging ways, the book convincingly argues that the crusade for equality undermines the core institutions of a free and prosperous society and drives us to a world of zero-sum, tribal conflicts."

—**Eric Mack**, Professor of Philosophy and Faculty Member, Murphy Institute of Political Economy, Tulane University

"*In All Fairness* is an insightful exploration of the tension between liberty and egalitarianism. Who will be better off if we opt for comprehensive redistribution and therefore against freedom? It's certainly not the poor. Read the book to find out why, especially if you think of yourself as an egalitarian!"

—**Sam Peltzman**, Ralph and Dorothy Keller Distinguished Service Professor Emeritus of Economics, Booth School of Business, University of Chicago

"Few matters bedevil American politics as do the need to find proper understandings of liberty and equality and the way government should endeavor to promote them. The authors of *In All Fairness: Equality, Liberty, and the Quest for Human Dignity* approach these matters from philosophical, economic, and historical perspectives, all to great effect. This rare volume is an intellectual feast that will repay repeated readings, whether the reader is a beginner or an expert."

> —**Kevin R. C. Gutzman**, Professor of History,
> Western Connecticut State University

"Equality is the theme, if not the obsession of our time. Yet it means very different things to different people. *In All Fairness* has brought together a range of scholars who explore the political, economic, and legal dimensions of different conceptions of equality dispassionately and seriously. Together they bring light to a subject that desperately needs it."

> —**Samuel H. Gregg**, Director of Research,
> Acton Institute for the Study of Religion and Liberty

"Every era has one or two hobgoblins that, by frightening the uninformed, increase the power of the state. One such hobgoblin today is economic inequality. Fortunately, we today have also the superb book *In All Fairness* that, if read widely enough, will reveal economic inequality to be the nonissue that it is."

> —**Donald J. Boudreaux**, Professor of Economics and Co-Director,
> Program on the American Economy and Globalization, Mercatus Center,
> George Mason University

"Among the many important lessons in the book *In All Fairness*, one of the most powerful is that when governments implement policies designed to create more equal outcomes, those policies compromise individual liberty but rarely result in a more equal society. Every chapter of this volume offers readers a thought-provoking analysis of the concept of equality and the challenges involved in public policies to address inequality."

> —**Randall G. Holcombe**, DeVoe Moore Professor of Economics,
> Florida State University; author, *Liberty in Peril: Democracy and Power in American History*

In All Fairness

INDEPENDENT INSTITUTE

In All Fairness

Equality, Liberty and the
Quest for Human Dignity

Edited by **ROBERT M. WHAPLES,**
MICHAEL C. MUNGER *and* **CHRISTOPHER J. COYNE**

Foreword by **RICHARD A. EPSTEIN**

INDEPENDENT
I N S T I T U T E
OAKLAND, CALIFORNIA

Independent Institute
100 Swan Way, Oakland, CA 94621-1428
Telephone: 510-632-1366
Fax: 510-568-6040
Email: info@independent.org
Website: www.independent.org

Cover Design: Denise Tsui
Cover Image: ER09 via Getty Images

Library of Congress Cataloging-in-Publication Data Available

Credits on p. 309

Contents

Foreword
The Theoretical and Practical Pitfalls in Egalitarian Thought
Richard A. Epstein

THIS EXCELLENT VOLUME offers an incisive, indeed, decisive, critique of modern egalitarian thought, whose intellectual strength remains weak even as its popularity becomes ever greater. No foreword can do justice to the arguments presented, all of which are strong in the two dimensions that matter most in policy work—a clear sense of theory, and a clear empirical grounding that tests the theories in question. The book's individual chapters all share those characteristics. To be sure, there is, out of necessity, some useful overlap in their content, but the overall conclusion is inescapable. Whatever the abstract appeal of egalitarian arguments, they cannot survive the institutional, political, and economic pressures of any complex society.

In writing this foreword I cannot go through all these arguments in the detail they deserve, but it is important to give some attention to the common strands that make *In All Fairness* cohere. My point of departure is clear enough. All of the authors, either explicitly or implicitly, adopt some form of classical liberalism as the benchmark from which they criticize the egalitarian moment. I believe that this is indeed the correct approach for dealing with any fundamental question of political theory. Classical liberalism, like egalitarianism, offers at its very root a social conception of the various rules and practices that, taken together, supply the foundation for a just society. In so doing, classical liberalism starts with a relatively narrow conception of harm that includes just these four elements: force, fraud, breach of promise, and the creation of monopoly power.

To be sure, each of these elements requires a good deal of work to explicate in detail, but for ordinary people seeking to live their lives, the first three of these guidelines easily translate into commands that everyone can understand

and respect. Don't hit, don't lie, and don't break your promises. Keep on the right side of these social divides and a law-abiding citizen has no reason to worry about the second-order complications that arise only after people hit, lie, and break their promises. The fourth of these commands, dealing with the prohibition against monopolization, has its well-understood images from ordinary language: someone is trapped in a corner, or over a barrel, or has no leverage. All of these can arise in daily lives when one person has a bargaining advantage—or to use the physical image, "leverage"—over another. But those sources of power tend to be ephemeral and localized, so they rarely lead to permanent or major social disruptions, given that it is easy, especially today, to obtain, even in remote locations, substitute goods and services in the unlikely event that some firm tries to exert monopoly power. For all the hullabaloo, there are no reports that any couple has been unable to obtain a wedding cake from some asserted monopolist. It is only when the inquiry shifts to common carriers and public utilities, who serve millions of customers, that the institutional implications of monopoly power loom larger. There is no pat solution to these problems, but the basic formula, which receives little attention from libertarians, is that these firms—no ordinary individual has that kind of power—cannot refuse to deal with potential customers. Instead, they have an obligation to serve all comers on fair, reasonable, and nondiscriminatory terms, or, as is commonly said, FRAND terms. Even that formulation does not exhaust the field, because some form of antitrust law takes over where the law of common carriers and public utilities leaves off. There are no efficiencies of scale for most ordinary businesses. Nonetheless, it is all too true that business firms are capable of colluding, and the law of antitrust, chiefly directed to monopolization and cartelization, seeks, with only partial success, to limit how private competitors can collude or (in some cases) merge their businesses in ways that decrease output and increase prices, generating social losses.

It would be foolish to pretend that the elaboration of these four pillars of classical liberalism is a simple task, for the opposite is surely true. But the difficulties in working through the complexities of this system are child's play in comparison with the gyrations that must be turned in order to counter the far broader definitions of wrongful harm that lie at the heart of any system of egalitarian thought. For starters, there are few egalitarians who wish to see the removal of the prohibitions against force, fraud, and monopoly. Only in the area of contract would they hedge their bets, and even there they understand that a modern system can never be put in the impossible position of eliminating categorically all voluntary cooperative effort, whether by exchange or partnership. But the actions that exhaust the playing field for the classical liberal are only the opening act in an egalitarian legal system that, on the protean matters of race, sex, and wealth, finds it necessary to respond to a far greater class of what they perceive as social harms. The egalitarian's concerns run the gamut from dramatic inequalities in wealth to status differentials and microaggressions, whose low intensity and high frequency pose major challenges to any system of legal or social regulation.

To start at the beginning, the huge opposition towards inequality of wealth reduces to one simple proposition: the diminishing marginal utility of wealth. That claim is surely true in the abstract: anyone who has a million dollars in wealth is far less concerned about the next dollar gained or lost than is someone who has only a thousand dollars. So, the impulse is to argue that some transfer of wealth, by state coercion if necessary, produces gains in overall social utility that justify the expenditure of the social resources needed to effectuate the change.

Unfortunately, the difficulties begin with the effort to operationalize this program. There is no a priori reason to believe that equal division of wealth will lead to an equal level of utility or satisfaction for different people with dramatically different temperaments and tastes—just how much wealth redistribution is necessary to rectify this social grievance? One obvious class of persons are people who have special needs, and who apparently can put greater claims on the resources of others—except perhaps when these transfers can do little to either ease pain or prolong life. But even if we put aside such extreme cases, it hardly follows that equal levels of wealth lead to equal levels of satisfaction across different people. Some people are, by some combination of nature, nurture, or happenstance, happy and are surrounded by friends. Others are morose and asocial. For these purposes, it is not the cause of these differences that matters. It is their very existence. To ignore these differences is to fail on the venture of equal outcomes. To attempt the needed calculations across millions of unique individuals whose subjective preferences can rise and fall like the tides is a fool's errand.

As a practical matter, many egalitarians try to overcome these difficulties with a broad-based progressive tax, either of income or wealth, on cash or other monetizable assets. But no legal system anywhere in the civilized world has ever tried to impose a tax on personal utility, happiness, or satisfaction. There are, moreover, powerful practical constraints that dictate the form of the tax in question. Progressive taxes are not easy to administer. To lower their effective rates, potential taxpayers will try to split income within families or with artificial entities. They will seek to convert ordinary income into capital gains. They will try to defer income into future periods, like retirement, where annual income is likely to be less. It is always possible to devise countermeasures for these stratagems, but any rules on timing and income splitting add to the overall complexity of the system. It is for this reason that classical liberals have always favored the flat tax, either on income or consumption, in order to minimize the political pressures at work to raise or lower tax rates, or create exclusions or preferential tax rates. As noted by Brian Gaines in "Taxes and the Myth of Egalitarianism," there is much popular support for the flat tax even in this egalitarian age.

In addition to its obvious simplicity, the flat tax scores highly on a measure that egalitarians tend systematically to underestimate: the effects of taxation on growth. Most egalitarians start with an unarticulated, but indefensible, assumption that it is possible to keep production and distribution in watertight compartments, so that anything done in the second will do nothing in the first. Yet that dangerous assumption ignores the simple proposition that taxation can stifle growth by reducing the net return on investment. Within the classical liberal tradition, this problem is attacked by devoting most (but not all) resources to the provision of public goods, which increases the likelihood that all people will benefit in roughly similar proportions. The instinct here is that taxation can overcome a prisoner's dilemma, identified long ago by Mancur Olson as the problem of "collective action,"[1] which makes it virtually impossible to fund (indivisible) public goods by voluntary contributions. But the fuller story also depends critically on how the tax revenues are spent. In principle, there would be little problem if each person in some ideal world derived from state action a benefit of the common good that exceeded his or her tax contribution. But that result is impossible to achieve completely. On all questions of political economy, it is never wise to let perfection be the enemy of the good. The problem will be reduced to the extent that some portion of the tax contributions are spent on return revenues. It will only be aggravated by purely egalitarian taxes in which none of the wealth taken goes back to provide public goods of benefit to the taxpayer.

At this point, there is a conceptual crisis in egalitarian thought. In its most naive formulation, the egalitarian approach aims to reduce the differences in relative endowments to zero for all people. The easiest way to achieve that end is for everyone to starve—equally. Egalitarianism can only avoid embracing that suicide pact by paying some attention to the total size of the pie (measured in dollars) from which personal utility can then be (imperfectly) derived. But it has long been understood that gains from voluntary transactions will rarely produce equal gains in dollars for all participants. Nonetheless most people happily enter into transactions that make them better off even if their trading partner—say a successful merchant—gains far more from entering into this and similar transactions. It is important to realize that market systems work because they articulate, as Aeon J. Skoble insists, negative and not positive rights.

These differences are key. Positive rights are those by which one person has a claim on another individual for the provision of some good like health care, education, or housing. Yet it is impossible to identify in advance which individuals should bear that burden for each, and impossible to identify how much should be supplied without a detailed knowledge of the available resources in society, which may well be reduced by the provision of these goods. As both James Harrigan and Ryan Yonk remind us, negative rights are a lot more powerful than they appear at first blush. These rights are given freely to everyone against everyone else, no matter how large or wealthy the population, through the simple injunction that no one can destroy or take the property of another. Within this framework, inequalities of wealth will, and should, emerge as a function of voluntary transactions that produce positive sums for their players. But the prospect of new entry—remember collusion is not allowed—will keep these profits in line. As people get wealthier, they will now have additional wealth that they can use in transactions with third parties, so that the *externalities* from these transactions will be positive and not negative. Nonetheless, powerful egalitarian forces work against this dynamic, for, as Nikolai Wenzel argues, much regulation works against the interests of the poor. To give but one example, the expansion of licensing requirements for routine trades and occupations, which are often done for the worst protectionist reasons, have their greatest negative effect on the poor. The antidote is economic growth, which as Ben O'Neill reminds us often does much to lift up the least fortunate among us. After all, the bottom portion of the economic distribution did not fare well during the eight years of the Obama Presidency, but under the relatively light-handed regulation of labor markets in the Trump administration unemployment levels have dropped for minority workers, young people, and even ex-cons, all without bolstering the programs of targeted benefits championed by progressives.

Indeed, lost in the egalitarian gloom is a simple powerful point made by Art Carden, Sarah Estelle, and Anne Bradley: even if the goal of equality is impossible to achieve, the goal of the alleviation of poverty is well within our power, if only we seek it. Indeed, the overall decline in global poverty is, as Johan Norberg reminds us in his book *Progress*,[2] one of the great untold stories of this age. This decline has been propelled by a set of positive-sum transactions that are only found in market economies. If we can boost wealth across the board, we will have as a society more wealth to give and fewer individuals below the subsistence level to whom it must be given, all without these massive government interventions.

There is, however, no similar cascade of gains for the egalitarian who faces the unhappy tradeoff of asking what reduction in wealth is appropriate to reduce inequality. The first victim in that campaign is likely to be, as William Watkins argues, a retreat from any principle of equality before the law. That goal is relatively easy to achieve within the classical liberal system, given the configuration of a set of rules targeted against force, fraud, breach of contract, and monopoly. It is not possible to maintain when the unique circumstances of each person along so many different dimensions each call for separate treatment. Yet the ability to make good on any egalitarian ideal is as remote as ever. And it is also necessary to recognize, as Jason Morgan stresses, that the constant concern with equal outcomes has as its first casualty the rule of law, which finds itself hard-pressed to survive the descent to inequality.

In his essay, Edward Stringham warns of the dangers of trying to control against the supposed dangers of inequality when in practice ordinary people tend for a wide variety of reasons to get rich at different rates, which become especially hard to measure when nonpecuniary benefits are taken into account. To give a simple example, suppose a stylized universe with only two people, A and B, who currently each have a wealth of 10: what does the egalitarian say about a voluntary transaction that increases the wealth of A to 20 and that of B to 12? The transaction is a clear Pareto improvement. But at the same time it increases the wealth disparity between the parties. Would an egalitarian prefer a system of coercion that restricts this voluntary transaction to one in which A goes to 15 if B goes to 13? The gap is narrowed, but is anyone confident that the five units of wealth lost by A justify the one unit of gain by B, especially if we do not know the overall wealth, let alone utility of both parties? And just how is this program to be carried out in larger markets in which hundreds of millions of people enter into billions of transactions generally?

Vincent Geloso and Steven Horwitz also give voice to these difficulties when they note how the risks of mismeasurement of well-being could easily overstate the problem of inequality, as, for example, by ignoring variations in wealth by location or over time. These errors are no second-order matters because, if the wealth (or other baseline) is miscalculated, a state system of coerced transfers could easily end up taking from the less well-off to support the more well-off, even if we ignore all the public-choice problems that stand, for example, in the path of any system of wages and price controls with its high administrative costs and massive economic distortions. Indeed, as Stephen Shmanske reminds us, we often resort to what he terms as "classroom egalitarianism" to avoid these difficulties, by acting as though a few neat blackboard diagrams can make all the real-world problems of implementation disappear. One good illustration of the dangerous power of these models arises in financial markets, where, as Robert Wright explains, the political pressure to create equality of outcome in residential mortgage markets led to the creation of risky loans by introducing "equal but extremely low mortgage-lending standards" that helped bring about the financial crisis of 2008, whose consequences are still felt today.

No matter how powerful the case is against full-bore egalitarianism, it is still critical to recognize, as does Michael Munger, that the claims for redistribution can never disappear, given the constant pressure to share the gains from market capitalism by making a set of Kaldor–Hicks moves that allow those below some line to gain a larger share of the social pie. For all its weaknesses, some (modest) progressive tax on income or wealth produces far fewer distortions than we have with any thoroughgoing egalitarianism. In addition, the classical liberal view of imperfect obligations is all too often forgotten today. These are obligations that are consciously keyed to move wealth from rich to poor. But they seek to do so, not by government coercion, but by a tradition of voluntary charitable giving, either in cash or kind, that is enforced only by individual conscience and social pressures. Individuals get to choose whom they help, and by how much, so long as they help someone else. Sometimes these gifts take the form of direct aid to the poor. Sometimes they are mediated through institutions that have just that end. Before one mocks this effort to respond to redistributive instincts, note the great institutions of higher education and medical care and research that were created by individuals who responded to these pressures. Fewer dollars go a lot further because these private donors face no administrative oversight and have strong incentives to watch how their money is spent. There is no way today that these efforts can displace public programs of redistribution, but they can supplement in a way that shows how market-oriented processes can sensibly address egalitarian concerns.

It should not be supposed, however, that the difficulties identified with ambitious regimes of taxation and regulation exhaust the problems that face the conscientious egalitarian, for they still have to deal with the implications of their extended definition of harms. The modern concern with racial theory involves at least two expansions in the definition of harm. The first of these comes from the willingness to impose liability for refusals to deal in competitive markets on an ever-growing list of specialized grounds: race, sex, age, sexual orientation, and disability for starters. In each of these cases, the problem of sorting out the mixed motives in any individual case leads to difficult conceptual and evidentiary problems.

It only gets worse. As Adam Martin reminds us, the next generation of racial theorists are not content to direct their attention to rectify discrete actions or statements that have racial content, express or implied. No longer does the party charged have to have any sense of antipathy or any belief in the subordination of the protected groups. It is now sufficient to brand as racist or sexist those socially constructed "invisible systems conferring racial dominance," or indeed any other form of -ism. That inquiry necessarily becomes far more expansive and intrusive for the intersectionality (i.e., interconnections) of the various forms of latent prejudices based on race, sex, sexual orientation, and age, which create overlapping territories of bad conduct. Yet since these offenses are apparently unseen to the naked eye, it will take especially diligent and intrusive prosecutors to pry into the business records and private lives of the many possible offenders against these norms. That oversight could easily become an appalling prospect if undertaken by the many public employees who may suffer from the same latent prejudices as their peers in the private market.

The difficulties do not stop here, for as James Otteson forcibly reminds us, the egalitarian seeks to offer redress not only from wrongdoers, but also from the ravages of bad luck, regardless of its cause. Otteson's simple example is the poor lovelorn man who loses out romantically when his intended finds someone else at the eleventh hour. Surely, the successful suitor owes nothing to the disappointed one. But if not him, then who else? His town, state, or the entire nation? And just how many compensable events of this sort are there? Yet if everyone is a victim, then one victim has to pony up to help another. But this is not the least of it because there are real mass disasters for which some sort of aid may well be relevant, and yet here the institutional challenge is to make sure that insurance mechanisms can be put into place to price these risks, for otherwise the moral hazard—such as building along the coastline—will aggravate the problem. The egalitarian program cannot cope with the monumental expansion in collective liability. The necessary oversight suggests that any systematic effort to implement this program will result, as Jeremy Jackson and Jeffrey Palm write, in a totalitarian regime whose bad consequences will do much to undermine its good intention.

The difficulties of course go further. These expanded definitions of harm all presuppose that we have victims even if we do not have wrongdoers. The insatiable demands of these systems will put enormous pressures everywhere else. The demands for equality will, as Peter Hill notes, necessarily infringe on what is in daily life one of the most important conceptions of equality—that all individuals are equal in the sight of God—which will be necessarily compromised if some people are made by secular forces to turn their own minds and bodies to help others.

In the end, we do not have a pretty picture. Even if we were to assume that governments had some powerful engine that allowed them to be single-minded in their devotion to their stated ends, the egalitarian system would still fall apart, a victim of its own overambition. Its goals in question are so large that they necessarily conflict with one another, so that in the end some second-order calculations will be needed to prioritize among these various claims, and to do so without the knowledge or resources to see the challenge through to the end. This implementation of this odd amalgamation of ends will not take place in a hothouse environment. It will be subject to huge political pressures, which, as public-choice theory reminds us, rarely leads to a happy ending. Instead, two dangerous outcomes are likely. The first is that the elites will take over the process so that the United States will come to look more like California—that is, as a place in which a small financial elite and a powerful upper-middle class of professionals will dictate a system that works to their advantage. The second is that these well-intentioned improvements will have (indeed, have already) increased the poverty rate for individuals at the bottom, who have substandard housing, long commutes, and few prospects for advancement. Exit becomes a harder option when the scheme goes national, and its full implications will only be greater as the set of goals expands, including issues of climate change, which, as the recent events with the Yellow Jackets in France show, have already sparked wide protests against increases in taxation and regulation. All the ingredients for this deadly stew are present in today's progressive agenda. Let us hope that books like this one will forestall what promises to be a dreadful day of reckoning.

Introduction

New Thinking on Equality, Liberty, and Human Dignity

Robert M. Whaples*

INEQUALITY IS AN exceptionally beautiful thing. Or maybe it's a terribly ugly thing. To most people, it depends on what is unequal and why it is unequal. Love it or loathe it, egalitarian sentiments and concerns about inequality are clearly on the rise in both politics and the academy.

Because of this renewed interest, our discussion includes perspectives that readers will find fascinating and unique. To set the tone for this comprehensive approach to the topic we begin with Adam Martin's view that modern egalitarianism rejects older thinking on the subject. Consider racism (or sexism or any type of anti-otherism). Martin argues that the old definition of racism was "individual conduct that is motivated by either *(a)* antipathy to other races or *(b)* a belief that those races are inferior." However, the New Egalitarians' definition, which has grown to dominate thinking in many parts of academia, is that racism equals "socially constructed, 'invisible systems conferring racial dominance.'"[1] Martin points out that accurately diagnosing the second type of racism requires "social scientific understanding of how social structures operate and . . . sufficient historical knowledge to judge how social structures have disadvantaged certain groups." Thus, it requires an immense of amount of knowledge and cannot be judged by laypeople, unlike the first kind of racism. It requires rule by experts. Second, he argues, these rent-seeking experts practice an intellectual style characterized by attempts to evade critical scrutiny, using vague and indeterminate terms and—more importantly—simply denying many of their critics standing to weigh in on the subject because,

*Robert M. Whaples is professor of economics at Wake Forest University and managing and co-editor of *The Independent Review*.

they argue, these critics are privileged by the system. Countering this obscurantism makes it especially hard for some to question the New Egalitarians' arguments—which increases their appeal in some quarters as they battle to make this new way of thinking the norm.

How did we get to this point, and where are we headed? James Harrigan and Ryan Yonk answer these questions with a conceptual and historical roadmap in "From Equality and the Rule of Law to the Collapse of Egalitarianism." They argue that in the early history of the United States, a direct line can be drawn from belief in human equality to the rule of law to an emergent regime based on negative rights as exemplified by Founding Fathers such as Thomas Jefferson, John Adams, and Thomas Paine. That line held for a century or so, but then the nation drifted to a regime predicated on positive rights and a corresponding large, powerful, redistributionist government exemplified by the ideas of the Progressives and Franklin Roosevelt. They argue that this shift in the American electorate's attitudes is playing out in an unsustainable manner. Policy makers are largely unconcerned with recapturing the original conception of equality because there is little profit for them telling the American public what it cannot have. Redistributive policies are enthusiastically supported by many voters, so policy makers roll back such policies at their own electoral peril. As a result, the nation is now drowning in egalitarianism. Because government has grown in both size and scope, the nation's financial situation has become dire. As the national debt grows beyond its limit, it will require an end, of sorts, to the redistributionist egalitarianism experiment. In the final analysis, a regime cannot be based on notions of both positive and negative rights because the former undermine the latter in every instance.

Many egalitarians argue that "brute luck" leads to unfair (because undeserved) inequalities, justifying redress. In "The Misuse of Egalitarianism in Society," James Otteson challenges this reasoning by showing—with the example of the undeserved bad luck of a student whose marriage plans disintegrate—that bad luck often results from "choices whose outcomes should be respected and not corrected." He demonstrates that policies that would match up with egalitarian goals "are far more difficult to craft than is typically envisioned" and shows that the likelihood that such policies will work the way we would ideally like them to is lower than generally imagined. Because it is impossible to eliminate all categories of luck—running from chance encounters between people who can help one another to unpredictable changes in the environment or in human society—Otteson advocates that an egalitarianism of respect for people and their decisions replace an egalitarianism of inputs or outcomes.

The egalitarianism embraced by classical liberals such as Otteson relies heavily on the concept of universal human dignity and moral agency. As Peter J. Hill explains, however, for most of history these beliefs about human rights were highly unusual. In earlier times, few defenses of human equality were even proffered, and slavery, one of the worst manifestations of inequality, existed for most of recorded history. In "Religion and the Idea of Human Dignity," Hill shows that the idea of universal human dignity and moral agency has its roots in a metaphysical concept—that all humans are the bearers of God's image. Western societies owe their commitment to human equality to the influence of Jewish and Christian ideas about human dignity. Modern liberalism also has benefited from Enlightenment-era thinkers who provided a way out of religious conflicts over heresy. Those philosophers grounded their philosophical views on universal dignity but also articulated a way of instantiating human equality in mores and laws that limit the use of power to enforce a particular definition of correct thinking.

John Rawls is undoubtedly the most influential modern thinker on fairness, but Michael Munger argues in "The Conceptual Marriage of Rawls and Hayek" that many readers misconstrue the implications of Rawls's arguments. Rawls was not a simple egalitarian advocating strict equality. F. A. Hayek shared Rawls's conclusion that using income redistribution "to ensure the welfare of the least well-off is a wealthy society's obligation," and Munger contends that we can synthesize Rawls and Hayek to become "Rawlsekians" by realizing that the obligation to ensure the welfare of the least well-off arises *because* the prosperity resulting from market capitalism allows gainers to gain enough to easily compensate the losers and still prosper. Munger warns that people who end up below average often protest procedurally fair voluntary transactions because they do not actually care about procedural fairness; they simply want more money. He explains that although capitalists may not deserve the profits that they reap, they reap profits only because they have reallocated resources to the benefit of consumers. Creating a system where work and risk-taking are massively rewarded is consistent with the asserted goals of the Rawlsian project because the poor have always prospered when capitalism is adopted, and "no country that has tried anything else has broken out of poverty."

Jeremy Jackson and Jeffrey Palm argue in "The Impossibility of Egalitarian Ends" that the ultimate goal of an egalitarian philosophy is an equal (just) distribution of resources. They outline the historical progression of the egalitarian philosophy and argue that, short of a totalitarian regime, the objective of an equal distribution is utterly impossible. The impossibility of an equal distribution of wealth is derived from the impossibility of redistributing *social* capital. It is fundamentally impossible to take social capital or a social network from one person and give it to another. Can the outlooks of children raised by loving, supportive parents be taken from them and transferred to children from neglectful homes? Yet social capital—the trust and norms of civic cooperation that are essential to well-functioning societies—enhances productive capabilities and labor-market returns. Jackson and Palm also extend this impossibility of redistribution to the recent focus on inequality in well-being.

In their essay, Art Carden, Sarah Estelle, and Anne Bradley ably argue that "we'll never be royals, but that doesn't matter." Their key point is that inequality doesn't really matter much in comparison to poverty, and the good news is that we are rapidly conquering absolute poverty around the world. "A society in which people are equally poor has far less scope for flourishing than one in which people are unequally rich"—as are Americans today. The largest exodus of humans out of absolute poverty in the history of our species, which we have recently witnessed, "has happened not because of redistribution from rich to poor but because of increased economic growth brought about by improved institutions and a new esteem for innovation." With enough force, we could equalize incomes and wealth through taxation, but we cannot forget how people respond to taxes. Many people are motivated by the pursuit of status, so "taxing income-generating production and utility-generating consumption will induce people to shift toward other ways of satisfying their wants . . . Closing off the financial means to status will lead people to seek status on other margins, but these margins are often not benign."

In "Taxes and the Myth of Egalitarianism," Brian Gaines uses public-opinion surveys to directly measure Americans' attitudes toward egalitarianism. Although it is widely believed that most Americans would prefer that the rich pay higher taxes than they currently do, he demonstrates that evidence of this preference in public-opinion surveys is quite weak. The clearest and sharpest questions reveal instead that Americans favor rather flat and low taxes and consider present tax rates on above-median incomes as suitably high or even excessive. Americans embrace equal treatment through (mostly) proportional taxation much more than through the equalizing of incomes or wealth via (highly) progressive taxes. When thinking about taxes, then, most Americans come closer to holding classical than modern liberal views.

Would you rather live in a society where incomes and wealth are relatively equal or in one where they aren't very equal? Although many people instinctively lean toward the first choice, Edward Stringham cautions in "Pushing for More Equality of Income and Wealth" that the choice isn't so simple. Make sure to take the questionnaire in his essay, through which he demonstrates that relative income/wealth and absolute income/wealth don't necessarily go hand in hand. He points out that if one measures equality in rich countries as access to particular technologies, "then we have much more equality than ever, even if relative income or wealth has diverged greatly." Then he demonstrates that one of the biggest problems with egalitarianism is that it negatively judges how people get richer at different rates, even if everyone in society is getting richer in the process. Although any policy marketed as "We want to keep everyone more equal and poor" sounds absurd, Stringham warns that many policies effectively do just that—as he amply demonstrates in the case of Social Security. Egalitarianism is often driven by envy and "encourages people to treat others' property as if it is not theirs." He concludes that modern egalitarian policies that reduce the rewards for increasing skills, working, or investing do not bring about the fully disastrous results of pure egalitarianism, but egalitarianism is still mildly disastrous and inhumane even in milder doses.

"Good and Bad Inequality" by Vincent Geloso and Steven Horwitz closes out the symposium. Clearly, last does not mean least in this case—this essay was strongly considered for the Independent Excellence Prize. This essay does more than any of the others to grapple with measures of inequality, which so fascinate economists and on which much of the recent policy push rests. Geloso and Horwitz begin by demonstrating that a significant portion of the recent putative rise in inequality results from mismeasurement. They highlight, for example, the importance of adequately measuring regional differences in the cost of living, considering changes in household size across the income distribution, and examining consumption inequality rather than focusing on pretax income. Their bigger point is that a rise in economic inequality might be a bad thing or might be a good thing. They accordingly divide recent changes into "good" (socially beneficial) inequalities and "bad" (socially harmful) inequalities. Good inequalities "result from the satisfaction of individual economic preferences or demographic changes and have no perverse impact on economic growth," whereas bad inequalities generally stem from government policies that push down the left tail of the income distribution (such as agricultural policies, zoning laws, and the war on drugs) while pulling up the right tail (such as bank bailouts and regulations that create barriers to entry into markets). They see the reversal of these bad policies as the appropriate focus of inequality reduction. In the face of harmful policies, as in medicine, we must "first, do no harm."

If Geloso and Horwitz had more space, they could have brought into their discussion additional measures of inequality as well. Each semester, to give my students a sense of inequality and the meaning of various Gini coefficient levels, I ask them to anonymously report how many pairs of shoes they own. The results are always fascinating. A few report that, like me, they own three or four pairs. The median is usually about a dozen, but there are always a few who own thirty or sixty or (occasionally) even one hundred pairs. The shoe Gini coefficient for my students is usually pretty close to the income Gini coefficient for the United States. However, when I ask them how many pairs of shoes they are currently wearing, the answer is always one for every single person—giving a Gini coefficient of zero. Whereas there are immense differences in shoe ownership, there is no inequality in shoe "adequacy."[2]

Life itself is far more important than shoes, income, or wealth. Sam Peltzman has shown that the inequality of life spans fell tremendously during the twentieth century in the United States and every other country studied.[3] Perhaps the modern preoccupation with income inequality has arisen because we have become much more equal in other things, such as life expectancy, literacy, and fulfillment of basic needs? These things were the low-hanging, nutritious fruit. Many of the authors in our symposium warn that we scale the ladder to pick pricklier fruit at our own peril.

It is important to examine the dimensions of inequality along with its causes and effects. Might it be useful to approach the topic from another angle by asking, "What is the *purpose* of inequality?" To consider this question, I contacted a couple of dozen colleagues at Wake Forest University who teach in a wide variety of disciplines—biology, economics, history, philosophy, political science, psychology, religious studies, sociology, and women's studies—and, promising them anonymity, asked them, "From the point of view of someone in your field, what is the purpose of inequality?"

Several were hesitant in answering. For example, one replied that "political scientists don't usually talk about inequality in terms of purpose. The focus tends to be on what *causes/creates* inequalities and what the *consequences* are for political power. So I've got to admit that I have trouble imagining what its purpose is." Another noted that "from the point of view of psychology, inequality would not be seen as serving any particular purpose per se."

Despite this hesitancy, the range of responses gives considerable food for thought. Some respondents had pithy answers, such as a historian who explained that inequality "is all about power. By deeming one group inferior, the other group is able to maintain all economic, political, and social power. So inequality justifies the rule of a minority over the majority. It also justifies the rule of one sex, race, ethnicity, or religion over others." A faculty member in women's studies echoed this view and concluded, after a discussion of Friedrich Engels and Gerda Lerner, that the "purpose of inequality today is still the same as it was in the past in many ways . . . maintaining power in social and in economic contexts." Several were blunt in their embrace of egalitarian assumptions, with one asserting that in an "egalitarian society such as ours, the starting point is absolute equality."

In contrast, a biologist explained that one reason animals are unequal in terms of size and other features is "to expand resource bases, and reduce competition for food, or [to] allow specialization" in getting food. Another biologist elaborated that "inequality is likely an inevitable feature of any complex natural system." Although he didn't see a purpose to this feature, he commented that because "the biochemical processes of cellular reproduction are subject to error, mutations are inevitable, and all large populations will therefore contain genetic variation. . . . Among humans, for example, dark skin near the equator protects folic acid, an essential metabolite, from destruction by ultraviolet light. In contrast, dark skin closer to the poles can prevent adequate synthesis of vitamin D, which is dependent on ultraviolet light. Presumably, genetic variation in our ancestors as they spread from our African birthplace . . . led to environment-specific variation in skin color." One might conclude that the function (purpose) of this inequality is—as the other biologist noted—to allow species, including humans, to flourish in a wider variety of settings and to create the greatest possible value out of limited resources.

A colleague in psychology noted that:

> [The] prevailing theories of group process assume that membership in groups contributes to important aspects of our self-concept—our social identity. Generally, we strive to maintain and obtain a positive social identity. Social comparisons among groups is one psychological mechanism by which we accomplish this goal—downward social comparisons to relatively 'inferior' groups . . . contribute to [an] enhanced sense of positive social identity, whereas upward social comparisons to higher status groups are a threat to positive social identity. However, these upward social comparisons can set the stage for upward mobility when group boundaries are permeable.

In this light, the purpose of inequality might be to make most people (except those at the bottom) have a positive self-image.

A sociologist noted that "most sociology . . . is premised on egalitarian ideals and so the idea that inequality has some purpose (other than the nefarious purpose of advantaging some people and disadvantaging others) doesn't get much consideration." One exception is the functionalist school of sociology, which contends that "stratification is functionally necessary to motivate people to undergo the sacrifices necessary to do certain functionally important jobs for which necessary talents are scarce." He cited Herbert Gans's essay "The Positive Functions of Poverty," which includes ideas such as "the existence of poverty makes sure that 'dirty work' is done."[4] This focus on the power of incentives will appeal to most economists, who would add that inequality is needed to get "clean work" done, too.[5] The supply of engineers, scientists, doctors, entrepreneurs, and others who do work that requires much training and effort would be fairly paltry if the rewards were scant.

This point is related to an answer supplied by a colleague in economics, who wrote, "One effect of inequality (in resources, skills, whatever) is to generate differences in relative prices, which provide opportunities for exchange and gains from trade." If you have studied comparative advantage and the gains from trade in models descended from David Ricardo, you may have noticed that if everyone has the same opportunity cost, then there is no comparative advantage, and no one gains from trading with each other. The immense gains we all get from trading with each other arise *because* we are unequal in our characteristics and talents—differences that may be innate or that we may have developed so that we can gain from trading with each other. The economics colleague quoted Jonathan Sacks, chief rabbi of Great Britain, who explains that "it is through exchange that difference becomes a blessing, not a curse."[6]

A scholar of religion argued that "from the Jewish–Christian prophetic perspective, inequality is a *symptom* of injustice, which God emphatically stands against. So the 'purpose' of inequality, we might say, is that it raises the 'red flag' of injustice and should arouse the appropriate responses of compassion, care, and giving. Perhaps that is one answer to your question."

Finally, a colleague in philosophy turned this idea around by arguing that God is the source of inequality. He explained that from his Thomistic point of view,

> most fundamentally, the purpose of inequality in creation is to show forth the Goodness of God. Roughly put, the perfection of Creation consists at least in part in goodness being displayed in all of its various degrees. Conversely, the universe would not be perfect if it displayed only one degree of goodness. It displays all degrees of goodness, even lesser goods. God in his wisdom has decreed the *distinction* of things, one from another. . . . Man differs formally from salamander. . . . These distinctions entail inequality—the elements are less perfect than plants, plants less perfect than animals, brute animals less perfect than rational animals (man). So God as the source of the distinction of things is the source of their inequality.[7]

Since God created people unequal, he must have had a purpose in mind. Perhaps one purpose of inequality is that it can allow us to gain the happiness of heaven by knowing, loving, and serving God in this world. Perhaps the purpose of inequality is to teach us humility, to instill in us the ability to accept things from others, to encourage and oblige us to practice generosity and kindness.

In summary, many scholars see no real purpose of inequality. Others, such as some of my colleagues discussed earlier, see in inequality only the nefarious purposes of those who presumably wield power. A few, such as biologists and economists, often find more beneficial purposes in inequality. The philosopher can see even deeper purposes.[8]

Lay philosopher C. S. Lewis considers the modern egalitarian impulse in his essay "Screwtape Proposes a Toast." The scene is in Hell at the annual dinner of the Tempters' Training College for young devils. Screwtape notes that

> democracy is the word with which you must lead them by the nose. . . .
> And of course it is connected with the political ideal that men should
> be equally treated. You then make a stealthy transition in their minds
> from this political ideal to a factual belief that all men *are* equal. . . .
> As a result you can use the word *democracy* to sanction in his thought
> the most degrading . . . of human feelings. . . . The claim of equal-
> ity, outside the strictly political field, is made only by those who feel
> themselves to be in some way inferior. . . . [One] therefore resents every
> kind of superiority in others; denigrates it; wishes its annihilation. . . .
> Under the name of Envy it has been known to humans for thousands
> of years. But hitherto they always regarded it as the most odious, and
> also the most comical, of vices. . . . The delightful novelty of the present
> situation is that you can . . . make it respectable and even laudable—by
> the incantatory use of the word *democratic.*[9]

As Lewis avers, our differences could teach us humility and other virtues, but the culture now seems rigged so that our inequalities instead teach us outrage and vice.

Inequality is exquisitely beautiful, but it can also be grossly ugly. Because this is true, the question becomes how we should properly respond to it. Will our response to it be ugly, say by envying or injuring those who have ended up with more than we have or by belittling and mistreating those who have less? Or will we see the dignity in all people—great and small—and treat others with respect, cooperating with them to fulfill that promise by achieving the virtue, prosperity, and peace that we all desire?

PART I

Problems with the Modern Philosophy of Egalitarianism

I

How "Experts" Hijacked Egalitarianism

Adam G. Martin*

F. A. HAYEK argued against social justice understood as distributive justice, especially in its egalitarian form. Among his many complaints was the idea that egalitarian morality was not suitable for a Great Society in which we regularly interact with strangers rather than only with a small group.[1] Egalitarianism is an atavistic impulse from our evolutionary past in small tribes of hunter-gatherers. Our socially evolved morality, by contrast, enables us to interact with strangers by adhering to general and *abstract* rules. These rules allow us to expand social cooperation *to the extent* that they are simple rules that *apply to all* and do not require us to make detailed judgments about what we owe others. The *social morality* that facilitates cooperation with unknown strangers is distinct from the instinctual, small-group morality that still dominates our more intimate relationships.

Equality before the law or informal norms is a desirable quality of social morality, but concern with equality of outcomes would undermine the functionality of that morality. By creating a sphere of individual liberty within the boundaries set by abstract rules, social morality enables us to act on our individual knowledge. Hayek's work stresses the economic benefits of allowing individuals to act on their local knowledge of time and place. Mario Rizzo builds on this argument, claiming that there are important moral benefits as well.[2] Regardless of the particular moral philosophy individuals follow, they can instantiate moral principles appropriately only when they are free to act on their beliefs about their particular circumstances. These beliefs might stem

---

*Adam Martin is assistant professor of agricultural and applied economics at Texas Tech University and political economy research fellow at the Free Market Institute.

from individual conscience, Aristotelian judgment, or some other vision of individual moral capacity. This Hayekian approach to social morality makes room for both universals and particulars: general, abstract rules facilitate interactions with strangers but also enable the use of subjective individual knowledge and require the use of individual moral judgment.

A different form of egalitarianism has recently become a noticeable political force: egalitarianism focused on identity. This family of egalitarian views is often referred to by terms of abuse such as *political correctness,* and those who believe it are demeaned as *social justice warriors. Identity politics* is one manifestation of these ideas but predates them and is also a tactic used by other groups. To avoid the polemical and misleading connotations of these terms and to highlight what is truly distinctive about this strain of thought, I refer to it as "New Egalitarianism." The New Egalitarians are focused on eliminating inequality predicated on race, gender, sexual orientation, and other identifying characteristics of traditionally disadvantaged groups.

A distinguishing feature of the New Egalitarianism is its focus on *structural inequality.* This focus is distinct from a focus on pure material deprivation associated with luck egalitarianism and from the widely shared belief that bigotry against particular groups is unjustified. New Egalitarians argue that systemic inequality stems from deeply rooted social structures that do not rely on overt prejudice.[3] It is not correct to say that they focus exclusively on equality of outcomes, but they do tend to cite systematically unequal outcomes as evidence of inequality of treatment. But New Egalitarians tend to believe that correcting these inequalities requires positive action (and not mere procedural equality), so it is fair to say that they have a thicker vision of equality in mind than Hayek's classical liberal view.

Certain aspects of the New Egalitarianism are appealing. It asks how different groups can live cooperatively together, a question that all liberals should take seriously. Some New Egalitarian views sound like invisible-hand explanations of inequality rather than naive constructivism. Although these concerns are valid, New Egalitarians articulate them in terms of a peculiar set of tendentious social scientific claims that, upon reflection, have troubling implications.

The most distinctive feature of New Egalitarianism is the way it draws on critical theory and related schools of thought such as Marxism, structuralism, and post-colonialism.⁴ Though there are differences between these schools of thought and between thinkers within them, there are important commonalities. Most notably, they all tend to emphasize functionalism, the belief that "social practices of the most varied kind can be explained by their tendency to maintain the hegemony of dominant groups."⁵ The goal of theory in these schools is to shine a light on forms of domination, in contrast to existing ideologies, which try to excuse or cover up domination. Critical theorists in particular argue that the point of social theory is emancipation, not just explanation.

New Egalitarians operate with an often implicit mental model of society drawn from critical theory. This essay argues that implementing the New Egalitarianism requires transforming social morality into an *obscurantist epistocracy*. The New Egalitarianism requires a set of moral experts to make judgments about right and wrong actions rather than to rely on either individual conscience or widely understood social rules. And this epistocracy, the rule of those with knowledge, is obscurantist in that it seeks to question the standing of critics rather than the substance of their claims.

I do not directly challenge the *substance* or the *truth* of New Egalitarian ideas but rather raise concerns about their implementation. As a consequence, I do not focus my critique on any one New Egalitarian thinker, for there are important differences in various thinkers' ideas. My argument parallels F. A. Hayek's description of how socialism creates a "road to serfdom."⁶ Hayek's critique does not depend on socialist moral ideals being mistaken; he merely points out what implementing central planning in a world of disagreement and imperfect intentions would require. Similarly, my goal is to sketch out some of the consequences of implementing the New Egalitarianism for the sorts of imperfect people that inhabit our world. If what we want is a social morality appropriate for beings like us, the aspirations of the New Egalitarians should be deeply troubling.

Epistocracy

Consider two definitions of racism, Racism 1 and Racism 2. One might draw parallel distinctions between Sexism 1 and Sexism 2 or Homophobia 1 and Homophobia 2. Everything I argue about conceptions of racism carries over to those issues and to others, but I use the term *racism* as a token for all issues surrounding group identity.

> Racism 1: Individual conduct that is motivated by either *(a)* antipathy to other races or *(b)* a belief that those races are inferior.[7]

> Racism 2: Socially constructed, "invisible systems conferring racial dominance."[8]

Racism 2 is the idea that critical theory and related schools of thought have brought to debates about social equality. New Egalitarians differ in what account (if any) they give of *how* structures generate inequality, but this is the common thread that has gained prominence in recent years. Racism 1 is what the person on the street recognizes as racism. Those who think that Racism 2 deserves special attention—including proponents of the New Egalitarianism—acknowledge that Racism 1 is still the dominant definition and lament that it is so difficult to teach students about racism.[9]

Racism 1 refers to intentions. Most individuals think that morally like cases should be treated similarly. What is morally troubling about Racism 1 is that characteristics that seem morally arbitrary, such as skin color, lead to differences in treatment. Conversely, if differences in treatment arise for good reasons, they are not necessarily objectionable. If employers base hiring decisions strictly on the consideration of talent, Racism 1 is not in play, even if this practice results in patterns of racial inequality. Avoiding Racism 1 fits well within a Hayekian framework that stresses the generality of social rules. It also relies on individual moral judgment: individuals can evaluate their own behavior to determine whether they have acted in an objectionable way. There may be a tendency for these judgments to be incorrect or unconsciously biased, but that does not change the fact that Racism 1 is a moral category that can in principle be deployed by individuals to judge and improve their own conduct.

Not so with Racism 2. *Accurately* diagnosing Racism 2 requires *(a)* social scientific understanding of how social structures operate and *(b)* sufficient historical knowledge to judge how social structures have disadvantaged certain groups. Recall that Racism 2 refers to "invisible systems" that prop up members of some groups at the expense of others. There is nothing mystical about claiming that these social structures or the processes that they govern are invisible.[10] But although there is nothing intrinsically suspect about invisible causes of inequality, explaining *how* structures cause inequality requires social science. The causal effects of social structures do not reveal themselves to the senses or to our everyday experience but rather only through careful theorizing and the analysis of empirical evidence. And if our goal is to right actual inequalities, it is not enough that our causal stories are plausible. It is not even enough that they are true. They must also account for a significant portion of the racial inequality that exists. In the real social world, many causes cooperate to produce broad-scale social patterns such as racial or gender inequality. New Egalitarians themselves recognize this factor, describing the "intersectionality" of how different forms of oppression—racism, sexism, and so on—are related to each other in myriad and subtle ways.[11] So a true account that explains only a small part of racial inequality is not terribly helpful when trying to correct that inequality. Ascertaining the causes of inequality, judging the relative importance of different causes, and understanding how these causes interact ultimately require a great deal of specialized knowledge, one that can plausibly be possessed only by *experts*.

Consider a partial list of technical terms that the New Egalitarians employ that are either not part of everyday parlance are used in a specialized way: *ally, appropriation, cisethnic, cissexual, domination, erasure, intersectionality, kyriarchy, lived experience, mansplaining, marginalization, microaggression, patriarchy, rhizome, subaltern, tokenism, triggering, victim blaming, white supremacy, whiteness.* This list only scratches the surface. My aim in mentioning them is not to question their usefulness for discussing some important questions but only to point out how specialized they are. The development of this sort of terminology requires specialists, and learning it requires access to these specialists.[12]

The reliance on experts helps explain why the New Egalitarianism thrives at universities. Universities provide a forum where scholars trained in critical theory, feminist or postcolonial philosophy, multiculturalism, or structuralism can introduce students to this vast lexicon, in addition to retraining them to think in terms of Racism 2 rather than Racism 1. Consistent with an understanding of racism as structural, New Egalitarians usually speak of battling racism as a matter of *education*.[13] Moral persuasion—appeals to individual conscience—is adequate only as a tool for combatting Racism 1. But individuals require education to grasp the structural cause-and-effect relationships that constitute Racism 2. Such education consists not in an appeal to commonly shared moral sentiments but to specialized expert knowledge. It is more like physics or economics than it is like Sunday school.

Contrast this approach with Hayek's view of social morality. Individuals need rules precisely because they *cannot* know all the consequences of their actions. The broad contours of invisible-hand processes can be understood, but the specific ways in which individual actions interact to produce large-scale social patterns defies precise prediction. Most importantly for Hayek, this limitation extends to expert knowledge as well. Experts are incapable of designing a moral code that can underwrite widespread social cooperation among strangers. So the existence of genuine experts—those that have a correct understanding of how social structures operate—does not extinguish the need for abstract, general rules to govern individual conduct in an extended order.

It is beyond the scope of this paper to convincingly establish whether Hayek's critiques of constructivism and distributive justice are relevant for New Egalitarians. Hayek's understanding of social orders as largely spontaneous processes would probably undermine a great deal of New Egalitarianism, which tends to draw on very different social theories. Hayek's work would seem to indicate that the New Egalitarianism—by insisting on thicker forms of equality—is morally atavistic. New Egalitarians are animated by an ethos that focuses on substantively benefiting particular groups of individuals. This sort of morality is suitable for intimate orders such as families and organizations within a broader social context. Complex, richly detailed sets of social rules have their place in such small-group interactions, but when applied to entire societies and cultures, such a morality is nonoperational because it requires that individuals have far more knowledge than they can possess in order to evaluate the effects of their actions.

But even if Hayek is wrong that rationally designed social morality is a nonstarter, it does not change the fact that New Egalitarianism requires a class of social scientific experts to combat systemic oppression. In this view, individual conscience is of little help if racism exists primarily due to invisible social structures. To know whether an action is racist or not—at least for as long as invisible systems of oppression continue to exist—an individual must ask someone who knows. The New Egalitarianism requires a moral epistocracy: those with special knowledge determine what morality requires.[14]

Obscurantism

Obscurantism is an intellectual style characterized by attempts to evade critical scrutiny. Jon Elster identifies precisely the sorts of critical theory that inspire the New Egalitarians as a form of "soft obscurantism."[15] My aim here is not to attack obscurantism as a practice but to highlight the particular forms and functions of New Egalitarian obscurantism. Obscurantism can take many forms, including the use of vague or indeterminate terms. To the extent that New Egalitarianism relies on these terms, labeling it "obscurantist" would be redundant with labeling it "epistocratic." Components of New Egalitarian thought may be obscurantist in this sense by relying on obscure terminology. But important aspects of New Egalitarianism try to be comprehensible. New Egalitarians typically want to be understood (hence their calls for education).

New Egalitarian obscurantism evades criticism by denying the *standing* of critics. Critics need to "check their white (or male) privilege," the argument goes. By default, those who benefit from the invisible structures of Racism 2 have no epistemic access to oppression because they have not experienced it. I refer to this argument as the Knowledge Response. Alternatively, critics may be labeled "deniers" or "apologists" who prop up oppressive social structures. I refer to this argument as the Harm Response. These two accusations—the Knowledge Response and the Harm Response—can manifest in the "liberal intolerance" springing up on college campuses that many critics have lamented.[16] The substance of a critique is secondary; what matters is the action of critiquing New Egalitarian ideals. If criticizing is inappropriate because of the speaker's epistemic or moral standing, then there is no reason to engage with the substance of the criticism.

Consider each of these obscurantist tactics in turn, beginning with the Knowledge Response. The concept of privilege may or may not be a helpful tool of social scientific explanation. But when applied to participants in a discussion, it removes any need to address the content of a privileged interlocutor's claims. The privileged person cannot access the "lived experience" of those who have suffered from oppression. This lack of access entails a lack of standing to object to New Egalitarian ideas. Privileged individuals need to be educated about the invisible structures that generate oppression. But even if the critics in question are not white males, their disagreement is evidence of "internalized oppression," an expression indicating that oppressed groups come to accept and perpetuate the social structures that oppress them.[17] If either the privileged or the internally oppressed persist in questioning certain New Egalitarian ideas, the argument goes, it is only proof that they need more education or that they are acting in bad faith.

Critics of New Egalitarians sometimes mistake the Knowledge Response approach for a naive, freshman-level philosophy brand of relativism. Although New Egalitarians may think that some statements that people take as fact are culturally relative, they also believe that there are objective truths about real forms of oppression. They seek to raise "awareness" about structural forms of inequality. The appeal to lived experience and privilege is more like the classic Marxist idea of false consciousness.[18] Social structures condition how individuals view the world, including their perceptions of oppression. New Egalitarians are not dismissive of any concept of truth, but only of those ideas that deny or even challenge their own accounts of oppression.

The Harm Response is more severe in both its claims and its consequences. The New Egalitarianism rests on an often implicit set of social scientific claims, mostly imported from critical theory. Despite subtle differences between New Egalitarian thinkers, they employ some common themes. Most important is the idea that the interests of disadvantaged groups are *insufficiently articulated*. Oppression can persist precisely because it is invisible. The most famous article in postcolonial theory asks the question, "Can the subaltern speak?"[19] The critical theorist's role is to reveal these invisible structures of oppression. Ideologies that support existing systems of oppression are forms of "epistemic violence" that undermine the emancipatory project of critical theory.[20] Failing to recognize this set of background assumptions has led many critics to argue that the New Egalitarianism seeks to protect members of disadvantaged groups from being offended. But what New Egalitarians are really worried about is that the oppressed will continue *to be silenced*. Their interests will remain unarticulated, and so they will continue to be marginalized and oppressed.

A recent episode is illustrative. Commenting on the election of Donald Trump as president of the United States, political theorist Mark Lilla argued in a *New York Times* op-ed that "identity liberalism"—what I dub the New Egalitarianism—has gone too far.[21] He maintained that attempts to lift up historically disadvantaged groups should be situated in a broader democratic ethos that emphasizes commonality rather than difference. Focusing on identity runs the risk of alienating those who are part of historically privileged groups and can provoke a resentful backlash. Lilla's Columbia colleague Katherine Franke responded to him on the *Los Angeles Review of Books* blog.[22] Franke accused Lilla of enabling white supremacy, of "mansplaining" the women's rights movement, and of blaming disadvantaged groups for Trump's election. Franke claimed that Lilla was not only wrong about identity politics but also wrong in a way that perpetuates oppression. Lilla's actions were part of the same "ideological project" pursued by the Ku Klux Klan.

The views that the New Egalitarianism inherits from critical theory generate a series of cascading harm claims. Bigoted motives are not a necessary condition for acting in a racist manner. Any action that reproduces or props up invisible structures of oppression is racist in its effects. Moreover, denying the reality or significance of oppression—for instance, by claiming that some observed inequalities are due to anything but white supremacy—serves to silence criticism of oppressive structures. Denialism is thus also a form of racism. But it does not stop there. Imagine that I have a critique of Racism 2 that will actually convince people to dismantle some structures of oppression. Imagine further that you agree that oppression exists but disagree with my diagnosis or my proposed solution. You are still being racist because it is effects and not intentions that matter. You have committed Lilla's sin, which was not to dismiss the reality of oppression but to disagree about how to achieve progress. Even *tolerating* criticism, it is thus argued, may reinforce structures of oppression.[23] If New Egalitarian social theory is right, the *act* of undermining an emancipatory critique—*even a false one*—must be oppressive.

New Egalitarian obscurantism is not dishonest in the traditional sense. It consistently applies a view of how oppression is generated and sustained in addition to the belief that theory should be emancipatory. Taken to the limit, instances of the Knowledge Response and the Harm Response can take the form of what Harry Frankfurt dubs "bullshit."[24] Bullshit is distinct from deception or fraud in that the speaker is not trying to distract from the truth but rather is indifferent to whether what he or she is saying is true or not. The goal of New Egalitarian arguments is first and foremost emancipation from oppression. Although broad truths about historical forms of oppression matter, New Egalitarians advance particular claims because these claims serve definite functions in the process of emancipation. Insofar as oppression is propped up by bad ideology, shutting down that ideology is more important than appealing to standards of social scientific rigor (that themselves may be an ideological cover for oppression). The fact that the New Egalitarianism concerns itself with altering complex social structures—knowable only by experts—through collective action increases the incentive for bullshit: "Bullshit is unavoidable whenever circumstances require someone to talk without knowing what he is talking about. Thus the production of bullshit is stimulated whenever a person's obligations or opportunities to speak about some topic are more excessive than his knowledge of the facts that are relevant to that topic."[25]

Frankfurt goes on to argue that bullshit might be associated with a desire for signaling internal sincerity. This may be true of New Egalitarian speech, in which strong signals of sincerity help solve collective action problems. Mobilizing sufficient support to change practices, even at a relatively local level such as a university, requires overcoming the free-rider problem. Willingness to adopt habits of speech and action that are peculiar to outsiders may help serve as a filtering device for identifying willing participants in demonstrations, protests, and other actions meant to challenge existing practices.

Sustained solutions to collective action problems can also have a dark side: they often involve stigmatizing a common enemy group. Hayek argues that consistent mistreatment of minorities in collectivist societies is no accident.[26] It is necessary to motivate individuals to go along with the broader group. Recent work in evolutionary biology reaches similar conclusions. Humans' ability to band together is due in part to our ancestors' propensity for battling competing groups of other humans. The New Egalitarians have settled on White Males as an identifiable Other that needs to be overcome. It would be surprising if this approach did not engender a backlash because New Egalitarians have handed those who disagree with them a ready-made solution to their own collective action problems. The possibility of backlash again calls to mind Hayek's concerns about socialist morality: it is entirely functional in a world of small, violently competing tribes. But tribalistic morality, even when it is aimed at emancipation rather than at conquest, can undermine the generality that is the basis for extended social cooperation.

Another victim of New Egalitarian obscurantism is a sense of proportionality regarding the harms of actions construed as oppressive. Recall that an action is oppressive if it perpetuates, covers, or props up invisible social structures that generate systemic inequality. These structures are *historical* in the sense that individuals can be born into them. When we hold an individual morally responsible for Racism 1, we focus on the harm that his or her actions directly cause. By this standard, racist speech is at most emotionally offensive, a breach of manners. Racist talk becomes a very serious moral issue only when it is joined to more concrete actions. But when we hold an individual responsible for perpetuating Racism 2, our gaze is drawn to the myriad historical injustices that disadvantaged groups have suffered. To contribute to Racism 2, even through mere speech, is to support *the same* social structures that underwrote slavery, genocide, and other moral horrors.[27] This difference in how we conceive of the harm perpetrated by individual actions helps explain why New Egalitarians react so strongly to speech and why their critics find these reactions hyperbolic.

Conclusions

When put into practice, the New Egalitarianism—that which seeks a thick version of equality for members of various social groups—relies on an obscurantist moral epistocracy. New Egalitarians would probably object to this claim. But whether a pristine version of New Egalitarianism would be more democratic or not does not tell us how such a moral code will operate with human beings as they are.

Both epistocracy and obscurantism flow naturally from the substance of New Egalitarian thought. According to this school of thought, experts are needed to fashion a new vocabulary that reveals the invisible sources of oppression. Obscurantism is needed because the consequences of speech are momentous. Because the stakes are high, the response to those who perpetuate oppression—whether intentionally or not—must be salient, authoritative, and decisive. There is no shame in shutting down arguments, New Egalitarian thinking goes, just as there is no shame in outmaneuvering an enemy on the battlefield.

It is not clear how to respond to these argumentative tactics in a constructive manner. If disagreement is dismissed as epistemically or morally unwarranted merely because it is disagreement, there is not much room for a productive conversation.

Nonetheless, it is vital to understand the distinctive characteristics of this new phenomenon. By taking New Egalitarian ideas seriously, liberal social scientists and philosophers may be able to offer a constructive alternative that recognizes the reality of historical and cultural oppression but seeks to empower the disadvantaged through freedom of association and disassociation rather than through a reversion to our atavistic instincts.

Acknowledgments: I thank Daniel D'Amico for the helpful feedback he provided.

2

The Misuses of Egalitarianism

James R. Otteson*

WHAT IS THE problem we wish to solve when we try to construct an egalitarian society? On certain familiar assumptions, the answer is simple enough. If we agree on what the proper conception of egalitarianism is and how it would apply to the people in our society, if we know all the relevant information about people's lives and the ways in which they depart from the proper egalitarian benchmark, if we have knowledge of the resources available to us that might be marshaled and allocated, and if we know the mechanisms by which these resources might be reliably reallocated according to the proper egalitarian benchmark, then the problem that remains is purely one of logic: the best use of our available resources is implicit in our assumptions. At that point, establishing an egalitarian society, under the assumption that it is what we want, is merely a matter of will: Do we want to effectuate such a society or not?

With apologies to F. A. Hayek, after whom the previous paragraph is modeled, the problem of constructing a properly egalitarian society is, alas, not so simple.[1] There are many difficulties that combine to frustrate our attempts to establish an egalitarian society.

In this article, I discuss some of the political-economic difficulties. By focusing on "political-economic difficulties," I accept for the sake of argument that an egalitarian society (properly conceived) is desirable, and I address three issues related to the practical instantiation of creating or taking positive steps toward creating such a society: (1) many cases of so-called brute luck, which

---

*James R. Otteson is Thomas W. Smith Presidential Chair in Business Ethics and professor of economics at Wake Forest University.

for many commentators leads to unfair (because undeserved) inequalities justifying redress, actually result from choices whose outcomes should be respected and not corrected; (2) political and economic policies that would match up with our considered egalitarian goals are far more difficult to craft than is typically envisioned; and (3) the likelihood that such policies, even when well crafted, will work in practice the way we would ideally like them to is lower than typically envisioned. I close by suggesting an alternative conception of egalitarianism—namely, egalitarianism of respect.

Luck Egalitarianism

Based on the amount of attention it has received, perhaps the most engaging topic in egalitarianism is luck: what it is, how to recognize it, how to (or whether we can) disaggregate its effects from those brought about by nonluck factors, and what to do about it.[2] Eliminating luck and its effects in people's lives altogether, however, is impossible. There is no way to eliminate all categories of luck running from chance encounters between people who can help one another to unpredictable changes in the environment or in human society. Might we, however, be able to dull or mitigate the effects of luck? Yes, but it is a very long way between saying that "some effects of luck seem unjust or unfair" to asserting that "we now know how to solve that problem"—or indeed even to saying, "we now have figured out how to plausibly address that problem."

There is in fact a chain of difficulties. We first have to specify what luck is and agree on a description of it that specifies under what conditions it is unfair. Luck egalitarians routinely distinguish what they call "option luck" from what they call "brute luck": the former comprises inequalities that arise as a result of choices people make, such as voluntary gambling; the latter comprises inequalities that result independently of agents' choices, such as accidents of birth, natural disasters, and so on. Luck egalitarians differ on whether people should be compensated for bad option luck, for bad brute luck, for both, or for neither.[3] As I argue later, however, the distinction between option luck and brute luck, which initially seems promising, turns out not to be dispositive in relatively routine, everyday cases. Even assuming that we can come to a satisfactory description of the morally relevant sense of unfair luck, we then have to figure out how we can recognize the presence of unfair luck in actual people's lives—not in hypothetical thought experiments, but in the lives of real people. The next stage of the program would be to develop policies to address or mitigate the effects of unfair luck that address or mitigate what we want addressed or mitigated and not something else—policies that *(a)* will not make the problem worse or create other unintended problems and that *(b)* can be effectuated by the actual people likely to be administrators of the relevant government agencies and not by superhumans.[4]

Before we get to this policy stage, however, we face a prior difficulty: the inequality that is often taken as reflective of luck is a symptom that has many causes. The difficulty is not just that we can measure inequality in many different ways but also that inequality is caused by many things—luck is one, but it is by no means the only one. Suppose there is a species of causal agents, call it category L, that plays a role in effectuating a species of effects, category R. But there are many subspecies of L: $L_1, L_2, L_3, \ldots L_n$; and there are many subspecies of R: $R_1, R_2, R_3, \ldots R_n$. To make the causal argument, one would have to show that the particular subspecies of L that one is discussing is what has led to the particular subspecies of R that one is targeting. That is very hard to do. But our situation is actually worse than that. First, we cannot be sure whether the various subspecies of L that are conceptually distinct are also ontologically distinct—that is, whether our conceptual distinctions match up with the distinctions in reality. Second, each actual instance of R will have been brought about by many causes, one (or some) of which might be in the category of L at issue, but we cannot know *(a)* how many other Ls might have contributed to the R we are targeting or *(b)* what proportion of the relevant R is accounted for—in fact, not in theory—by the particular subspecies of L we are discussing. Causal ascriptions are difficult and delicate. They may hold in the hypothetical cases we construct, but such cases typically imagine that all else is held constant and ignore how the relevant situations might have arisen historically. There is hence a substantial gap between such hypothesized scenarios and their application to real people's actual situations that renders many of our narratives about connecting Ls to Rs otiose—simply just-so stories.

Let us stipulate for the sake of argument, however, that (1) there is such a thing as undeserved bad luck and that (2) it can give rise to justified disappointment on the part of the disaffected agent. In what follows, I raise three considerations against the luck egalitarian (LE) position, even granting both (1) and (2). First, I argue that in many common, everyday cases it does not follow that the disaffected agent is owed anything by anyone. Second, I argue that the main political-economic proposals for reducing or mitigating inequality would not plausibly address the cases of undeserved bad luck and justified disappointment about which luck egalitarians are concerned. And third, I argue that the standard LE argument is incomplete because it fails to take into consideration relevant trade-offs and opportunity costs.

Bad Luck and Justified Disappointment Resulting from Unobjectionable Choice

Let me illustrate the first consideration with an example. Jack and Jill are college seniors who have been dating for some time. Jill is coming to think that she might be in love with Jack; Jack, for his part, also believes he loves Jill. On a Sunday evening, Jack calls Jill and asks her to dinner the next Saturday evening. She agrees, and he tells her it is going to be *special*. When Jack says that, Jill begins to wonder whether Jack intends to ask her to marry him. She decides that if he asks her, she intends to say "yes." On Monday, Jack goes to a jewelry store and buys an engagement ring. Also on Monday morning, Jill is in class; on her way out of class, while happily thinking about the impending Saturday evening date and its potential future ramifications, she gets stopped by . . . Joe. Joe missed what the professor said at the end of class and asks Jill if she could fill him in. When Jill looks up at Joe, their eyes meet, and there is a spark. Joe asks her if she wants to get a coffee; she says yes. They talk and enjoy their conversation. After several hours of talking, they decide to get some dinner. Then they talk, walk around the quad, and talk some more. They eventually realize that they have been talking all night long. The sun is coming up over campus. Joe looks at the sunrise, he looks at Jill, and he says, "Jill, I've never met a person like you before. I can't believe I'm saying this, but, let's get married—right now. Let's elope." Though numerous predictable thoughts begin to whir in Jill's mind, she replies, "Yes." They agree to elope.

Now think for a moment of poor Jack. Did he suffer undeserved bad luck? Obviously yes: in the very week that he plans to ask his longtime girlfriend to marry him, her meeting a new person whom she suddenly decides to marry is clearly bad luck. Is the resentment Jack no doubt feels justified? Again, obviously yes. He and Jill have a history, and he had reason to believe they might spend the rest of their lives together. But what can Jack do about it? Can he sue her for compensation for the future companionship and affection he expected to get from her but now will not? Can he seek redress for the children he wanted to have with Jill but now will not? Can he seek reparation for the time, energy, and effort he put into the relationship with her, all of which now has come to an unexpectedly fruitless end? The answer to all of these questions is "no." Jack suffered undeserved bad luck and is experiencing a disappointment that I think we all would agree is justified, but he has no right to Jill. He has no right to her affection, her love, or her time. She is a free moral agent, and she thus gets to decide with whom she will spend her time and to whom she will give her affection, even if that means Jack or anyone else is reasonably disappointed.

Is Jack owed something from anyone else? If you are a friend of Jack, your friendship might require you to console him or offer sympathy. Perhaps you take him out for a beer and talk things over with him. You might introduce him to another possible mate. Any of those extensions of beneficence are acceptable, but what would not be acceptable is to visit some harm, injury, or cost on Jill or Joe. Does *society* owe Jack something? Should we endorse policy that would require Jill or uninvolved others to compensate Jack? Should we endorse policy that would seek to prevent people like Joe from meeting or speaking to people like Jill? Again, the answer to these questions is clearly no—and for the same reason as that given earlier: Jill is a free person, entitled equally with anyone else to give or withhold her affections to or from whomever she chooses. If she had already entered into a contract (such as marriage) with Jack, or if she had made some promise (express or perhaps even implicit) to Jack, the situation might be different. But in the scenario proposed, no such contract was executed, and no such promise was made.

I suggest that the same reasoning holds in many other realms of human social life. Suppose you regularly go to Coffee Shop A (CSA). Then one day Coffee Shop B (CSB) opens up across the street. You discover that you like its offerings better than those of CSA. Perhaps other CSA customers similarly decide they like CSB better; perhaps this change in preference eventually puts CSA out of business. Now, did the owner of CSA suffer undeserved bad luck? Yes: it was unlucky that another coffee shop opened across the street. Is the disappointment of CSA's owner justified? Yes: it seems entirely reasonable that she should be disappointed that her plans for keeping her coffee shop in business indefinitely into the future are now threatened. And if she should lose her business, this will cause significant displacement and difficulty in her life that she did not want or anticipate as a result (at least in part) of bad luck she did not seem to deserve. But does she have any rights to press against the owner of CSB or against the customers who have now chosen to stop patronizing her coffee shop? No. Just as Jack has no right to Jill, the owner of CSA has no right to those customers or to their resources, and she has no right to make them choose otherwise than they would on their own—or to visit harm or cost on them if they choose otherwise than she wishes they would. They are free moral agents, entitled equally with anyone else to choose with whom to associate or whom to patronize.

I argue that these examples indicate that having established that a person suffered undeserved bad luck and that he or she is experiencing justified disappointment do not, even when combined, suffice by themselves to establish that the person is owed compensation. An assumption my argument makes is that all of the persons involved—including not only the disaffected person(s) but also those who made choices leading to the scenario under which the disaffected persons are unlucky and disappointed—are equal moral agents and thus deserve to have their choices respected as much as anyone else's choices.[5] I also assume that there was no contract or promise (explicit or implicit) in place that would obligate anyone to act in a way differently from what they chose. If there were such a promise in place, then a disaffected person might be owed compensation—from the affecting parties, if not from anyone else.

Note that the "great stress [egalitarians place] on the distinction between the outcomes for which an individual is responsible—that is, those that result from her voluntary choices—and the outcomes for which she is not responsible—good or bad outcomes that occur independent of her choice or of what she could have reasonably foreseen"[6]—does not defeat either the Jack-and-Jill scenario or the coffee shop scenario. The unfortunate results for Jack and the owner of CSA result from the voluntary and unobjectionable choices made by Jill and Joe and by prospective coffee shop patrons, respectively, and both

Jack and the owner of CSA presumably engaged in their respective enterprises knowing that others' choices could frustrate their hopes. Thus, on the standard "option luck" view, they are responsible for the consequences of their voluntary choices. At the same time, the specific negative consequences suffered by Jack and the owner of CSA occurred independently of their own choices—they resulted from others' choices. Thus, those consequences would qualify as "brute luck" for them, and yet Jack and the coffee shop owner are still entitled to no compensation.

The Difficulty of Crafting "Responsibility-Catering" Policy

The second consideration I wish to raise regarding the LE argument again begins by accepting two starting points: (1) there is such a thing as undeserved bad luck, and (2) it can give rise to justified disappointment on the part of the disaffected agent. Here, however, this consideration further stipulates an additional premise: (3) the disaffected agent is owed compensation of some kind and from someone. Whereas the previous consideration questioned whether a disaffected agent is indeed owed something, this consideration concedes that point and instead asks another question: How can we reliably compensate the disaffected agent? What political-economic policy might we endorse that could *(a)* reliably pick out of a large and diverse population which individuals meet criteria (1), (2), and (3) and *(b)* reliably get the proper compensation to them instead of to other people?

Elizabeth Anderson writes, "Luck egalitarianism relies on two moral premises: that people should be compensated for undeserved misfortunes and that the compensation should come only from that part of others' good fortune that is undeserved."[7] My argument from the Jack-and-Jill and coffee shop scenarios questioned whether undeserved misfortunes alone entail that compensation is required. Suppose, however, that we have demonstrated satisfactorily that in a particular case compensation is indeed owed. The second part of the LE position, according to Anderson, is that the relevant proper compensation is due "only from that part of others' good fortune that is undeserved." Anderson goes on to claim that luck egalitarians "take from the fortunate only that portion of their advantages that everyone acknowledges is undeserved."[8] Putting aside the not inconsiderable likelihood that there may in fact be *no* portion of others' advantages that *everyone* would acknowledge is undeserved, we must ask: How can we know what part of others' good fortune is in fact undeserved—not in theory or in hypothetical cases, but in the lives of actual people? And further: How can we design a policy that would have a chance of reliably determining and responding to that undeserved good fortune?

The LE position requires that differentials in luck lead to differentials in relative success in life: people with good luck tend to have levels of success that are both greater than that of people with bad luck and at least in part attributable to the luck.[9] The next step in the LE argument is to devise policy recommendations that could make some headway in compensating for the differential levels of relative success between those experiencing good luck and those experiencing bad luck. Since the LE position addresses both luck and equality, it must seek policies that tend to equalize the effects of luck on people's lives. Such policies can address inputs or outputs: they can seek to equalize funding—for, say, education in an attempt to minimize the effect of luck pertaining to where one happens to be born or in what school district one happens to be raised—or they can address outputs by seeking to equalize relative levels of success—for example, by applying what one might call a "luck tax" on those who have benefitted from favorable luck and then redistributing the proceeds to those who have suffered from unfavorable luck. I argue, however, that neither of these methods has a reasonable chance of reliably picking out those people who meet criteria (1), (2), and (3) stipulated earlier or reliably getting the proper compensation to those we believe deserve it and not to others who do not deserve it.

Policies applied at either the federal or state levels are general and thus must treat populations as being composed of relatively homogenous and fungible units. An input-based policy of providing, say, some equal level of funding per pupil to every school district cannot be sensitive to the fact that a single level of funding would be significantly more impactful in some places than in others and significantly more impactful in some people's lives than in others'. Even more particularized policies of, say, discounting the funding according to localized costs of living are, in addition to being more difficult to administer (and thus introducing more potential opportunities for actual implementation to differ from what was intended),[10] nevertheless still unable to discriminate among those individuals in the intended population who have had good luck and those who have bad. Some people in poor areas have better luck than others; the same is true in wealthy areas. Even if a greater proportion of those in the former areas have bad luck than those in the latter areas, nevertheless a general policy of providing any particular level of funding will fail to pick out which individuals have suffered bad luck and which have enjoyed good luck. It will instead treat individuals in the relevant populations according to some specified and relatively objective criterion, such as income or wealth. But no policy can be designed to address luck directly because there is no way to directly equalize luck in people's lives—only some of the consequences of luck. Thus, any actual policy will inevitably fail to be responsive to morally relevant differences in different individuals' circumstances.[11]

A similar problem besets other general redistributive polices. A universal basic income, for example, or a progressive income tax assumes, if it is to be justified on LE grounds, that all of the people within the respective tax or welfare groups it distinguishes have experienced the same levels and kinds of luck. But that cannot be known from afar. Moreover, the assumption is also almost certainly false: no two people—even two people from similar demographic backgrounds, even two people within the same family—experience the same levels of luck and have the same consequences from luck in their lives. So a general redistributive policy will have the effect of compensating some people who have suffered bad luck (the intended target of benefit) as well as some people who have not suffered bad luck (who would hence become undeserving beneficiaries). It will also draw from the resources of both some people who have enjoyed good luck (the intended target of the "luck tax") and others who have not (who would hence become undeserving victims).

Although it is relatively clear how we can capture in general rules things such as assault, theft, and fraud, it is not clear how we can capture in similarly general rules things such as *"this proportion of this person's (lack of) success in life is due to undeserved luck"* because any general rule we design to pick out and redress undeserved luck will end up in practice being blind to morally relevant distinctions in individual circumstances. It will thus wind up wrongly punishing or rewarding at least some people for circumstances that were not due to luck. One might perhaps think that merely stipulating a principle of redressing only those cases of bad luck that ought to be redressed could solve this problem. This might be, for example, Anderson's response. She proposes what she calls "democratic equality," which she claims "guarantees all law-abiding citizens effective access to the social conditions of their freedom at all times."[12] But her claims about what her democratic equality "guarantees" do not address how it could plausibly do so via policy, especially since such policy would have to be administered by people with incomplete knowledge of localized circumstances and with mixed and often idiosyncratic incentives that can lead them to act in ways that depart from the policy designers' intentions.[13] Thus, Anderson's argument simply stipulates the political-economic problems away rather than addressing, let alone solving, them.

Is a Proposed Redistribution Worth the Cost?

The third consideration I raise against the LE argument is that it fails to consider relevant trade-offs and opportunity costs. Richard Arneson claims that "the absolute value of the gain that further aid can provide the [disaffected] person might vary from enormous to piddling,"[14] but he fails to ask what else the contemplated aid might do. We live in a world of scarce resources and opportunity costs. This means that any resource distributed to one location cannot go elsewhere. To know whether a proposed distribution is beneficial overall, we need to know what the alternative uses of that resource are. Compensating one person for his bad luck entails depriving others of benefit, and it might easily be the case that the benefit denied to these others may outweigh the benefit granted to the compensated person.[15] Allocative arguments are certainly easier to make if we assume scarcity away, but it is not clear that such arguments warrant political-economic consideration: *all* logically consistent allocations are possible without scarcity.

Arneson also argues that if "we hold that equality is valuable for its own sake," then with respect to "worsening the condition of those who have more without making anyone else better off, and without bringing it about that those whose condition is worsened are now worse off than others, we must hold that at least in one respect the state of affairs just described is better than the one it displaces."[16] But the conclusion does not follow. Granting that equality is valuable for its own sake does not entail that it is the *only* thing valuable for its own sake, and trade-offs will almost certainly be required in a finite world with scarce resources. Perhaps community, happiness, liberty, and virtue might also be valuable for their own sakes.[17] However we would prioritize these values, we cannot maximize for all of them at the same time. So it is not enough to say that because equality is valuable for its own sake, it therefore follows that we should maximize for it. We further need to know *(a)* why equality is the *only* thing valuable for its own sake, a claim that seems prima facie implausible given other candidates that also seem valuable for their own sakes, or *(b)* what the relevant trade-offs would be and why and when they are worth making (which includes a reckoning of the opportunity costs of the relevant trade-offs). These are crucial but crucially missing elements in the LE argument.

Egalitarian Respect

Anderson criticizes other luck egalitarians on the grounds that they are concerned "only with the distribution of goods themselves" instead of being "concerned with the relationships within which goods are distributed."[18] This criticism points to an important moral claim: a proper conception of equality should, whatever else it does, endorse an equal respect for the dignity of all. It is not an egalitarianism of luck, of wealth or income,[19] of capacity,[20] or of outcomes:[21] it is an egalitarianism of respect. I believe this conception is a critical moral principle, indeed a foundational principle of any political economy worth contemplating.[22] But it points in a different direction from that in which Anderson wants to take it. Rather than entailing that the state ensure everyone "[has] the means to do what one wants,"[23] it entails instead that we respect the choices people make—even when those choices lead to unequal outcomes or to consequences that the choosers did not want. That is the point of the Jack-and-Jill and coffee shop examples: Jill's choices led to consequences Jack did not want, just as the choices of patrons who preferred CSB to CSA led to consequences that the owner of CSA did not want. But respecting the equal dignity of all requires that we respect their choices, even when some others do not like or do not benefit from those choices, and that we grant to no one preemptive rights to others' time, talent, and treasure. If we accept, moreover, an Adam Smithian "negative" conception of justice as requiring respect for people's persons, property, and voluntary promises, then this egalitarianism of *respect* follows from an egalitarianism of *justice*.[24] This egalitarianism, I submit, is one that is worth defending and one that has the considerable additional benefit of being achievable.

Acknowledgments: I thank Adam Hyde and Matthew Phillips for their comments on an earlier draft. Thanks also go to David Bery, who provided crucial research assistance for and discussion of the ideas in this paper. Remaining errors are mine.

3

The Conceptual Marriage of Rawls and Hayek

Michael C. Munger*

WE MAY VALUE equality for all sorts of reasons. It's cute when two runners, after a long race, cross the finish line holding hands and intentionally finishing together. But suppose that we see *inequality*. Are we allowed to "fix" things? Are we *obliged* to fix things, so that failing to act is actually a moral mistake? Is the impulse to decry inequality born of envy ("You have more than I do; you should share!") or charity ("I have more than you do; I should share!")?

For much of political philosophy, the most salient work on egalitarianism derives from the work of John Rawls. But Rawls was no simple egalitarian. He advocated contingent inequality, in fact, consistent with the "difference principle." Allowable inequalities must be "reasonably expected to be to everyone's advantage, and attached to positions and offices open to all."[1]

The problem is that any Pareto improvement, or move that makes at least one person better off and no one strictly worse, might satisfy this restriction. How should society distribute the gains from one of these many *possible* Pareto improvements, compared to (admittedly inferior) equality? Must we make interpersonal utility comparisons to select the "best"? Rawls advocates "justice as fairness" as the criterion for choosing. Given that citizens (even reasonable citizens committed to reaching agreement) disagree about the good and the nature of the ideal society, the answer is to reach agreement on fair procedures.

The advantage of the difference principle, from this perspective, is that it narrows down the set of allowable Pareto improvements. By Pareto, everyone

---

*Michael C. Munger is director of the Philosophy, Politics, and Economics Program and professor in the Departments of Political Science and Economics at Duke University.

must be better off than in a state of pure equality, but according to the difference principle those *least* well-off must enjoy the *greatest* improvement. As Rawls put it, "[S]ocial and economic inequalities, for example inequalities of wealth and authority, are just only if they result in compensating benefits for everyone, and in particular for the least advantaged members of society."[2]

The power of Rawls's argument comes from finessing direct interpersonal comparisons and focusing instead on rules. In stating the difference principle, Rawls sets out these requirements: "Social and economic inequalities are to be arranged so that they are . . . (a) to the greatest benefit of the least advantaged; and (b) attached to offices and positions open to all under conditions of fair equality of opportunity."[3] Also, "an inequality of opportunity must enhance the opportunities of those with the lesser opportunity. . . . *General Conception*: All social primary goods—liberty and opportunity, income and wealth, and all the bases of self-respect—are to be distributed equally unless an unequal distribution of any or all of these goods is to the advantage of the least favored."[4]

In this essay, I want to investigate "egalitarianism" as a concept of social justice and to ask whether a synthesis of two apparently incompatible viewpoints, that argued by Rawls and that argued by F. A. Hayek, is possible (and possibly desirable). One might object that those who have objected to the very notion of social justice make the project doomed at the outset. But a number of authors have considered the possibility to be fruitful.[5] As evidence, I can cite Hayek himself, from *Law, Legislation, and Liberty*:

> Before leaving the subject [of "social" justice,] I want to point out once more that the recognition that in such combinations as "social," "economic," "distributive" or "retributive" justice[,] the term "justice" is wholly empty should not lead us to throw the baby out with the bath water. Not only as the basis of the legal rules of just conduct is the justice which the courts of justice administer exceedingly important; there unquestionably also exists a genuine problem of justice in connection with the deliberate design of political institutions, the problem to which Professor John Rawls has recently [this passage was published in 1976] devoted an important book. The fact that I regret and regard as confusing is merely that in this connection he employs the term "social justice." But I have no basic quarrel with an author who, before he proceeds to that problem, acknowledges that the task

of selecting specific systems or distributions of desired things as just must be *"abandoned as mistaken in principle, and it is, in any case, not capable of a definite answer. Rather the principles of justice define the crucial constraints which institutions and joint activities must satisfy if persons engaging in them are to have no complaints about them. If these constraints are satisfied, the resulting distribution, whatever it is, may be accepted as just (or at least not unjust)."* This is more or less what I have been trying to argue in this chapter.[6]

One problem is the definition of the term *egalitarianism* that I want to use—because the question is whether "social justice" allows or even requires concerns for egalitarianism to be central. One common distinction is between concern for strict "equality of outcomes" as distinguished from "equality of opportunity." To get an idea of the relative importance of these concepts over time, examine figure 3.1, an Ngram from Google's database. As the figure shows, "equality of opportunity" was the dominant concept from 1890

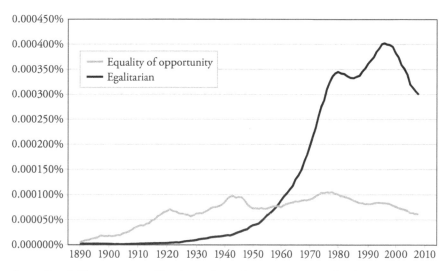

Source: Google Ngrams, at https://books.google.com/ngrams/interactive_chart?content
=egalitarian%2C+equality+of+opportunity&year_start=1890&year_end 2010
&corpus=15&smoothing=3&share=&direct_url=t1%3B%2Cegalitarian%3B%2
Cco%3B.tl%3B%2Cequality%20of%20opportunity%3B%2Cco%22%20width
=900%20height=500%20marginwidth=0%20margin height=0%20hspace=0%20
vspace=0%20frameborder=0%20scrolling=no.crolling=no.

Figure 3.1. Google Ngram: Frequency of Use of the Terms
Egalitarian and *Equality of Opportunity*

through the middle 1950s, after which "egalitarian" became much more common. By 1970, "egalitarian" had eclipsed the older concept; since then, the two ideas have diverged in importance, so that "egalitarian" has become the main concern, at least in Google's published sources.

In the remainder of this essay, I first consider problems of "fixed systems of justice" where egalitarianism is paramount and then consider the implications of truly voluntary exchange and profits for the welfare of "the least well-off."

Insecurity, Inequality, and Fixed Systems of Justice

Can a capitalist system, with state actions yet to be determined, satisfy Rawls's "justice as fairness" conception? What transactions, activities, and wealth distributions would be allowed?

In a market system, profits result from redirecting resources toward producing things consumers want and need. *Large* profits are signals that before the entrepreneurial activity there were *substantial* resource misallocations, implying large costs and losses for consumers. We pay the cost of the profits as a way of grasping the far larger societal benefit of greater output, higher-quality products, and much lower prices. Confiscating profits, unless it can be done by surprise, eliminates the incentives for entrepreneurship and perpetuates resource waste and misuse.

However, it may be justified, as Hayek famously argued, to create a social safety net, redistributive taxation, social insurance, and assistance to ease the plight of workers in a declining industry, though never to trap them in that industry by protectionism or subsidies.

> There are two kinds of security: the certainty of a given minimum of sustenance for all and the security of a given standard of life, of the relative position which one person or group enjoys compared with others. *There is no reason why, in a society which has reached the general level of wealth ours has, the first kind of security should not be guaranteed to all without endangering general freedom; that is: some minimum of food, shelter and clothing, sufficient to preserve health. Nor is there any reason why the state should not help to organize a comprehensive system of social insurance in providing for those common hazards of life against*

which few can make adequate provision. It is planning for security of the second kind which has such an insidious effect on liberty. It is planning designed to protect individuals or groups against diminutions of their incomes.[7]

Hayek's point is, in a way, identical to Rawls's: social insurance and income security to ensure the welfare of the least well-off are the wealthy society's obligation because the wealth and prosperity result from a system—in this case, market capitalism—that allows gainers to gain enough that they can compensate the losers and still prosper.

So we might (with both Hayek and Rawls) endorse a move from a hypothetical starting point *(a)* (pure equality) to a realized institutional state *(b)* (market system with social safety net to protect the least well-off). And the extent of the social safety net would be a matter of public agreement, in a way to be made clear in a moment. If I am right, then it is possible to propose a "Rawlsekian Synthesis" that accepts both Rawls's and Hayek's principles and goals without compromising either thinker's claims.

What would be *impermissible* is to justify a coerced move to yet a third state of the world *(c)*, where further redistribution and punitive tax policies are undertaken to "fix" the realized society of position *(b)*. The reason this is impermissible in the Rawlsian framework is self-evident: it is *only after we know our status in the realized society* that we wake up one morning and decide that position *(b)* is not what we (the least well-off) wanted after all.

The problem is that if voluntary transactions are to be allowed, income inequalities are inevitable. A continuous process of readjustment—not just *(c)* but then *(d)* and before long *(e)*—would be required, based on information no one could have behind the "veil of ignorance." And that is the reason that people who end up with below-average levels of income or wealth protest procedurally fair voluntary transactions: they don't actually care about procedural fairness; they just want more money.

Robert Nozick famously responded to Rawls by focusing on the justice of voluntary exchange and a different kind of (un)fairness.[8] Nozick objected that institutions in the realized "just" state would not be just after all but would require further, perhaps continuous, redistribution of income. He was willing to accept, for the sake of argument, that Rawls's justification for redistributing wealth was that otherwise the realized distribution was *not fair.*

But Nozick responded that such redistributions could not be *just*. First, voluntary transactions would over time have cumulative effects of creating inequalities that Rawls would deem unfair. Paradoxically, each of the individual transactions that led away from a fair distribution was *by itself* just and beneficial to both parties. Why punish a middleman who had actually provided benefits to each partner in each transaction?[9]

Second, the possessors of wealth holdings have property rights in that wealth. These rights include the right to have and to use the property as well as the right to transfer the property. Rawls would either violate the right to possess property by taking it or violate the right freely to transfer the property, taking the fruits—in other words, profits—of those transfers. I call such fruits "profits," as is common in the economics literature.

As an illustration, Nozick famously used a particular person: professional basketball star Wilt Chamberlain.[10] The example is well known, so I do not describe it at length here. But the point was that many people, even relatively poor people, might be willing to pay the marvelous Chamberlain to see him play. They are happy to pay the money and are happy with the result.

The question is whether the "new" distribution, after allowing people to pay Chamberlain, is unjust. If one answers yes, then one must believe either that the citizens who paid extra are not competent judges of their own welfare or that the transactions themselves are unjust in ways the state must overrule. Either way, a state that would force redistribution to return to the initial fair distribution is "outlawing capitalist acts between consenting adults."[11] That violates both Rawls's liberty principle and many people's moral intuition about an important side constraint on what government can regulate.

This point is important. It means that the internally coherent Rawlsian must outlaw transactions that would benefit both parties or else must reverse transactions after the fact, returning the money spent by the buyer after taking it by force from the seller. The argument is powerful, but I have always wondered that Nozick chose such an odd and narrow example. Wilt Chamberlain was nearly supernatural; using him as an example does not justify normal commerce.

A much more useful example, at least in my opinion, is the fable of the "Itinerant Padre" that R. A. Radford described.[12] This example is not well known, so I cover it at a bit more length here.[13] The point, lest it be obscured, is that because voluntary exchanges make both parties better off, allowing those who are least well-off to have access to exchange improves their welfare. Access to voluntary exchange may well be, for the least well-off, the difference between death and survival. By that logic, access to markets improves the welfare of the least well-off by more, thus satisfying Rawls's principle. Now, the example.

During World War II, British economist R. A. Radford was captured and placed in a German prisoner-of-war camp. Radford noticed the universality of exchange in various camps, and, as an economist, he knew that voluntary exchange makes both parties to the exchange better off. The interesting thing about the prison camp setting was that each prisoner had precisely the same endowment, the contents of a Red Cross packet: tinned milk, jam, butter, biscuits, tinned beef, tinned carrots, chocolate, sugar, treacle, and cigarettes.

Now, if I like two carrots more than one milk, and you like one milk more than two carrots, we can trade. There is no increase in the *total amount of food* in the area, but the *total welfare of the group* and the welfare of each of the two individuals are improved. Any law or restriction requiring that we all have the same distribution would be quite harmful. And such a restriction would harm the most those who have the least because the first few trades yield the highest marginal utility. Because the least well-off start with such a low base of utility, even small increases represent a dramatic increase in their welfare.

Nevertheless, even if trade and exchange are good actions on one's own behalf, what about middlemen? Aren't *they* a problem? After all, in Nozick's example the exchange was direct: the fans paid, Chamberlain received, and both were better off. Suppose someone specialized in such activities, profiting by creating exchanges without producing new value. Would that deviation from the "fair" distribution be defensible?

Radford describes a priest with a sharp eye for exchanges: "Stories circulated of a padre who started off round the camp with a tin of cheese and five cigarettes and returned to his bed with a complete [Red Cross] parcel in addition to his original cheese and cigarettes."[14]

Interestingly, the prisoners in Radford's camp thought that the resulting distribution (padre gets an extra Red Cross packet) was unjust. They had no quarrel with any of the individual transactions, only with the consequent wealth differences. This is the paradox Nozick was getting at: If we start at a just distribution but allow trade, how can an unjust *aggregate* result come from many *individually just* transactions? And if we don't allow trade, aren't we harming those who are least well-off?

Let's grant that every exchange makes both parties better off. That still doesn't establish how a third party, in this case the itinerant padre, can "earn" profits. It depends on what you think the alternative is. Truly voluntary transactions create value for buyers and sellers, and profits are the reward for facilitating transactions *that otherwise would not take place*. The padre might find Allan, who would pay six (or fewer) cigarettes for a tin of beef, and then look for someone such as Barry, who would sell a tin of beef for three (or more) cigarettes. Of course, if these two consumers had *happened* to meet each other, they would have exchanged directly. But finding just the right person to trade with is time-consuming at best and may not happen except by chance. The padre, by searching across trades, *arbitraged* the difference: he could sell the beef to Allan for five cigarettes after buying it from Barry for four. Thus, both Allan and Barry are better off by at least one cigarette, and the padre "profits" one cigarette. If there are many such trades, the padre would have large profits, but these profits are a sign of his having helped many of Rawls's "least well-off."

Truly Voluntary Exchange

The idea of "truly voluntary" exchange comes up often enough that in an earlier paper I tried to formalize both the concept and its definition.[15] I used a neologism, coining the word *euvoluntary,* borrowing the Greek prefix *eu-,* meaning "well" or "truly." *Euvoluntary* exchange requires

1. Conventional ownership of items, services, or currency by both parties

2. Conventional capacity to transfer and assign this ownership to the other party

3. The absence of regret, for both parties, after the exchange, in the sense that both receive value at least as great as was anticipated at the time of the agreement to exchange

4. No large-scale or dangerous uncompensated externalities or costs imposed on third parties without their consent[16] (consent would have to

be explicit and elicited under circumstances that otherwise approximate euvoluntary exchange)

5. The coercion of neither party in the sense of being forced to exchange by threat ("If you don't trade, I will shoot you!")

6. The coercion of neither party in the alternative sense of being harmed by failing to exchange ("If I don't trade, I will starve!")

Categories 1–4 are standard requirements for a valid contract in the common law.[17] Likewise, categories 5 and 6 can be summarized as "no duress," also a requirement for valid contracts under the common law. The fifth requirement is a routine aspect of "voluntary" acts for political scientists. In the political world, "power" means a person (group) can impose his (its) will on others through the threat of violence.[18] That is the sense of the term *coercion* in category 5.

What, then, of profits and the income disparities associated with market processes? Is not the pursuit of profit the goal of capitalism?

Absolutely not, and to say that is to fundamentally misread the argument for capitalism. Capitalism is that system run by entrepreneurs for the benefit of consumers, using market prices as signals. Profits and income inequality are by-products of entrepreneurs' attempts to serve consumers. Wouldn't it be better to allow market processes to produce things but then later to equalize the results by taxing away profits?

It seems tempting to think the answer is "yes." John Stuart Mill certainly thought so.[19] Mill argued that something like a capitalist system is necessary for efficient *production* of goods and services. But the *distribution* of wealth that results from leaving market processes to work without interference is still contingent on state action. Therefore, "free-market" distribution is just as arbitrary as any other distribution the state might select. The state *must* choose, so why not choose the best distribution from the perspective of the society as a whole?

Rawls likewise envisions a sphere where government action is focused primarily on *protecting* liberty (including property rights) and then a separate sphere where government action creates a just redistribution of income, as if these two arenas could be separated.[20] The key problem with this formulation is visible clearly in Mill's formulation and is strongly implicit in Rawls. In

Mill's words, "The things once there, mankind, individually or collectively, can do with them as they like."[21]

"The things once there . . . ." Really? We have no basis for assuming that "the things" will be there unless prices and profits can perform their directive functions. Without the promise of profit, *the things are not there*. In fact, the things are not even things but rather ideas that no one has ever thought about.

A Simple Experiment as an Example

To illustrate the problem of time and the original position as a lottery, I do a classroom experiment. I give each student one "scratch off" ticket from the North Carolina Education Lottery. I ask that the students not scratch off until we decide how we might divide the winnings.

The students are presented with two choices: each person can keep his or her own ticket and accept the profits, recognizing they were due to chance alone, or we can agree to pool all the winnings and divide them evenly among the fifty or so students in the class. After discussing this for a few minutes, we vote. Having done this in several classes, I can say for sure the result is always the same: a large majority favor keeping whatever each person's ticket gives him or her.

I then ask the students to scratch off their tickets. Before class, I enlisted the aid of a "confederate" with some acting experience, so, on cue, she jumps up and starts yelling (quite convincingly), "I won $10,000! I won $10,000!" and runs out of the room.

After a moment of silence, one of the students asks, "Can we vote again?" I nod, and almost all of the students vote this time to distribute the lottery winnings equally. Remember, most of these students had voted that each should keep his or her own winnings *before* the values of the lottery were revealed.

Then the confederate comes back in, and I explain what happened. The room gets very quiet. I'm not sure if the students are embarrassed. But I do know that behind the "veil of ignorance" they vote for equality of opportunity. In the world of realized institutions, they vote for equality of outcome.

It is time to consider the role of profits and the argument that entrepreneurs are "just lucky" and haven't earned the extra wealth that profits represent.

Profits

The advantage of markets is that they make each consumer the boss of his or her consumption decisions, with an ability to use subjective judgments to decide whether he or she is "better off." In a capitalist economy, resources are directed by prices toward their highest valued use. "Value" means the values voted on by consumers, aggregated through the system of supply and delivery. The self-interest of the owners of factors of production and of finished products leads them to direct these articles toward the highest price (value) activity they can discover.

This process of "discovery" operates imperfectly, but that is because the informational requirements of matching production and delivery to an enormously complex set of consumer demands, demands that are constantly changing and being updated, is difficult in the extreme. Much of this information is local or "impacted" in the sense that it is not generally known, or (as with the padre in the prisoner-of-war camp) the information is hiding in plain sight but available only to those who happen to be looking for it.

Profits are the ex post rewards to those who look hardest and most energetically or who perhaps out of sheer dumb luck happen onto the correct answer. Profits are the result of taking a resource out of one use and redirecting it toward an alternative use that consumers prefer.

Ludwig von Mises's statement on this subject is instructive:

> Profits are never normal. They appear only where there is a maladjustment, a divergence between actual production and production as it should be in order to utilize the available material and mental resources for the best possible satisfaction of the wishes of the public. They are the prize of those who remove this maladjustment; they disappear as soon as the maladjustment is entirely removed. In the imaginary construction of an evenly rotating economy there are no profits. There the sum of the prices of the complementary factors of production, due allowance being made for time preference, coincides with the price of the product.[22]

But how much profit is necessary to allow entrepreneurs to carry out this function of directing resources to their higher values uses? Might profits be excessive? And won't the excessive profits improve the welfare of some arbitrarily selected (i.e., "chosen" by market forces) entrepreneurs who are illiterate, undeserving jerks? Mises goes on to make a distinction about what we might think of as "excessive": "The greater the preceding maladjustments, the greater the profit earned by their removal. Maladjustments may sometimes be called excessive. But it is inappropriate to apply the epithet 'excessive' to profits."[23]

Profits accrue to redirecting resources in response to consumers' "orders." If resources are badly misdirected compared to what consumers want, then the profits can be quite large. But no one knew about the misdirected resources or the profit opportunity until the entrepreneur proved their existence by making profits. Anyone could have done it, perhaps, but that particular entrepreneur *did* do it.

The problem with this reasoning is that it stops short. The income differences are indeed *morally* arbitrary, but they are by no means *consequentially* arbitrary. And Rawls's central justification for income inequality is not moral but consequential. It is stated in terms of benefits to those who are least well-off. Capitalists may be lucky, at least in part. But even if they do not fully *deserve* the profits they reap, it does not follow that the state or "the people" deserve those gains instead. By creating a system where work and risk are rewarded handsomely but where the benefits in terms of lower prices and useful products for the least well-off are distributed across the entire population, capitalism advances the asserted goals of the Rawlsian project. No country that has adopted capitalism has failed to prosper; no country that has tried anything else has broken out of poverty. We all should be Rawlsekians now.

4

The Role of Negative Rights

Aeon J. Skoble*

CONTEMPORARY DISCUSSIONS OF social justice often elide the distinction between justice in outcome and justice in process. For example, institutions such as the right against self-incrimination in criminal trials or the right to vote are ones that provide justice in process. People typically do realize this, even though it's conceivable that they could lead to unjust outcomes (guilty parties escaping punishment; bad candidates elected). But more often, the category "social justice" is invoked in the context of justice in outcome. For example, that there is wealth inequality is frequently cited as a failure to achieve justice. So, on this view, institutions that redistribute wealth are intended as ones that provide justice in outcomes. In this essay I hope to show why incautious blurring of the distinction between process and outcome makes justice harder to achieve. Some institutions may turn out to be self-undermining. Egalitarianism as an ideal can be served by a robust conception of rights, but this in turn requires a philosophically coherent account of both rights and egalitarianism. Equality before the law turns out to be a necessary condition of social justice, but insufficient where institutions have incentives to overlook or ignore it.

Our legal system features rights. In the legal context, rights are legally enforceable claims established by the political framework. We also speak of rights in the moral context. Rights in this discourse are not justified by the political framework—e.g., when we speak of a government's human rights abuses, we are not concerned with whether the treatment is allowable by that nation's laws, but with whether those laws comport with a philosophical theory of

---

*Aeon J. Skoble is professor of philosophy at Bridgewater State University.

rights. My argument is primarily about the moral theory of rights, although of course there is overlap, as we would hope that the rights we are said to have or not have in the political/legal order are based on a philosophically coherent account of moral rights.

I argue we should understand rights as rationally justifiable moral claims. We each have a rationally justifiable moral claim to be treated as equals in our social status; that is, the structure of the political/legal order cannot justifiably assign positions of authority or power to Smith that could not be enjoyed by Jones. Smith can have no rights over Jones that Jones does not have over Smith. The usual caveat to that claim is "except by mutual consent," but this presupposes that Smith and Jones are moral equals. So the fundamental moral equality we ascribe to them is the rationale for the legitimacy of the equal liberty they enjoy. In other words, the underlying moral equality justifies the claim of equal rights, not the other way around. This is relevant to the way institutions are structured, informally as well as formally—for example, if a law seems well-intentioned and neutral, but is in fact used to disproportionately disadvantage some segment of the population, then we can say that rights are not being fully respected.

Perhaps ironically, democratic processes are not a guarantee of equal rights in the fuller sense I am describing here. Democratic processes are not sufficient for protecting equal rights or for promoting prosperity, largely due to factors such as voter ignorance, bias, and corruption. An outcome can be democratically justified, yet profoundly inegalitarian with respect to rights. People can therefore inadvertently fail to be working towards social justice, despite their intention to do so, by being inattentive to these matters. Clarifying the meaning of social justice thus requires a philosophically coherent account of what rights and equality actually mean in a moral sense; otherwise those concepts are likely to be misapplied in the political/legal order.

Rights can be understood as correlating with duties (Smith's right being related to Jones's duty), and this helps illuminate the common distinction between positive and negative rights. If Smith has a positive right to X, it means that Jones has a duty to provide or relinquish X. If Smith has a negative right to X, it means that Jones may not interfere with Smith's pursuit of X. In the latter case, what does the placeholder "Jones" actually signify? Everyone. It would not be a "rationally justifiable moral claim" unless everyone had a moral duty of noninterference towards Smith. But then what does "Jones" signify in the former case? It cannot there be referring to everyone, because that would imply that Smith had a right to 7.5 billion Xs. That means that the placeholder refers to some particular person who has this duty, or to no one. If no one has that duty, then Smith doesn't have such a right. Under what set of conditions, then, could the placeholder refer to a particular person? One possibility is that Smith has a contractual arrangement with Jones which stipulates their rights and duties towards each other. In this case, both placeholders "Smith" and "Jones" must refer to individual people—people who have entered into such a contractual arrangement. Neither placeholder could be "everyone," as contracts are agreements between persons. Under a contractual arrangement like this, Smith's right clearly fits the description of a rationally justifiable moral claim, given that both agreed to the contract. But if Smith doesn't have a contractual relationship with a particular Jones, then the placeholder "Jones" cannot refer to anyone, unless we arbitrarily pick someone to be the bearer of this duty nonconsensually. As the latter would not be rationally justifiable, we can conclude that Smith cannot have a positive right to any X outside of a contractual arrangement.

In the last sentence of the previous paragraph, I asserted that it wouldn't be rationally justifiable to impose nonconsensual obligations on Jones to provide something for Smith. That presupposes a missing premise, of course: the moral equality of Smith and Jones. It's because Smith and Jones are moral equals that it would not be rationally justifiable to treat one as a nonconsensual servant to the other. Conversely, it's precisely a claim that Smith and Jones are unequal that underwrites the relationship between a feudal lord and a serf, or a master and a slave. The moral inequality of persons presupposed by those systems is the rationale for the legitimation of the nonconsensual service obligations. Presupposing, on the other hand, the moral equality of persons, it can then be seen why a nonconsensual service obligation would be not rationally justifiable—it would fail the simplest test of universalizability.

Treating Smith and Jones as equals requires equal respect for their rights, which according to the argument I've outlined here means respect for their equal negative rights and respect for their consensual contractual arrangements. This is justice in process: we regard Smith and Jones as equals, and we design institutions of the political/legal order to treat them equally. However, this is where an incautious conception of egalitarianism can become self-undermining. If we look at an outcome, rather than a process, say a wealth disparity between Smith and Jones, and conclude that egalitarianism requires redistribution from one to the other, we would be obliged to undercut the sense of egalitarianism already established. Jones's positive right to be provided Xs by Smith has already been shown to be incompatible with Jones and Smith being moral equals. Demanding justice in outcome may thus entail violation of the morally more fundamental justice in process. The seeming contradiction of the preceding sentence suggests that defining social justice by outcome rather than process is not coherent. Justice can't logically entail injustice. Yet wealth inequality does cause people to assume injustice. This may be due to the confusion about process and outcome. The wealth disparity between Smith and Jones may well be causally related to process injustice. For example, if Jones is a serf and Smith is a feudal baron, or, less anachronistically, if Jones is a member of an ethnic minority which is barred by law from entering higher-paying occupations and Smith is a member of the group to which no such restrictions obtain. In this case, we would be missing an important aspect of the inequality if we focused on the wealth inequality and not on the legal inequality, for the latter is the cause of the former. The true injustice is that Smith and Jones are not treated as equals by the political/legal order. Their wealth disparity is a symptom, not a cause, of the more fundamental inequality.

But what about wealth inequality under conditions of moral and legal egalitarianism? If we are moral equals, and live in a political/legal order with institutions that treat us as such, we will surely end up with wealth inequality. This is because treating Smith and Jones as equals means equal respect for their rights, which, again, means respect for their equal negative rights and respect for their consensual contractual arrangements. It's a virtual certainty that this will result in wealth inequality, since different people have different skills which are valued differently by others. The better shoemaker will command a higher price for shoes, the most popular singer will sell more records, the world-record athlete will be sought for endorsements. And the numbers matter: if a million people pay Smith a dollar each for what Smith does, and a hundred people pay Jones a thousand dollars each for what Jones does, Smith becomes considerably more wealthy than Jones, despite the fact that each individual person values Jones's work much more highly than Smith's. But Jones is not being treated unjustly in these circumstances. The best way to actually treat everyone as equals, then, is to protect rights equally, the protection of negative rights and the respect for consensual contractual arrangements that classical liberalism is known for—social justice in process, not in outcome.

A more troubling conundrum arises, however, when some of the institutions of the political/legal order overlook or ignore the moral equality of persons that justice requires. We see this phenomenon when some segments of society actively conspire to gain privilege at the expense of others, or when poorly chosen policies have unintended consequences that produce this real breakdown in process justice. It would be an obvious violation of equality to have a rule forbidding a class of the population from pursuing an occupation, such as "Women are not permitted to become physicians" or "African-Americans are not permitted to become attorneys." Yet a similar effect is attained via occupational licensure regulations and wage floors. Laws such as these inhibit people of fewer means from advancing, thus perpetuating and exacerbating a wealth disparity. It appears to the incautious observer that this is merely outcome injustice, when in fact it is process injustice. By overlooking the fact that the wealth disparity is caused by a process injustice, effective solutions are obscured from view. It would be as if I had a pain caused by a nail in my foot, and I kept taking painkillers but ignored the nail. The pain wouldn't actually go away, and I would conclude that the painkillers were insufficient and take stronger ones. Similarly, in an attempt to eradicate drug use, minority populations are disproportionately incarcerated, thereby ensuring that they remain marginalized. To ameliorate this sort of injustice, then, requires not heavier doses of painkillers, but removing the nail. It may not be an injustice that Smith is wealthier than Jones, but it is an injustice if Jones is impoverished due to a political/legal order which does not treat the rights of all with equal respect.

Another related conceptual confusion that leads to inadequate solutions is the conflation of disparity per se with injustice. Imagine a state of affairs (*a*) in which Smith earns $90,000 per year and Jones earns $20,000 per year. Now say we could change things either such that (*b*) Smith earns $50,000 per year and Jones earns $30,000 per year, or (*c*) Smith was earning $200,000 a year and Jones $60,000 a year. In (*b*), the inequality has been greatly decreased. In (*c*), the inequality has increased considerably. But plainly (*c*) is better for Jones than (*a*). What Jones should want, and what we should insist on, is a set of social institutions which allows for transitions from (*a*) to (*c*). In other words, the inequality of wealth between Smith and Jones may be a concomitant of tangible *increases* to Jones's well-being. This presupposes that the institutional arrangements that allow for Jones to get wealthier are also the ones that allow for Smith to get *a lot* wealthier. I suspect that this is precisely what market economies do, although my point here is that *whichever* set of institutions promotes (*a*) to (*c*) shifts would be in everyone's best interests, as opposed to either (*a*) to (*b*) shifts or the status quo. If it *is* what market economies do, it would have the added advantage of instantiating social justice as I have defined it: the genuine egalitarianism of a political/ legal order of equal respect for everyone's negative rights and equal respect for their consensual contractual arrangements. By "contractual arrangements," I do not refer to hypothetical social contract ideals which presume consent, but actual arrangements made by real individuals with actual consent and the mutual benefit that typically accrues.

If we are interested in social justice, we should be interested in discovering which institutional arrangements in a political/legal order map to the moral equality of persons. If treating everyone as moral equals means respect for their rights and for their consensual contracts, this entails abolishing laws that fail to treat everyone as equals or which do not respect people's contractual arrangements. Restrictions on transactional freedom, especially those which place a disproportionate burden on already-marginalized groups, will fail to respect rights and exacerbate their impoverishment. What's challenging is seeing beyond the symptoms to the actual disease. We see a wealthy person in a mansion, and then a poor person in a shack. What is bad is the poverty of the second person, not the disparity between the two. (After all, no one sheds a tear because the person with $5 million isn't as well off as Bill Gates.) If we can alleviate the poverty, the disparity should become less important.

Two things we must avoid, however: addressing one inequality by introducing a new one, and failing to remove the source of the problem. If we try to remedy wealth inequality by coercive redistribution, barriers to entrepreneurship, and wage floors, we will be committing both mistakes. First of all, these mechanisms fail to respect people's rights to choose what they do with their lives. To coercively require or forbid action is to direct one person's actions towards another's will. This makes the first subordinate to the second, not equal. Second of all, these mechanisms do not speak to the source of the problem. Ironically, by focusing on the inequality and not the poverty, the inequality persists: the poor person receives some amelioration, but is still regarded as unequal and facing the same barriers to advancement and the same stigmas.

Some might object to this model of justice by saying that its reliance on rights is a smokescreen that masks oppression. But that's an odd sort of objection: saying that oppression is bad is simply the converse of saying that freedom is good. People are typically impoverished by oppression, so we should all agree that removing oppression, i.e., increasing freedom, would be a good thing. But getting in the way of that agreement is the idea that the impoverishment of Jones is *caused by* the wealth of Smith. In non-rights-based systems, this may in fact be true: Smith could be a slave owner, or a feudal baron, or someone in today's world with sufficient political influence to get special privileges, either through direct transfer or protection from competition. In cases like these, justice requires eliminating those privileges—but not just for Smith. The very mechanisms that apportion those privileges have to go. In other words, it's not that *Smith* is unfairly shielded from competition, but that *anyone* can have that kind of pull in the first place. The complaint that the rich have an undue influence over political favors is legitimate, but it is clear that the more effective solution would be the abolition of those favors. As long as there are spoils to be obtained, someone will obtain them. Rather than worry about who has the right sort of access to secure special privileges, better to end special privileges. Besides being more effective, this is also consonant with the idea of equality of persons. The very concept of "special privilege" suggests an inequality. If the special privileges are part of the political process, then it's a violation of equality of persons. But if Smith's wealth is not the product of special influence with the political process, nor obtained by violating the equal rights of others, then it's false to claim that Smith's wealth is the *cause* of Jones's poverty.

When we talk about "systematic inequality" or "cycles of poverty," we are typically referring to the products of *violations* of equal rights, not the result of respect for equal rights. It is therefore a mistake to conclude that the solution to wealth inequality is further political inequality. Wealth inequality by itself is not objectionable, but poverty and oppression and political inequality are. If alleviating poverty resulted in greater inequality, as in the thought experiment earlier, it would be a good thing, not a bad thing. And there's good reason to think removing political inequality would help and not hinder that effort. Equal respect for a robust conception of negative rights and freedom to contract is the kind of egalitarianism that is most conducive to bringing about the social justice results people say they want.

So what, concretely, would be the right steps to egalitarianism? Egalitarianism as an ideal can be served by a robust conception of rights, but I have tried to establish that this requires a philosophically coherent account of both rights and egalitarianism. I have argued that equal respect for the negative rights of all persons is morally more fundamental than wealth egalitarianism, and that in general, justice in process is more consistent with that respect than justice in outcome, which would contradict it. The concrete steps suggested by this model are one, to remove all barriers to entrepreneurship, wage floors, special protections for the well-connected, and legal inequalities among persons; two, to rethink coercive redistribution as a solution to poverty, seeing it as treating a symptom and not a cause; and three, repealing laws that are either designed to target, or inadvertently target, some groups disproportionately, such as incarceration resulting from the war on drugs or warrantless surveillance resulting from the war on terror. Real egalitarianism results from the absence of both special privilege for the well-connected and inadequate protection of rights for the not-so-well-connected. Real equality is the equal protection of everyone's negative rights and respect for their contractual arrangements.

The Impossibility of Egalitarian Ends

Jeremy Jackson and Jeffrey Palm*

ONE OF THE many dangers of the modern egalitarian philoso-phy is that it hides its true objectives behind the guise of social justice. Adher-ents would insist that they reject the materialistic values of their free-market foes. However, not far below the surface commitment to relational equality and disruption of social hierarchy lies their true motive: material equality. The modern egalitarian is shifting from a focus on equality of relationships to a focus on equality in quality of life and more comprehensive measures of well-being.[1] Whether the egalitarian desires to create policies that lead to equality in distribution of wealth or to equality in well-being, it does not mat-ter. Both are impossible ends. Inequalities in wealth and well-being are due in part to inequalities in the distribution of social capital, which can be neither removed nor transferred from one individual to another. Thus, inequalities in wealth and well-being are the inevitable result of a system reliant on humans autonomously making decisions.

The Origins of Egalitarianism

Egalitarianism as an academic school of thought did not actually begin to concretize until the post–World War II era, although certain basic ideas go back as far as biblical times (equality of souls but not "earthly" equality).[2] Many of egalitarianism's roots are traceable to a particular understanding of the philosophy of altruism: the idea that a person has but two options in

---

*Jeremy Jackson is director of the North Dakota Center for the Study of Public Choice and Private Enterprise. Jeffrey Palm is an undergraduate fellow at the North Dakota Center for the Study of Public Choice and Private Enterprise.

life—to sacrifice one's self in the service of others or to sacrifice others in the service of one's self.[3] From this understanding of altruism, egalitarians derive a fundamental misunderstanding of "the zero-sum game." Because they mistakenly think of all goods and services as slices of a (finite) pie, they deduce that for one person to gain, another must lose. From this either–or conception of altruism, egalitarianism concludes that the only moral thing to do is to sacrifice one's self in the service of others.[4]

Karl Marx himself was no egalitarian, yet many of his ideas have helped to shape modern egalitarianism. His focus on conflict and the exploitation of the subjugated worker, derived from his misconceptions of the labor market and the means of production, contributed to the mid- to late-nineteenth-century push for a shorter workday and higher wages.[5] This push then fed into Otto von Bismarck's creation of the first modern welfare state in Germany in an effort to combat Marx's more revolutionary socialism. Anthony P. Mueller states that "social policy was foremost national policy and the social security system was primarily an instrument to lure the workers away from private and communitarian systems into the arms of the State."[6]

By the early 1940s, which saw the publication of the Beveridge Report in the United Kingdom in 1942 and Franklin Roosevelt's suggestion of the "Second Bill of Rights" in 1944, contemporary crystallization and acceptance of the principles of "distributive justice" had taken place.[7]

Philosopher John Rawls, another one of egalitarianism's most prominent historical standard bearers, was himself not strictly an egalitarian. However, his seminal work, *A Theory of Justice*, is counted among the most foundational of contributions.[8] In this volume, Rawls explains his most influential concept, the "difference principle," which "gives expression to the idea that natural endowments are undeserved."[9] Rawls felt (as do the so-called luck egalitarians) that just because a person is more intelligent or a naturally gifted musician or better looking or raised with better values, or something else, it does not entitle him or her to be better off than others. To Rawls, being more successful than others by using one's natural endowments (or by any other means) can be justified only if people who are worse off are made better off because of that success.

On the face of it and according to their own descriptions, egalitarians have differing ideas with respect to defining the concepts "justice" and "equality."

However, all schools of egalitarian thought lead to the same ultimate goal: distribution.

Most egalitarians do not actually advocate equality of outcomes because most realize that a rigid insistence on the tall being made short or the intelligent being made less so would lead to disastrous consequences. What they want is what they consider to be "fair" distribution.[10] So their basic notions of equality hinge on whether distribution is just or in the case of relational egalitarianism that societal relationships are just. However, before discussing the two broad categories of luck egalitarianism and relational egalitarianism, we must say a few more words regarding the concept of justice.

To many libertarians and classical liberals, the claim that a free market, an impersonal mechanism governed by the laws of nature, is either just or unjust is absurd. This claim is evidence of a complete misunderstanding of how the market functions. As Hayek aptly points out, such claims amount to nothing other than anthropomorphism.[11]

However, those who advocate free markets certainly cannot claim to have ever actually *seen* them. Much of the egalitarians' perceptions of injustice are the symptoms of the very root causes that such advocates devote the bulk of their work to exposing, refuting, and denouncing. This feature of the justice problem is twofold: on the one hand, egalitarianism incorrectly concludes that the corruption observed is simply the way free-market capitalism works; on the other hand, some market advocates inadvertently defend the corruption as though it were free-market capitalism. It is imperative to acknowledge that which is *correctly* perceived as unjust as such and simultaneously to point to its being but a symptom of *corruption* that is rooted in *government intervention* in the market. It must always be stressed that this corruption is *not* a product of free-market capitalism because it then becomes possible to illustrate the clear distinction between calls for justice that are grounded in reality and those that are founded on anthropomorphism.

Unfortunately, this distinction does not usually carry much weight in the view of the egalitarian, who frequently finds it completely irrelevant. As David Kelley points out, every form of "social justice" rests on the belief that individual ability is a social asset, a collective good.[12] John Rawls wrote, "Injustice, then, is simply inequalities that are not to the benefit of all."[13] On this point, Rawls and Hayek tend to agree. "The most common attempts to give meaning to the concept of 'social justice,'" states Hayek, "resort to egalitarian considerations and argue that every departure from equality of material benefits enjoyed has to be justified by some recognizable common interest which these differences serve."[14]

Luck egalitarianism—what Murray Rothbard refers to as "old" or "classical" egalitarianism—is more *overtly* concerned with distribution of income and wealth.[15] It holds that no one should have to be worse off just because they were born into unfortunate circumstance or were the victim of a natural disaster or made a mistake in business or are unintelligent or something else. Rothbard terms this egalitarianism "old" because modern-day egalitarians have realized the limitations of using the mere poverty of individuals as moral leverage for their demands for justice.

Relational egalitarianism (sometimes referred to as "democratic egalitarianism") has been discovered to be a much more effective means of moral intimidation when it comes to insisting that justice be done. Rothbard terms this viewpoint "new group egalitarianism." The significance of the "group" distinction will become clear as we delve a bit deeper into its meanings.

The new-group egalitarians are concerned primarily with social hierarchies—specifically, *domination and subjection, honor and stigmatization,* and *high and low standing in the eyes and calculations of others* (calculations as in government policy, for example).[16] However, one must always remember that these egalitarians employ this technique to rationalize, justify, and effect their ultimate goal of distribution. Sometimes they assert that just distribution is what is necessary in order to bring about just social relationships. At other times, they assert that policies to affect just social relationships are necessary to bring about just distribution. Whether the cart comes before or behind the horse makes little difference; the end result is always governmental use of violence, coercion, and central planning to affect distribution (of other people's money).[17]

Groups such as ethnic minorities, genders, laborers, elders, the young, and virtually any other group conceivable conveniently fit into one or more of the social hierarchies listed earlier.[18] New groups are readily added to the seemingly endless list whenever anybody says the magic word *injustice,* and anyone who would oppose (re)distribution to one of these groups must be considered an oppressor. Rothbard sums it up nicely by paraphrasing Joseph Sobran: "[I]n the current lexicon, 'need' is the desire of people to loot the wealth of others; 'greed' is the desire of those others to keep the money they have earned; and 'compassion' is the function of those who negotiate the transfer."[19] The insidiousness of relational egalitarianism lies in its approach to distribution. Egalitarians have erroneously concluded that the cause of economic difficulties is rooted in the unjust social hierarchies. Therefore, it follows (they conclude) that in order to affect just distribution, they must design a system that eliminates the unjust social hierarchies.[20]

Although unjust social relationships certainly cause an incalculable amount of (often catastrophic) damage, the currently fashionable notion that these relationships are the root causes of economic difficulties rather than the other way around is incorrect.[21] Economic difficulties can always be shown to be the ultimate root causes of the unjust social hierarchies or relationships. They arise as resentment for being treated unjustly, as rationalization or justification for treating (or having treated) others unjustly, as a means of securing the ability to treat others unjustly in the future, and so on. Upon observing social injustices, we should ask ourselves what motives the perpetrators might have for their unjust conduct. The origins of the injustice are never arbitrary. They are economic. They may be completely immoral and thoroughly unjust, but the fact remains that they exist because the perpetrators hope to derive some benefit from them.[22]

Sources of Inequality

Regardless of its rhetoric, at its core egalitarianism has as its main goal the elimination of wealth inequality. It has been argued that wealth inequality itself comes from one primary source: capital.[23] Yet capital itself can be placed into many categories. Physical capital includes the factories, buildings, computers, land, and infrastructure that are ultimately used as the inputs to production. Human capital comes from the knowledge and creativity possessed by human beings that gives them the capability to contribute to production. Commonly overlooked but increasingly important is the concept of social capital, which refers to the "trust and norms of civic cooperation . . . essential to well-functioning societies."[24] To the extent that wealth can be taxed and redistributed, the egalitarian would argue that the desired end of equality of distribution is achievable.

Physical capital and the income stream it produces can be taxed from one individual and transferred to another. Thus, egalitarians conclude that any wealth inequalities perpetrated by differences in the distribution of physical capital ownership can be remedied by the well-intentioned taxing powers. To this end, proposals have advocated a sweeping global tax on wealth and expansion of the estate tax.[25] However, taxation and redistribution of wealth will be able to produce sustained equality in wealth only under a limited set of circumstances. A wealth tax can be effective if the only sources of wealth inequality are inequalities in the distribution of physical capital. If there are other sources of wealth inequality, such redistribution will not be possible with a simple tax system and will be effective only under continuous management by a totalitarian regime. "So long as the belief in 'social justice' governs political action, this process must progressively approach nearer and nearer to a totalitarian system."[26]

Wealth inequalities caused by differences in the distribution of human capital are more difficult yet not impossible for the state to overcome. Although it isn't possible to directly take one person's human-capital stock and give it to another, it is possible to tax the wage income derived from some persons' human capital in order to provide educational opportunities for others.[27] However, an increasing amount of evidence has shown that the labor market rewards and punishes certain noncognitive traits, including personality, with wage differentials.[28] An individual's psychological traits and characteristics cannot be instilled in others through mere education. The family also plays a significant role in the development of human capital, which makes it even more difficult for redistribution to be effective.[29] Rawls himself states that the family, with its effects on the development of the natural capacities, will ultimately always stand in the way of "equal chances of achievement," unless a solution is found that will "mitigate this fact."[30]

Perhaps most problematic for the egalitarian goal of equality of distribution are the differences in wealth and income that are perpetrated by social capital and networks.

Wage earnings aren't derived solely from an individual's human capital. Douglas North argues that informal social norms and culture are critical to an understanding of the sources of prosperity.[31] One way that this idea has been evidenced and measured in the literature is through the concept of social capital popularized by the works of Robert D. Putnam.[32]

Social capital itself has proven difficult to define, with no one definition being agreed upon in the literature. Emily Chamlee-Wright defines it as "a complex structure made up of community norms, social networks, favors given and received, potluck suppers, book groups, church bazaars, and neighborhood play groups."[33]

Even with the complexities and difficulties in measurement associated with social capital, a large empirical literature has shown that social capital and networks add significantly to an individual's labor earnings.[34] Human capital and social capital often function as substitutes.[35] Yet not much is known about the production of social capital, unlike about physical capital, with its capacity for direct redistribution, and about human capital, with its capacity for indirect redistribution. We may in a limited sense be able to tax some of the labor returns to social capital, but it is yet unclear how that tax income can be used for the creation of social capital.[36] Although we know that there are great benefits to both the individual and society at large from social capital and that societies don't flourish in its absence, we don't have a well-developed theory or policy on how to create social trust and cohesion. Perhaps the most obvious policy recommendations (as evidenced by the empirical relationships) are among the most illiberal because social capital is known to be highly related to racial, ethnic, and religious homogeneity.[37] As it turns out, people trust those who are most like them.

There is also an empirical literature that links free-market institutions to measures of social capital and trust. Although some of the results in this literature are mixed,[38] several papers suggest a positive and causal relationship between economic freedom and social capital.[39] In this light, it is possible that inequalities caused by gains from returns on social capital may to some degree be the kind that Rawls deems acceptable. Social capital brings about benefits to society as a whole. Yet those benefits are not spread equally among all of society's members but accrue in increased quantities to those with the more favored social network. The inequality of incomes and wealth could be taxed away, but this increase in taxation and redistribution decreases economic freedom, with a resultant deleterious effect on social capital. These inequalities serve the "social good." Attempting to redistribute them away may cause the benefits that all receive to disappear.

Given the impossibility of equality of distribution, the only option available to meet the egalitarian end of equality of distribution is complete totalitarianism. Only when every facet of each individual's life is completely controlled by the state in a continuous manner can equality be achieved. If the system is ever left to operate on its own, inequality in distribution will be the result.

New Directions for Egalitarianism

As discussed in a previous section, relational egalitarians may not see equality of wealth as their most desired outcome. They instead desire equality of social relationships. To them, equality of wealth has been the most direct path to achieve this desired end. However, new trends are developing.

There has been increased attention in the economics literature on the failings of policies that target economic growth and income in an effort to make lives better off. This argument has been the apex of the emerging literature on the economics of happiness. Ever since the publication of Richard Easterlin's work, which popularized the Easterlin Paradox, some of the literature has set out to explain why increases in a country's income do not correlate with higher levels of self-reported happiness among its citizens.[40] Indeed, now even former Federal Reserve chairman Ben Bernanke argues that "GDP is not itself the final objective of policy."[41] The better objective is well-being (happiness), and the egalitarian now has a new direction for policy in promoting equality of well-being. Many advocate augmenting the national measurement of gross domestic product with a national happiness accounting.[42]

In shifting the policy focus away from wealth inequality and toward inequality of well-being, a host of interventionist policies are opened up to the egalitarians' disposal.[43] Subjective well-being measures are regarded as comprehensive measures of quality of life, and they have many correlates. A nonexhaustive list of correlates[44] includes variables such as income,[45] education,[46] environment,[47] materialism,[48] mortality,[49] employment,[50] personality,[51] and even social capital and trust.[52] The shift in focus away from income and toward a more broadly defined well-being measure can open up a Pandora's box of progressive policy proposals.

However, the egalitarians' search for policies to attain equality of well-being may in fact lead to the unraveling of well-being itself. A large literature demonstrates that autonomy of individual choice leads to greater subjective well-being,[53] and an ever-expanding literature links high economic freedom to greater subjective well-being.[54] The problems this literature presents for the goals of redistribution are in addition to the inherent difficulties in distributing such fundamental determinants of well-being as personality traits and psychological characteristics. Perhaps a more pervasive problem for proponents of policies for happiness is that of adaptation.

Adaptation in the happiness literature refers to humans' innate ability to adapt to new circumstances. In fact, one explanation of the Easterlin Paradox is that increases in income can fail to create increases in happiness because people rapidly adjust to their higher incomes. Although there may be an initial temporal boost in happiness from increased income, the effects do not persist in the long run. Adaptation also explains why poor and impoverished countries sometimes report much higher levels of happiness than might seem reasonable.[55] People have a baseline equilibrium level of happiness, and any deviations from that baseline are short-lived. If well-being inequalities are taken to be meaningful, then any policies implemented with the intention of combating them must target an element of well-being that isn't subject to adaptation. Among the correlates of subjective well-being, social capital is often referred to as a prominent candidate policy target that is immune to the problems of adaptation.[56] Thus, if egalitarianism pursues equality in the domain of well-being, it will still find itself trying to accomplish an impossible task in determining the distribution of social capital.

Conclusion

Although egalitarians may be reluctant to admit their focus on equality of distribution in philosophical debate, this singular policy focus has emerged even among the so-called new-group egalitarians with their emphasis on social hierarchy. Equality of social relations, they assert, must begin from the establishment of economic equality of wealth. Unfortunately for these egalitarians, wealth and well-being are partly determined by the distribution of social capital. Social capital is distinct from physical capital and human capital in that it can neither be removed from an individual nor imputed to another. A sovereign's inability to distribute social capital results in an impossible equality of distribution in wealth or well-being short of totalitarian control of the entire system.

PART II

The Historical Development of Egalitarian Ideas

6

Religion and the Idea of Human Dignity

Peter J. Hill*

CLASSICAL LIBERALS BRING much to the debate on modern egalitarianism, in particular their understanding of the overriding importance of moral agency and universal human dignity. Many classical liberals ground their understanding of human equality in natural-rights theory, whereas others reach similar conclusions about equality through consequentialist arguments, such as rule utilitarianism.[1] Whatever the basis for the concept of equal human dignity, it is important to understand that this understanding of the person is, in a historical context, a recent event.

For most of the recorded history of humankind, both mores and legal structures sanctioned differences in people. Not all humans were seen as moral agents capable of self-directedness. Slavery was almost universally sanctioned. Legal distinctions based on ethnicity, race, gender, and social class were justified as inevitable and appropriate. This essay traces out the evolution of belief from fundamental human inequality to universal equality.

The roots of human inequality lie deep in human history. Although a strong advocate of the virtuous life, Aristotle (384–322 BCE) believed that such virtue could be achieved only by certain members of society, certainly not by slaves and women: "There are species in which a distinction is already marked, immediately at birth, between those of its members who are being ruled and those who are intended to rule. . . . Again, the relation of the male to the female is naturally that of the superior to the inferior—of the ruling

---

*Peter J. Hill is professor emeritus at Wheaton College and senior fellow at the Property and Environment Research Center.

to the ruled. It is thus clear that, just as some are by nature free, so others are by nature slaves."[2]

Aristotle was not unique in his sanctioning of slavery. In early history, there were almost no defenders of human dignity outside of the Jewish world,[3] and in fact slavery was so common that articulating a reason for slavery was not even considered important. According to Thomas Sowell, "Aristotle had attempted to justify slavery, but many other Western and non-Western philosophers alike took it so much for granted that they felt no need to explain or justify it at all."[4] Other social differentiations based on ethnicity, gender, race, or social background likewise required no moral justification but were accepted as facts of life.

So if human equality and the rule of law have not been generally accepted until recently, what has caused this dramatic change in our basic anthropology? As in biological evolution, survival of the fittest has been a strong influence in cultural evolution. Nevertheless, belief structures can have a dramatic impact on the course of cultural evolution.[5] The economist Dani Rodrik argues, "Much human behavior is driven by abstract ideals, sacred values, or conceptions of loyalty that cannot be reduced to human ends."[6]

Two prominent thinkers, intellectual historian Larry Siedentop (2014) and French philosopher Luc Ferry (2011), argue that it took a metaphysical concept, seeing individuals as created in the image of God, to overcome the almost universal belief that people are fundamentally unequal. Despite its origins in early Jewish history and then in Christian anthropology, the concept of human equality took a long period of time to work its way into philosophical and political thinking before finally becoming fully ingrained in modern thought. Today almost everyone starts the discussion about egalitarianism with the assumption that all people should be free moral agents and that equality before the law is one of the most basic ways of expressing and defending that moral equality.

Luc Ferry argues that Christianity represented a dramatically different worldview than Greek philosophy because it contested the Greek aristocratic idea of differential human endowments and hence potentialities. "In direct contradiction [to Greek philosophy], Christianity was to introduce the notion that humanity was fundamentally identical, that men were equal in dignity—an unprecedented idea at that time and one to which our world owes its entire democratic inheritance. But this notion of equality did not come from nowhere."[7] "But with Christianity," Ferry explains,

> the idea of a common humanity acquired a new strength. Based on the equal dignity of all human beings, it was to take on an ethical aspect. As soon as free will becomes the foundation of moral action and virtue is located not in natural, "unequal gifts," but in the use to which they are put, then it goes without saying that all men are of equal merit. Humanity would never again be able to divide itself (philosophically) according to a natural and aristocratic hierarchy of beings: between superior and inferior, gifted and less gifted, masters and slaves. From then on, according to Christians, we are all "brothers" on the same level as creatures of God and endowed with the same capacity to choose whether to act well or badly. Rich or poor, intelligent or simple: it no longer holds any importance. And this idea of equality leads to a primarily ethical conception of humanity. The Greek concept of barbarians—synonymous with a "stranger" (anyone not Greek)—soon disappeared to be replaced by the conviction that humanity is ONE. To conclude we could say that Christianity is the first *universalist* ethos; *universalism* meaning the doctrine or belief in universal salvation.[8]

Although Ferry recognizes the historical influence of Christianity on philosophical thought, he is an atheist and hence does not spend much time discussing the actual theological doctrines that produced this radical departure from conventional thought. In reality, it was Judaism that provided the original foundation for dignity for all because of the concept of the *imago Dei,* a concept that is also crucial to Christian theology and anthropology. If all humans are bearers of the image of the omniscient, omnipotent God of the universe, then social and political equality are logical necessities of that concept.

If Jewish and Christian thought is responsible for the modern concept of human equality, why the long lag between the time this idea originated and the time it and institutions changed? Intellectual historian Larry Siedentop, like Ferry, sees the spread of Christian thinking as disruptive to the Greek and Roman idea that some are born to command and others to obey. Siedentop recognizes, however, that changes in fundamental concepts, such as the revolution in moral equality, require a long period of time to realize their full impact: "Centuries would be required for the implications of Christian moral beliefs to be drawn out and clarified—and even more time would pass before long established social practices or institutions were reshaped by these implications."[9]

The Jewish belief in human agency and moral equality manifested itself in many forms. That God chose to reveal his plan for humankind through a particular people, the Israelites, makes the universal claims of human dignity somewhat less obvious, but the creation account provides the metaphysical grounding for human dignity for all. The fundamental concept is in Genesis 1:27: "So God created man in his own image, in the image of God he created him; male and female he created them."[10]

According to Joshua Berman, the Pentateuch, which is the first five books of Hebrew scripture, describes a social order that recognizes human dignity and that was much different from the order prevailing throughout the ancient Near East.[11] Political and social hierarchy had strong metaphysical legitimation in the non-Israelite world, but the theology of the covenant in the Pentateuch rejects this hierarchy. In one of the most radical texts in ancient political economy, God asks for a commitment from all the Israelites, not just from their leaders. Even though Moses was the spokesperson for the people, the actual covenant was between God and all of the people, including the women and children.[12] Berman argues that "it is in the covenant, properly conceived, that we may discern a radically new understanding of the cosmic role of the common man within the thought systems of the ancient Near East, one that constituted the basis of an egalitarian social order."[13] The request of a commitment by all members of the society implies a strong sense of universal human agency, the ability of all to decide when asked to decide yea or nay to a moral proposition.

For Siedentop, "Christian moral intuitions played a pivotal role in shaping the discourse that gave rise to modern liberalism and secularism."[14] He sees the Apostle Paul as the primary intellectual force in the development and spread of the concept of moral equality and moral agency of all people because Paul provided an ontological foundation for the concept of the individual. His Damascus Road encounter with Christ gave him clear instructions that the gospel message was relevant to all humanity because Christ's death and resurrection were atonement for all sinners everywhere. Through his travels throughout the Mediterranean world and his numerous letters to the various churches, Paul built upon the Jewish concept of universal dignity. The argument that the Christian faith was open to everyone also meant that all humans are moral agents, capable of choice and responsible for those choices. "Faith in Christ requires seeing oneself in others and others in oneself, the point of view which truly moralizes humans as agents."[15]

Among many New Testament texts that articulate the idea of human dignity for all, one of the most explicit is Paul's declaration, "There is neither Jew nor Greek, there is neither slave nor free, there is no male and female, for you are all one in Christ Jesus."[16] Jesus himself made the claim that his atoning sacrifice was for all of humanity: "For God so loved the *world,* that he gave his only Son, that *whoever* believes in him should not perish but have eternal life."[17]

Although Christians' moral practices often did not reflect the concept of universal human dignity, various spokespersons and numerous church documents would reiterate that theme again and again. Augustine, the great theologian who followed Paul, strongly articulated the concept of universal human dignity through his emphasis on the universal fallenness of humankind and the absolute necessity of God's grace for all.[18] Once again, this argument represented a sharp break from Greek and Roman thought, which denied human equality and drew sharp distinctions between classes, races, and sexes.

As Christianity spread throughout the Mediterranean world, new forms of human association arose. Monastic orders, quite prevalent by the fourth century, were a uniquely egalitarian social order, open to all believers no matter what their class or status. They also gave new meaning to the concept of work, changing it from an activity of servile status to an exercise of human dignity and worth.[19]

Women also formed cloisters, sometimes as separate communities and sometimes as "double monasteries," where female and male monks lived in the same monastic premises.[20] Women's choices to join such orders meant recognition of their own moral agency, something not possessed by most women throughout ancient history. For instance, Aristotle saw women as incomplete or deformed men and hence not truly human in the sense of having the ability to make moral choices.[21]

The Roman Catholic Church's concern for the poor and disenfranchised was an important step in the recognition of universal human dignity. Hospitals for the care of the needy were an important part of monastic life. The laity were taught that charity was one of the highest of virtues: "certain ways of life, and entire social classes of people, could no longer simply be dismissed as incorrigible or irredeemable."[22] Hildebrand of Sovana (1028–85), who became Pope Gregory VII, declared that rulers would be judged according to what they had done for "all souls."[23] Knights were also expected to respect property rights, especially those of the powerless.[24] According to Kevin Madigan, a "prodigious volume of spiritual and secular charity [was] received by the poor and anguished in the high and middle ages [*sic*]."[25]

The fact that the Christian worldview was responsible for the concept of equal human dignity does not mean that the believers always acted in a manner consistent with an egalitarian belief structure. There was a continual tension between the revolutionary doctrine of the *imago Dei* and actual social practices. For instance, it was a remarkable statement of human agency that slaves were accepted into the community of faith from the beginning of Christianity, but Christians nevertheless still held slaves for more than a millennium. Gregory (335–95), bishop of Nyssa, made a strong plea for the immorality of slavery, but it took another fourteen hundred years for his arguments to gain substantial traction in the Christian world.

Jeffrey Grynaviski and Michael Munger (forthcoming) give a detailed account of how Christians in the nineteenth-century American South were able to provide a rationalization for slaveholding.[26] That ideology was eventually defeated militarily by the Union armies and intellectually by the tenets of modern liberalism. The abolitionist argument that a Christian could not in good conscience favor slavery was also an important influence. Today it is impossible to find Christian arguments for slaveholding.

In the sixteenth century, Spain's colonization of South America clearly violated the rights of the indigenous people.[27] During the religious wars of Europe from 1524 to 1648, Protestants and Catholics had little compunction about killing each other.

Despite the fact that the social order did not fully reflect the idea of human dignity, numerous voices articulated the concept and were responsible for its eventually becoming a part of standard political thought. In 316, Constantine

(306–337) banned the branding of criminals on the face, for "man is made in God's image."²⁸ Hildegard of Bingen (1098–1179) was one of the most influential women of her age. She was an articulate defender of orthodox Christian belief but protested vehemently against the burning of heretics because the heretic was also made in the image of God.

The authority of law and especially the concept of natural law, a law distinct from the state's legal apparatus, were strengthened by the ongoing development of canon law. Moral equality before the law was a basic presupposition of canon law, and its elaboration from 1050 to 1300 made it the first modern legal system.²⁹ According to Brian Tierney, "By 1200 the canonists had created a language in which natural rights theories could readily be expressed."³⁰

Scholasticism, a system of thought that used reason to articulate and formalize principles of human ordering, also advanced the concept of human dignity, largely through the development of the natural law.³¹ There were differences among the Scholastics, especially ones such as Thomas Aquinas (1225–74) and William of Ockham (1287–1347), regarding the exact content of God's law, but they all affirmed humans as agents of free will with the ability to discover truth.

The church's natural-law and natural-rights doctrines were an important part of political thought long before the modern era, but they were more forcefully articulated and more successfully applied to cultural structures with the coming of the Protestant Reformation. One of Martin Luther's primary claims was the dignity of all humans as expressed in his tract "The Freedom of the Christian."³² Because we all stand equal before God, human equality is divinely constructed, not humanly constructed. Luther (1483–1546) did not develop a strong case for political freedom; in fact, after the Peasant's Revolt of 1525, he emphasized strong political authority as necessary for an orderly society. Nevertheless, his argument for freedom of conscience was an important first step in the development of more general human rights.

John Calvin (1509–64) wrote eloquently about the importance of protecting other domains in life—including church, family, and commerce—from potentially selfish use of power in the hands of political rulers. This was another important step toward recognizing that people have political and economic rights. Theodore Beza (1519–1605), a reformer in the mold of Calvin, developed a more complete articulation of an appropriate political order that protected religious and economic liberty. Although Beza's writings represented new developments in political and religious thought, he drew upon centuries of Christian thinking. In the words of John Witte, Beza "called on five decades of Protestant and five centuries of Catholic teachings on law, politics, and society as well as the whole arsenal of classical and patristic sources."[33]

Although much of the early debate over religious liberty and individual rights occurred in France and Germany, the Netherlands fairly quickly became a hotbed for discussion about the importance of the image of God in formulating rules for the political order. Johannes Althusius (1557–1638) was probably the most important contributor to this debate. Althusius was an active pamphleteer, authoring numerous pieces on natural law and the liberties of individuals and groups.

Althusius started his theory of society and politics with an account of the state of nature—which he equated with human nature and more particularly with the nature of persons as creatures and bearers of the image of God. God created humans as moral creatures, Althusius argued, with natural law written on their hearts and consciences as well as "an innate inclination," "hidden impulse," and "natural instinct" to be "just and law abiding." God created persons as rights holders, vested with natural sovereignty, rooted in the supernatural sovereignty of God, whose image each person bears upon birth.[34]

Throughout the sixteenth and seventeenth centuries, religious toleration, a radical concept in Christian history, became a part of Dutch political life. "But the Dutch had also come to believe that religious toleration was the most Christian policy as well as the most politically effective policy."[35] Such toleration was based on the concept of the equal human dignity of all, despite differences in religious belief.

This period also witnessed a vibrant intellectual debate over the rights and duties of English citizens. Between 1640 and 1680, more than twenty-two thousand pamphlets, sermons, and tracts were published. The power of the sovereign, the protection of the rights of citizens, and the legitimacy of various laws and forms of governance were hotly contested.[36] As in the Netherlands, in England a major part of the political debate over human rights was driven by the articulation of the dignity of all people in the biblical doctrines of Christ's death for all humans and the universality of the image of God in every person. These doctrines were important influences on the move to the rule of law, contract enforcement for all market participants, and the opening of occupations and businesses to a wider range of people.

Although numerous theologians and philosophers were involved in the debate, one of the most important figures was John Milton (1608–74). According to Witte,

> [I]t was the great poet and political philosopher John Milton who pro-
> vided the most interesting integrative theory of rights and liberty. . . .
> Milton argued that each person is created in the image of God with
> 'a perennial craving' to love God, neighbor, and self. Each person has
> the law of God written on his or her heart, mind, and conscience and
> rewritten in Scripture, most notably in the Decalogue.[37]

Deirdre McCloskey provides copious details on the many ways in which the concept of universal dignity became a part of ordinary life.[38] Literature, language, Bible translations, church governance, and attitudes toward wealth generation were affected by this ideological revolution.

The gradual development of the concept of full-blown human agency and human equality created a natural tension with many of the claims of religious authority. If individuals are moral agents with the ability to choose from a large range of belief structures, what is the role of the church, which claims to articulate a unique belief structure as the path to salvation? Numerous Renaissance and Enlightenment thinkers struggled with this conflict, and the concept of equal human dignity gradually served to delegitimize the religious claims of absolute authority. Thus, the doctrine of equality, with its strong roots in Christian thought, came to be used against the church's claims to use political power to enforce its definition of heresy.

Thomas Hobbes (1588–1679) was one of the first to articulate in *Leviathan* an antireligious perspective on human ordering that was based on human equality.[39] According to Peter Berkowitz, "While Hobbes is not a liberal in the classic sense of the term, he should be seen as a major figure in the laying of the foundations of the liberal state. . . . Hobbes argued that human beings are fundamentally equal and endowed with certain natural and inalienable rights."[40]

John Locke (1632–1704) published *Two Treatises of Government* around 1689, the same year that the English Bill of Rights was adopted. He offered what would later come to be the predominant understanding of the rights proclaimed in that document, developing more fully the conditions under which a revolution was justified. He also developed a much more complete theory of natural rights than was embodied in the Bill of Rights of 1689. Locke argued for the application of natural law equally to all because all are equally God's creatures made to exercise dominion over the natural order.[41]

Locke also made a substantial contribution to the concept that the rule of law applied equally to all because of his principle of religious freedom.[42] Prior to Locke, political philosophy justified the use of the state's coercive power against heretics, with the reigning religious authorities responsible for defining heresy. This assignment of responsibility meant that there were always members of society who could not claim equal treatment under the law because of their particular set of religious (or nonreligious) beliefs. Locke said government should enforce the rules of justice and equity. As Greg Forster puts it, "If government plays favorites among religions in any way, it undermines the moral laws on which government itself is based, because those laws require the impartial administration of justice to all people."[43]

Montesquieu (1689–1755) also was an articulate defender of human equality, using a concept similar to the Rawlsian "veil of ignorance" to argue that rational human beings would not choose a system of slavery if they did not know which side of the ownership-owned divide they would fall.[44]

Hobbes, Locke, Jean-Jacques Rousseau (1712–78), and Montesquieu were important shapers of the philosophical groundings of the new liberal order. There were sharp differences among them as to where and how human equality existed and what constituted a just and workable social and political system, but they all integrated the concept of universal human dignity into their philosophies. These thinkers found a way of preserving the basic assumption of the Western religious beliefs about human dignity while avoiding the assumptions that led to the devastating consequences of the wars of religion over what constituted heresy. Siedentop argues that these Enlightenment thinkers succeeded in grounding modern liberalism "on the moral assumptions provided by Christianity. It preserves Christian ontology without the metaphysics of salvation."[45]

Conclusion

The move from a widely accepted concept of human inequality to a belief in universal equality was a long process of cultural evolution. Judaism and Christianity provided a metaphysical concept, all humans are bearers of God's image, that shaped that evolutionary path. Enlightenment thinkers advanced the argument for equal human dignity by articulating the principles of a social and political order based on human agency, but with stringent limits on the power structures' ability to define and enforce a particular concept of heresy. Thus, classical liberals, with their well-developed arguments about human equality as the appropriate basis for the modern polity, are heirs to a long process of intellectual and cultural evolution, a process that has been influenced by both religious and secular thinkers.

7

A Descent from Equality
to Egalitarianism

Jason Morgan*

EQUALITY IS A touchstone of political discourse. Nearly every polity idealizes equality in some way, and the promise to increase it (often framed negatively as "reducing inequality") is the most common trope in the political idiom. From Lucius Sicinius Vellutus in 494 BCE, galvanizing the plebeians with calls for greater political equality with patricians, to Bernie Sanders in 2016 CE, rallying disaffected crowds under the standard of greater equality of income and attacks on accumulated wealth, appeals to "equality" run like a bright thread through the fabric of political history. Equality is invoked and idolized, its delayed arrival is lamented, and its enemies—both real and alleged—often have cause to fear for their possessions, their livelihoods, and even their lives. There is no more fundamental element of politics than equality: it has been on the lips of office-seekers since the advent of politics itself.

But what is equality? The more the word is spoken, the less it appears to be understood. Even when "equality" has been deployed in specific historical circumstances—under the banner of the Jacobins in France, for instance, or the Levelers in England, or even the Taiping armies in Imperial China—it is a word so amorphous, so malleable in the mouths of men, as to be almost without any meaning at all. And yet, taken as a whole the word "equality," used as it has been in a broad panoply of contexts for thousands of years, underwent a substantial change during the nineteenth and twentieth centuries. What the Romans and the Greeks, the Roundheads and the Yellow Turbans, meant by "equality," various though those iterations of the concept may have been, is fundamentally different from what is meant by the term today.

---

*Jason Morgan is a 2016 Mises Institute Fellow.

In this essay, I will argue that the mental technology of equality—the techniques of thought and the deep grooves of mass psychology upon which political leaders tacitly rely when summoning the spirit of the term—has changed radically over the past two hundred years. What we continue to call "equality" is, now, actually better understood as "egalitarianism." The distinction is important. Equality, whatever it might denote, has always been a potent political promise made and implemented by elites. This is key, because equality is impossible to bring about without the application of external violence, whether actual or threatened. Egalitarianism, though, is the endless quest for equality internalized by a governed people and made self-actuating: Foucauldian "governmentality" programmed to cycle through an endless loop of equality-seeking as a way to render populations more pliable by demagogues, who for practical reasons prefer to rule by suggestion and propaganda rather than by brute force.

Using the ideas of Giorgio Agamben and Carl Schmitt, I then go on to argue that egalitarianism creates the conditions for the "state of exception," a permanent political emergency that removes virtually all checks on the prerogatives of a sovereign. Equality's inevitable failure thus helps legitimate the hegemony of those least well-disposed to rule justly. I conclude by offering an alternative view of inequality, namely, that it is best countered not by the enforcement of its opposite, but by the Misesian entrepreneur, who finds opportunities in discrepancies and helps to bring prosperity for all out of the ineffable diversity of the human condition.

Political leaders almost always adopt a non-Misesian tack. This is because, for politicians, equality is not a chance to educe the greater common good, but a means by which to shore up the state's control over a population. Perhaps the most notable early explication of this understanding of equality as a pretext for eliminating rivals to a given regime comes from the Greek historian Herodotus. In his *Histories*, Herodotus tells the story of Periander and Thrasybulus, the former a budding tyrant in Corinth who seeks the advice of the latter, the experienced tyrant of Miletus. By plucking the heads off of the tallest, ripest, choicest grain in his field, Thrasybulus indicates to Periander's messenger that the secret of a successful tyranny is the willingness to use violence in order to eliminate the superior people from a realm, thereby preventing the emergence of rivals to a tyrant's rule.[1] Enforced equality has a long pedigree as a method of preserving the privileges of the elite.

Nor was the usefulness of equality unknown in the East. Even richly stratified societies made full use of equality as a tool of social control. The caste system in India, for example, was really one of layered equality, with each superior layer benefitting from the stability beneath it, which arose as a function of meticulously enforced uniformity of social standing within each caste. And in China, the *baojia* system of rule provides a classic example of a government attempting to impose equality upon an economically and socially diverse population. The baojia system was originally designed as a more efficient means of tax collection and law enforcement. Significantly, the architect of the system was Wang Anshi (1021–1086), a Sung Dynasty statesman who advocated currency debasement and centralized economic planning. Even more significantly, it was the autocrat Zhu Yuanzhang, the founder of the Ming Dynasty, who re-deployed the baojia system in 1381 as the *lijia* system. Zhu Yuanzhang had a transformative vision of society and was determined to remake his empire accordingly. Unlike the baojia system, the lijia system aimed to have the Chinese people internalize the need for order and govern themselves. In an outcome familiar from history, Zhu initiated purges and mass executions when his attempts to impose unnatural equality on his subjects failed.[2]

Following the collapse of the Roman Empire in the West, equality before God became the common theme of Christian Europe. This largely prevented the tumultuous quest for equality in the political or social contexts. As jurist Sir Henry James Sumner Maine points out in his comparative work *Ancient Law* (1861), medieval Christendom was ordered by status, and compacts between individuals were entered into on the basis of inequality. Those compacts were covenants, sealed by vows and oaths, binding each party's honor in accordance with his station in life. Later, as status lost its grip on social dominion and equality before the law became the ideal, covenants gave way to contracts, entered into by equals who agreed to fulfill a set of very specific obligations laid out in a written document. Contracts were blind to social status and served only to bind man to man on strictly delimited terms, and no further. Equality before God allowed men to enter into covenants as social wholes; contracts denatured interactions into pragmatic, short-term arrangements of coincidental convenience.

This shift from status to contract reflected a wider change in the West. The change was fundamentally anthropological. During the European Middle Ages, human beings had been understood relationally. Just as Confucius had argued in the fifth century BCE, medieval Europe, too, defined the individual in terms of his position within his world. A man was a serf or a lord, a knight or a noble, but never merely a "citizen."[3] This was, in short, a feudal conception of the human person, one of deep intersubjectivity and relationality. Gradually, though, this social milieu broke down. The rise of wealthy merchant cities in Italy and northern Europe presented alternatives to the feudal social arrangement, while the localized theological disaffections of Martin Luther, used more often than not as a pretense for political gamesmanship, spiraled into a full-blown rejection of the religious hierarchy itself.

By the end of the eighteenth century, monarchy, too, was under attack. The old social order was falling apart. The "great chain of being"—the attempt to situate humanity within a grand vision of the ordered cosmos—dissolved.[4] The paradigm that took its place was one of radical individualism to be policed by the social aggregate, or else by a state strong enough to enforce the general will. The philosophies of Jean-Jacques Rousseau, Thomas Hobbes, and John Locke are, at heart, programs for imposing discipline on the stochastics of atomized individuals all claiming the perfect political equality promised them by demagogues mounting a challenge to the *ancien régime*.

The revolutions in France and in the New World—North America, of course, but also the Caribbean and Central and South America—were the high-water mark of equality as the handmaiden of liberty. However, the "equality" that was touted from the Bastille to Boston to the armies of Simon Bolivar carried a primarily negative valence. Those clamoring for equality during the age of transatlantic revolutions were sons of liberty, to be sure, but their more immediate task was to tear down the bastions and symbols of inequality that they saw all around them. In Europe, the most obvious target for this anti-inequality zeal was the aristocracy, cartooned as portly sensualists living in gross luxury while the peasantry starved to death. In the Caribbean and Central and South America, the targets were the slaveowners and landholders, the more business-minded wielders of aristocratic power who were oppressing the populace, not so much with opulence and social status as with inhumanity and greed.

And in North America, the champions of liberty sought equality within the confines of the Anglo-Saxon law. The American Revolution was nothing if not the culmination of the long march from status to contract. The American colonists were fond of attacking King George III as a tyrant, but what they really wanted was not for King George to donate his ermine robes to the poor in order to alleviate their suffering, but rather for King George's Parliament to admit the Americans to the bar of civil discourse as equals before the law. Parliament and the king did not do this, of course, and so the Americans sought equality on their own terms, in a rebirthing of the common law on the shores of the western Atlantic.

Once the revolutions had reached a natural stopping point—once the ties with the Old World had been severed in North America, the hacienda owners sufficiently chastised and dispossessed in Latin America, and the new masses of "citizens" grown sick of bloodshed, terror, and the burdens of Napoleonic empire in Europe—the promoters of equality were forced to shift from a negative, attacking mode of discourse into one that necessarily promised something more substantial than the dismantling of the strongholds of privilege. In the United States, the bogeyman of slavery engendered the final phase of the legal revolution begun by the 1776ers: robust equality within the episteme of the law—"substantive due process"—for all men regardless of ethnic origin, and then, by the early twentieth century, for all women, too. But once the last real adversaries of political equality had fallen, political leaders began to see that the next targets of the equality juggernaut might be the politicians themselves. It was therefore when political equality had gained its greatest victory that it began to be sublimated into an entirely different phase: egalitarianism.

It has often been remarked that equality is an unrealizable goal. Even if it could be arranged such that every person in a given society were provided with exactly the same resources—money, housing, educational background, and so forth—within a short period of time this engineered equality would be undone. Some would use their windfall as seed capital, creating businesses, improving their property, or staying up late to master a new subject or skill. They would purchase land, practice austerities, make advantageous trades, and generally exhibit what Eugen von Böhm-Bawerk and Hans Hermann-Hoppe have called "low time preference."[5] Others, however, would display all of the hallmarks of "high time preference." They would use the boon of free income and materials as an excuse to take a permanent vacation. They would prefer leisure to industry, and it would not be long before their land was overgrown, their property was ruined, their families were hungry, and their children were running about unsupervised and uneducated. In short, one man would redouble his efforts and work even harder than before, while his neighbor would rise at noon, waste the day in diversionary trifles, and consume his unearned capital. True equality is a chimera, at best. The notion of "equality" is a perennial slogan of politics precisely for this reason.

The frustration born of this unalterable tendency towards greater entropy in the absence of countervailing hard work would soon be the end of any political group that promised to overcome it. Every rejiggering of the social landscape in order to create equality would be rendered futile within a few days at the longest, and would need to be taken up again (and again and again). The solution to this dilemma—i.e., between the usefulness of "equality" as a tool of political control and the hazards of preaching "equality" without sufficiently prominent totems of inequality to attack—was the transformation of equality to egalitarianism, the internalization of equality's unreachable telos.

In *Discipline and Punish*, philosopher Michel Foucault wrote of the need for a "panopticon" allowing a political authority to constantly monitor a population for signs of subversion.[6] In "Security, Territory, and Population," however, Foucault spoke of "governmentality," the process by which a people unwittingly obviate the necessity of the panopticon by learning to govern themselves through the appropriation of the authority's program of command.[7] Egalitarianism is the marriage of equality and Foucauldian governmentality. Under egalitarianism, a political group—the larger the better—polices itself through the endless advocacy of the impossible goal of full and lasting equality. Once initiated, egalitarianism takes on a life of its own, as people begin to apply the undefinable metric of "equality" to aspects of their own shared existence that the authority would never have dared to subject to his suzerainty. Whereas past tyrants used equality to bludgeon their political rivals, today, populations show little need to be governed by the club and the lance. Egalitarianism has so eroded the cultural and social underpinnings of societies that cohesion unto revolution is now a virtual impossibility.

The objection has been raised, however: what is wrong with all of this? It is frequently argued, for example, that equality has helped attenuate racial discrimination. Without equality, it would be 1860 in perpetuity. Minorities would have little to no political standing and would be subject to gross violations of their civic and natural rights. Or, the line of argument frequently extends, what about marriage equality? Is it not true that equality has ended institutional governmental bigotry against non-heterosexual partnerships? What was once reserved for a certain segment of the population is now open to all. Inclusivity, surely, is better than exclusivity, we are often reminded. And as far as women's suffrage goes, attacks on equality sound suspiciously like attacks on women's ability to participate in the political process. In short, what can one possibly have against equality? And, isn't it far-fetched to claim that equality—or, now, egalitarianism—is just a tool of political manipulation? The deconstruction of equality, one often hears, is little more than a veiled attempt to undermine the hard-won progress of the modern age.

These arguments are compelling when set within the swift-moving stream of current events. However, when time is afforded for a bit more reflection, it becomes clear that such arguments, well-intentioned though they may be, are in fact backwards. For, it is not that equality has elevated humanity out of the pit of discrimination and bigotry. Rather, it is that equality has eroded, to the point of indistinguishability, the standards of human dignity and excellence in human endeavor that had long been benchmarks for truly respecting the human person in his or her entirety.

One key to understanding how equality is antagonistic to humanity in its fullness can be found in the writings of Aristotle. In both the *Nicomachean Ethics* and the *Eudemian Ethics*, Aristotle holds that every virtue is pursued for the sake of some other end, but that living well in happiness, or *eudaimonia*, is the only thing pursued for its own sake.[8] Health, for example, is sought out in order to attain eudaimonia, but happiness is always its own reciprocate. The doctrine of equality, however—and in particular egalitarianism, which refuses to specify the terms in which we are all to be made equal—reworks Aristotle's insight. It is no longer living well in happiness, but equality itself, which is to be sought for its own sake. Equality, in other words, usurps man's proper ends, which leaves a given polity virtually defenseless against political manipulation. A man who does not know where he is going is dangerously liable to be led astray.

Consider, for example, the change which took place between the Declaration of Independence, in 1776, and the Gettysburg Address, in 1863. In just "four-score and seven years," the political ideal had swung quite dramatically, from an Aristotelian "pursuit of happiness" enshrined in the Declaration, to an incipient egalitarianism that sidelined the pursuit of happiness in favor of the pursuit of equality *qua* equality. "Government of, by, and for the people" is tautological. We are made for more than mere self-reference and political collectivism. Abraham Lincoln may have been invoking noble sentiments in his solemn battlefield speech, but in transposing the individual search for happiness with the collectivist search for equality, he was inadvertently condemning the American slaves to a life of spiritual impoverishment even as he sought to free them from their physical bondage. On the cusp of liberation from slavery, Americans of all situations were thrust into the burgeoning unfreedom of mass politics, typified by a pursuit of equality that regards other men, and not higher ideals, as the measure of all things.

Indeed, this transposition is hardly noticed anymore, so thoroughly has happiness been reduced to a secondary, dependent variable. Once this mental shift has been accomplished, the dominoes rapidly fall. The mental scaffolding of the good life, the notion that mankind may attain some measure of happiness by following the principles of reason and ordered action, comes crashing down. Seen in this light, equality is not wings for ascending the heights of our human potential. It is a millstone, dragging everyone down to the lowest common denominator. Equality does not liberate; it tyrannizes, by destroying standards of good, better, and best, replacing them with the iron rule of absolute uniformity.

This egalitarianism of the shallows now reigns in nearly every aspect of modern life. Take the arts, for example. The Western canon of great artistic achievement is unmistakable prior to the nineteenth century. The canvases of Velazquez, Raphael, Rembrandt, and El Greco, the sculpture of Praxiteles and Michelangelo, and the architecture of Athens and Rome are the artistic nerve centers of our aesthetic existence. Viennese art historian Alois Riegl (1858–1905), however, argued that there are no objective standards by which to judge art. *Kunstwollen*, a word that Riegl created in order to describe the mere impulse to create something, refocused art history away from evaluation and towards an inflexible relativism. Egalitarianism, in other words, became the organizing principle of aesthetics.[9]

Perhaps the exemplar nonpareil of the anti-aesthetic impulse of equality, which destroys the pursuit of what Aristotle called *arête*, or excellence, is the United States federal government. Under the egalitarianism scheme of the American political class, the internalization of the neuroses of equality allows Leviathan to avoid direct confrontation and proceed with the quotidian business of overseeing a massive bureaucracy, tasked with managing the daily lives of some 320 million people down to the most exiguous minutiae. The pathological mediocrity of the federal bureaucracy is precisely coterminous with the telos of the egalitarian state. By preventing its "citizens" from imagining a better life than one spent filling out paperwork and complying with illogical and invasive regulations, the 'immanentization of the eschaton'[10] is achieved and the Aristotelian cosmos is turned on its head. For federal bureaucrats and, they hope, the legions they govern, the highest human good consists, not in happiness, but in submission to Kafkaesque absurdity.

The borders of this submission are continuously policed by those most invested in its continuation. What is solely worthwhile for the government about diversity, for instance, is that it creates an endless horizon of busywork in the pursuit of equality, while simultaneously guaranteeing that true equality will remain eternally out of reach.[11] This demolition of enterprise and independence, coupled with the incessant push towards collectivization, has one aim in view: crushing the individual.

In his *Managerial Revolution*, American political philosopher James Burnham, drawing on the earlier insights of A. A. Berle and Gardiner Means, showed that entrepreneurial capitalism in the United States was giving way to managerialism.[12] Personal oversight of a firm by its founder and owner, rooted in the regimes of private property and individual responsibility, was collapsing in the face of broad-spectrum collectivism and statism under the New Deal.[13] Egalitarianism undermines personal initiative and centrifugally casts liability for speculative business failure (losses) up to the highest level— i.e., the state—while centripetally drawing the fruits of speculative success (profits) down to those who have done the least work to achieve them. The individual, driver of economic dynamism, is intentionally isolated and sty-mied. In the middle of this process are the managers, faceless and nameless, with no personal stake in the firms they run, and actively working in tan-dem with the regulatory technocratism of a grasping central government.[14]

The essential element of the rise of the managerial society is anti-individualism. Anti-individualism also helps explain governmental reliance upon equality as a means of political control, and, a fortiori, the rise of egali-tarianism as the internalization of that control. But as Ludwig von Mises writes in *Human Action*, it is the individual who acts, even when actions appear to be carried out by larger groups, such as societies, corporations, or nation-states.[15] And the individual, in an economic context, acts catallactically, that is, in an endless series of exchanges with his fellow men. Each individual believes a given exchange will have some advantage or work towards some goal; other-wise, he would not enter into the exchange. In other words, humans act praxe-ologically, or with some future result in mind. But without "the inequality of men," as Mises puts it, there can be no action. Egalitarianism is the enemy of the acting individual, because inequality is the catalyst for individual choice.

The pursuit of equality is as futile as the pursuit of Mises's "evenly-rotating economy," in which all economic discrepancies are brought into equilibrium and full parity is achieved between supply and demand. In fact, the distinc-tion between equality and egalitarianism may be compared to Mises's dis-tinction between the plain state of rest and the final state of rest.[16] The plain state of rest happens when transactions among unequal trading partners are concluded and there is a temporary pause in economic interaction. This pause lasts until new states of inequality arise, which individual actors seek to balance out through further market activity. This is akin to the pursuit by governments or societies of equality. In limited circumstances and within certain parameters, equality may be temporarily achieved, such as, say, by collectivizing farms and allotting every farmer an equal area of land to work. But the process always requires violence or the threat of violence, and is never permanent. Regardless of the attempts made to enforce equality on a given population, inequality will always re-emerge over time. Under the final state of rest, however, the economy achieves perfect and permanent equilibrium. This state is fictional and impossible, as Mises explains.[17] Nevertheless, the impulse to approach this final state of rest is what drives economic interactions forward. "The market," Mises writes, "is always disquieted by a striving after a definite final state of rest."[18] This mirrors what happens when equality, imposed from outside and never more than fleeting in realization, sublimates into egalitarianism. Egalitarianism is the internal "disquiet" of a society to achieve the perfect, final state of equality, a state which never arrives and so must be hastened with ever-more draconian measures, which a society, in its mad quest for the unattainable, often chooses to impose upon itself.

Egalitarianism, then, engenders what Giorgio Agamben calls the "state of exception." The state of exception is an emergency brought about by a departure from the impossible norms of a utopian political philosophy, in turn necessitating the tyrannical rule of a strong leader who can overcome the state of exception and restore order to a given society.[19] The mass murders and totalitarian dictatorships of the twentieth century all conformed perfectly to this pattern. Indeed, egalitarianism may be likened to a spell that calls into political prominence those most hungry to exercise dictatorial absolutism, while also providing, under the state of exception (which as Schmitt showed was actually the amplification of sovereignty), the conditions necessary for carrying that absolutism out.

This grim portrait of the spread and consequences of egalitarianism need not be the sole definition of the subject, however. While it is true that egalitarian distraction has befogged the true meaning and end of political life for the past two centuries, this long night has not been without occasional beacons of orderly thinking. Among the most potent challenges to egalitarianism mounted during the nineteenth and twentieth centuries was the Austrian school of economic and political philosophy, for example. This loose coterie of thinkers forms a counterpoint to the anti-philosophy of the egalitarian managers and levelers, grounding epistemology not in aggregate behavior but in individual human action. This defiance of collectivism finds perhaps its most succinct expression in the aforementioned Austrian economist Ludwig von Mises's writings on the entrepreneur.

Mises defines "entrepreneur" as "acting man in regard to the changes occurring in the data of the market."[20] The entrepreneur, for Mises, is the "historian of the future" who is able to anticipate changes in the shared life of a given polity in ways that will allow him to provide better goods and services to that polity while profiting himself and his firm. The entrepreneur is the one who breaks apart from the stultifying atmosphere of imposed egalitarianism and stands alone, using a mind cleared of managerial mediocrity and striving toward the true political end—happiness. Where equality works to reduce multiplicity to uniformity, the entrepreneur embraces difference and meets it gamely by his own individual action. While inequality will always cause some to resort to oppression in the vain attempt to stamp it out, it will also inspire others to sharpen their own talents and use them freely in pursuit of higher ends.[21] Unlike egalitarianism, entrepreneurialism—which allows men to act in pursuit of "psychic profit"—is open to, even conducive towards, eudaimonia.[22] Mises's entrepreneur, using Aristotelian phronesis in search of higher-order goods, is thus the antidote to the now-global egalitarian regime.

The shift from equality to egalitarianism has been wreathed in violence. The statism of the twentieth century was predicated upon this change in governing technology, from external to internal enforcement of conformity. No ideological change has been bloodier or more ruinous of true freedom. But the Austrian school, and Mises's entrepreneur in particular, show a way to overcome egalitarianism by means of dynamic human action. The choosing, acting individual, and not the mirage of egalitarianism, is, after all, the one enduring political reality.

8

Why Redistributionism Must Collapse

James R. Harrigan and Ryan M. Yonk*

IN CONSIDERATIONS OF the American regime, the language of egalitarianism is never far from the surface. The reason for this is clear enough: the United States is the only nation the world has ever known to be founded on the principle of human equality. Thomas Jefferson's language in the Declaration of Independence, although familiar, bears revisiting. Echoing or even channeling John Locke, he wrote:

> We hold these truths to be self-evident, that all men are created equal, that they are endowed by their Creator with certain unalienable Rights, that among these are Life, Liberty and the pursuit of Happiness.—That to secure these rights, Governments are instituted among Men, deriving their just powers from the consent of the governed,— That whenever any Form of Government becomes destructive of these ends, it is the Right of the People to alter or to abolish it, and to institute new Government, laying its foundation on such principles and organizing its powers in such form, as to them shall seem most likely to effect their Safety and Happiness.[1]

Not only has this assertion become American dogma or even, in the words of Pauline Maier, "American scripture," it has resonated internationally as well, serving as the explicit or implicit framework for every revolution that has been undertaken from 1776 to the present.[2] From the antislavery, women's

---

*James R. Harrigan is senior fellow of the Institute of Political Economy at Utah State University. Ryan M. Yonk is assistant research professor in the Department of Economics and Finance at Utah State University.

rights, and civil rights movements in the United States to the Israeli Declaration of Independence (which in an early draft began with the words "When in the course of human events"³) to Ho Chi Minh's assertion of Vietnamese independence in 1945 (which he began with the sentences: "All men are created equal. They are endowed by their Creator with certain inalienable rights, among these are Life, Liberty and the pursuit of Happiness"⁴) the logic of the Declaration has been profoundly influential both at home and abroad.⁵

But although the first two paragraphs of the Declaration have undoubtedly been the most influential portion of the document, both in the United States over time and throughout the world, the strength of this influence obscures the comparatively longer portion of the document, the list of offenses committed by King George III against the American people. This middle section comprises roughly two-thirds of the total document and in some respects is a great deal more important than the theoretical underpinnings that begin the document in so high-minded a fashion.

In this section, Jefferson presents twenty-seven grievances against George III on the part of the colonies. These grievances range from the king's exercise of tyrannical authority to Parliament's inappropriate and unchecked meddling in colonial affairs to specific actions undertaken that the colonists felt amounted to acts of war. The list represents the sum total of colonial unhappiness in 1776 and includes grievances that had been festering in most cases for a number of years, dating to at least as early as the Sugar Act of 1764 and the Stamp Act of 1765. None of them, in the minds of the colonists, represented "light and transient causes," as Jefferson put it. Rather, they represented "a long train of abuses and usurpations, pursuing invariably . . . a design to reduce [the people] under absolute Despotism."⁶ Indeed, all twenty-seven grievances can be summed up as violations of the rule of law itself.

Further, the second part of the Declaration provides a clear illustration not only that the law must apply to all but also that some laws are so offensive to the notion of the equality that they represent an appropriate justification to break the ties that bind politically and to do so with violence.

Although the principle of human equality undoubtedly animated the revolution, it was combined with an appreciation for the rule of law, a combination that drove the conversation both before and after independence had been won. On the eve of the revolution, Thomas Paine made the case most clearly in his widely read pamphlet *Common Sense,* which was perhaps the single greatest summation of the American mind as the colonists moved toward revolution. He wrote:

> But where, say some, is the King of America? I'll tell you, friend, he reigns above, and doth not make havoc of mankind like the Royal Brute of Great Britain. Yet that we may not appear to be defective even in earthly honours, let a day be solemnly set apart for proclaiming the Charter; let it be brought forth placed on the Divine Law, the Word of God; let a crown be placed thereon, by which the world may know, that so far as we approve of monarchy, that in America the law is king. For as in absolute governments the King is law, so in free countries the law ought to be king; and there ought to be no other.[7]

The law is king in America, and indeed it is and must be so in any free country. And in the years that followed America's revolutionary period, a distinct and protracted effort was made to operationalize this concept. The principle of equality stood directly behind every attempt to bolster the rule of law at the expense of the rule of men.

John Adams was the first in the American colonies to refer to a government of laws when he described republics as "a government of laws, and not of men,"[8] in his seventh *Novangelus* letter of February 6, 1775, and he brought this thought to bear as primary author of the Massachusetts Constitution in 1780, which began with a bill of rights. In that bill of rights, Adams borrowed liberally from Jefferson's language in the Declaration, writing: "All men are born free and equal, and have certain natural, essential, and unalienable rights; among which may be reckoned the right of enjoying and defending their lives and liberties; that of acquiring, possessing, and protecting property; in fine, that of seeking and obtaining their safety and happiness."[9]

But in the preamble to the Massachusetts Constitution, Adams linked the rights that flow from human equality to the very purpose of government. Echoing Jefferson here, too, he coupled the role of government as protector of the people's safety and happiness, adding prosperity for good measure. But he also stressed the need for equity in the law-making process and for everyone to find security in the laws at all time. In short, he necessarily married egalitarianism to the rule of law.

The end of the institution, maintenance and administration of government, is to secure the existence of the body-politic; to protect it; and to furnish the individuals who compose it, with the power of enjoying, in safety and tranquillity [*sic*], their natural rights, and the blessings of life: And whenever these great objects are not obtained, the people have a right to alter the government, and to take measures necessary for their safety, prosperity and happiness.

The body-politic is formed by a voluntary association of individuals: It is a social compact, by which the whole people covenants with each citizen, and each citizen with the whole people, that all shall be governed by certain laws for the common good. It is the duty of the people, therefore, in framing a Constitution of Government, to provide for an equitable mode of making laws, as well as for an impartial interpretation, and a faithful execution of them; that every man may, at all times, find his security in them.[10]

The US Constitution, drafted some seven years later in Philadelphia in the summer of 1787, was similarly informed by the principles of human equality and the rule of law, although neither appears explicitly in the document. The logic of the Declaration of Independence was simply assumed, and the rule of law was the very project of the Constitution itself. Everything the delegates to the federal Constitutional Convention did was in pursuance of the rule of law for the young nation, and this goal could be undertaken only in a condition defined by general human equality.

What emerged from their efforts was an institutional government that was designed, following Jefferson, to effect the safety and happiness of the people. The negative-rights regime that emerged was perfectly consonant theoretically with the equality espoused in the Declaration, even if that stated egalitarian bedrock was, for many, more aspiration than reality. A condition of general equality could be fostered and ensured only by the rule of law, not by men. And the rule of law required that certain things be removed from the purview of government in the form of entrenched negative rights. And virtually every right asserted by the Founding generation was distinctly negative in nature.

The Bill of Rights illustrates this well enough with its opening phrase: "Congress shall make no law."[11] There are, quite simply, any number of things that government cannot legitimately do. As such, the line from equality to rights to the rule of law to institutional government results necessarily in a relatively small government. That is not to say it results in a weak government, which had been the problem under the previous Articles of Confederation. Indeed, according to Alexander Hamilton in *Federalist No. 23,* a government "at least equally energetic with the one proposed" was necessary.[12] The inherent friction between a limited government that could secure negative rights and an energetic or powerful government that could in both theory and fact do a great deal more would come to define the long-term expansion of positive rights in the United States. Just as a regime typified by negative rights leads necessarily to a small government that is by definition and nature limited, a regime typified or even featuring positive rights necessarily tends to the opposite.

This dual understanding of the rule of law and of the fundamental equality that precedes and therefore governs citizens' relationships to that law represents American scripture at its most pure. It is in their union that the American Idea is given its fullest and most eloquent expression, and their union has important practical implications for public policy. Equality that precedes law necessitates an understanding that the law must apply to all equally, and if all are equal before that law, they must also be equal in their liberty. Liberty thus understood necessitates a regime that is comfortable with and even features unequal outcomes. But once the United States dedicated itself to the pursuance of positive liberty in the name of compressing the range of outcomes experienced in the nation, different rules and a large, powerful government were the inevitable results. In pursuance of these goals, the government grew and became a threat to the liberty that egalitarianism made possible in the first instance.

The growth of the federal government over time has been unmistakable. At the time of the first census in 1790, there were 1,000 federal employees. By 1962, the first year data were systematically collected, the number had grown to 2,515,000. By 2014, the last year for which data are available, there were 2,726,000.[13] This growth is similarly reflected in the amount of regulation imposed on the American people. The first issue of the *Federal Register,* which contained 16 pages of official rules, was released in March 1936. By 2015, it had more than 80,000 pages. These are imperfect proxies, though, given the paucity of data in the early years of the republic regarding federal employees and the fact that the *Federal Register* was not even published for the first time until 146 years after the first census. A far better metric is federal spending relative to gross domestic product (GDP).

During the period from the Founding to the Civil War, spending relative to GDP was between 1 and 3 percent every year. From 1870 until World War I, spending relative to GDP again hovered largely between 1 and 3 percent. But from World War I on, a new pattern emerged, and we have lived in this new pattern ever since. A new plateau is evident after the Great War, and this level of government spending relative to GDP was roughly twice as high as it had previously been. The two world wars certainly obscure the trend, but beginning about 1930 a distinct upward trend of government spending is clearly evident. It was at this time that Americans' understanding of the proper role, size, and scope of government underwent a sea change that clearly found its intellectual roots in the Progressive Era, beginning at least as early as the publication of *The Promise of American Life* by Herbert Croly in 1909, but found its political purchase once the dust from the war had settled.

From that point forward, Americans came to understand the role of government not in terms of negative liberty, which had to that point yielded a government that rarely spent anything approaching 5 percent of GDP, to one that they conceived in terms of positive liberty. This new, more comprehensive kind of liberty would shake the very foundations of Jeffersonian equality, a vision of equality of opportunity, replacing it with one defined more in terms of equality of outcome than had been previously contemplated. And all of this would play out in the realm of public policy. The data tell a very clear story (see figure 8.1).

From the close of World War I on, the energy idealized by Hamilton overtook the egalitarianism espoused by Jefferson as a regime feature. And although the law from that point forward was still king in the United States, any pretense toward strict, fundamental equality was missing. Indeed, from the dawn of the Progressive Era, the government became deeply involved in deciding the question of who would have to forfeit some of their negative rights in the form of taxes on their property so that others might enjoy a new set of positive rights in the form of all manner of social welfare programs.

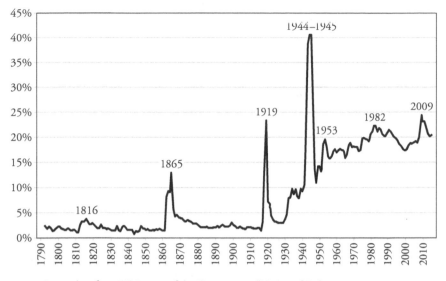

Source: Data taken from US Bureau of the Census 1949; "Historical Debt Outstanding— Annual" 2015; US Office of Management and Budget 2016; Johnston and Williamson 2017.

Figure 8.1. US Federal Government Spending as a Percentage of GDP 1792–2015

The language of this shift was firmly in place when on January 11 President Franklin D. Roosevelt offered a "Second Bill of Rights" in his State of the Union Address. The implication was clear: the negative rights enshrined in the Bill of Rights were no longer sufficient. Roosevelt announced "new" rights, including the right to a job; "decent" housing, food, clothing, and leisure; medical care; social security; and unemployment insurance. He even claimed the right of farmers to sell their products, which would give them "a decent living." Roosevelt did not indicate where the corresponding responsibilities to provide for these rights would come to rest, but the conclusion was unavoidable: some of the American people would be expected to provide for others.

What began as a demand for equality before the law rooted in individual natural rights gave way to a public-policy approach that focused instead on achieving particular outcomes for ever larger groups over time. Simply put, the goal was no longer to render all equal before the law; rather, it was to render social outcomes more equal over time or to work from egalitarian principles to what might be termed "equalitarian" principles. Roosevelt's positive-rights revolution was at hand, and it came at the expense of America's foundational negative rights.

Although Social Security, Medicare, Medicaid, and even the recent Affordable Care Act of 2010 receive the lion's share of the redistributionist consideration, with good reason, virtually any piece of legislation with a financial component illustrates the point. Each of the various and sundry agricultural subsidies in the United States, for example, is an attempt to guarantee some form of outcome equality. The current Agriculture Risk Coverage (ARC) program does so in the form of providing guaranteed base incomes to farmers.

The ARC program exists ostensibly to protect farmers from crop-price volatility by guaranteeing at least some revenue. Individual farms can elect to participate in ARC-County or ARC-Individual, which differ only in how payments are calculated. Under ARC-County, the program creates a "benchmark revenue" using five-year Olympic averages for a county's yield and marketing-year average price for a given crop. ARC-County guarantees 86 percent of that benchmark revenue to farmers who elect to participate in the program (as opposed to other, mutually exclusive programs). When actual county yield dips below that 86 percent, government payments make up the difference. ARC-Individual is essentially the same program but uses the individual farm's averages and actual yield rather than the county's. Both programs have payment rates capped at 10 percent of benchmark revenue.[14]

Although perhaps better than previous forms of farm subsidies, the ARC program includes important and damaging disincentives to good farm management. By guaranteeing subsidy payments for commodities based on historical yields and prices, government provides farmers protection against potential demand or yield reductions. And although the design of the policy (by setting the guarantee at only 86 percent of the benchmark, for example) is clearly intended to discourage negative behavior on the part of farmers, reducing incentives for any activity, in this case productivity, necessarily precipitates a reduction in that activity.

The ARC program is emblematic of modern American legislation. It may be a godsend to frugal but unlucky farmers, but its benefits also accrue to farmers in many cases precisely because those farmers made poor decisions. It does so at the literal expense of all American taxpayers in the name of an enhanced form of equality that goes well beyond the nation's founding and animating principle. The ARC is hardly unique in this respect. The United States as a nation has been walking this new road for so long that it is no longer all that new. And the American people have clearly come to expect it.

The genie will likely never fit back into the bottle. The impulse away from equality under the law toward a regime that aspires to something approaching equality of outcome, even if it achieves something only more akin to a mandatory minimum standard in all that it touches, is one that by definition appeals to a majoritarian impulse. Indeed, the only limitation on such regimes is the outer limit of how deeply the government can tax the people in the name of such programs. Here, a pragmatic concern ultimately trumps a theoretical one. As the sustained growth of expenditures relative to GDP illustrates, though, the United States has likely not approached that outer limit to this point.

Policy makers, of course, are largely unconcerned with recapturing the original conception of equality. There is no profit to them in telling the American public what they cannot have. Redistributive policies are in the end extremely well supported, and policy makers roll them back at their own electoral peril. The ARC is clearly an example of concentrated benefits and dispersed costs, but larger and costlier programs are just as well ensconced, enjoying broad appeal precisely because of their expected broad payouts. Social Security did not become "the third rail of American politics" by accident. Medicare and the Affordable Care Act are no different. Whether these programs benefit a thin slice or a broad swath of the American electorate, their continued existence seems assured no matter how deeply that continued existence undermines the founding principle of human equality or the subsequent principle of equality under the law.

Although the outer limits of what the American taxpayer will accept are yet unknown, the massive costs of these sorts of programs are well established. The ongoing problem with budget deficits in the United States and the concern about the $20 trillion debt that has resulted indicate at the very least that the nation is uncomfortable with the costs of such things. But this concern is a matter of degree. The American people are simply not uncomfortable with the idea of equalitarian policy making and have not been for nearly a century. This discomfort is not brought about by a disagreement of kind.

The ongoing question of these policies does not concern their conformity with the principle of equality but rather their sustainability. The federal debt is $20 trillion, but when unfunded liabilities are factored in, there is really a $120 to $200 trillion shortfall. Unfunded liabilities are simply financial promises the government has made to people in the future, the majority of which comprise future Social Security, Medicare, Medicaid, and veterans' benefits. Although estimating unfunded liabilities is difficult, requiring the estimation of future interest, inflation, population growth, and mortality rates, even the lowest estimates exceed the annual economic output of the entire planet. Sustainability is undoubtedly in question moving forward even if equality under the law is not.

The move away from egalitarianism has yielded a situation with no logical, theoretical limit. As laudable or desirable as equality in the form of social outcomes might have been or indeed might be, the difficulties that have emerged are simply undeniable. As the government has grown in both size and scope, and as the nation's financial situation has become more dire, it has become clear that the present growth trajectory cannot continue indefinitely. How far it can continue and what will ultimately stall its growth are still open questions.

Once the outer limit has been reached, though, some rational, political limit on the amount of redistribution will of necessity have to be implemented. America's political development has seen expenditures relative to GDP expand from well less than 5 percent throughout much of the nation's history to more than 20 percent presently. Throughout most of this period of growth, the United States has accrued an ever-increasing debt. Sooner or later a line will have to be drawn. And when that line is drawn, it will call an end, of sorts, to the equalitarian experiment. The problem is ultimately that there is simply no obvious principled limit, even if there might be a technical one. The American people might not be able to afford a certain percentage of GDP dedicated to these types of expenditures, but that is not to say there is a reason they should not be expected to forfeit their negative rights in the bargain. This question becomes simply a technical matter to be adjusted by policy experts over time, as so many political questions did beginning in the Progressive Era.

In the final analysis, a regime cannot be based on notions of both positive and negative liberty because the former undermines the latter in every instance. That said, there is no escaping politically some amount of redistribution in the name of the common good. The real question is how much of this redistribution a nation based on simple human equality can withstand. All evidence points to the fact that we are nearing that limit at present, and when unfunded liabilities are considered, we might have reached that limit some time ago.

The language of equality is never far below the surface in American political thought, but the nature of that equality undergoes consistent reinterpretation with each succeeding generation. Our present understanding, couched in the language of the Founders but derived more clearly from the Progressives, suffers from a lack of commitment on the one hand and a lack of resources on the other. We have come to the point where the problems of our current understanding of equality can be addressed only by using our former understanding of equality.

Theoretically, this outcome would be the best possible one. But it will not come to pass for such high-minded reasons. Like the melding of positive and negative liberty into an incoherent amalgamation of political thought, it will come to pass as a result of political expedience and necessity. As such, the human equality put forth as a self-evident truth by Thomas Jefferson and the rule of law rather than of men that necessarily followed will not be rescued. They will simply be resuscitated to some degree.

What will emerge will be some form of limitation on government, even if that limitation is not defined ultimately by clear formulations of human equality. As such, a government of laws in the purest sense is likely out of reach. What might well be possible, though, is a government that lives within certain prescribed limits, even if those limits are born of pragmatism rather than of principle. Compared to what we have had for nearly one hundred years and to what we are likely to have for the foreseeable future, this outcome might be the best possible one.

9

The Retreat from Equality before the Law

William J. Watkins Jr.*

IN *THE CONSTITUTION OF LIBERTY*, F. A. Hayek observed that "[t]he great aim of the struggle for liberty has been equality before the law."[1] The absence of special privileges for individuals or groups, according to Hayek, is key in distinguishing a free government from an arbitrary one.

In the United States, the idea of equality before the law is traced to the Christian influence on our institutions. Edmund A. Opitz, a long-time scholar in residence at the Foundation for Economic Education, described the United States as a Christian nation "in the sense that our understanding of human nature and destiny, the purpose of individual life, our convictions about right and wrong, our norms, emerged out of the religion of Christendom."[2] Undoubtedly, Moses's teaching in Genesis 1:24 that man is made in the image of God forms the basis for American adherence to equality before the law.[3] As image-bearers, each individual has an intrinsic value. This is especially so when, as the Apostle Peter teaches, we remember that "God shows no partiality" and accepts men from all nations who come in the name of Christ.[4]

Hayek also observed that "[e]quality before the law leads to the demand that all men should also have the same share in making the law."[5] This is especially so in the United States where popular sovereignty is the very bedrock of American constitutionalism. The classical liberal tradition and democracy intersect and require, according to Hayek, that decisions on the use of state power "ought to be made by the majority."[6] Hayek certainly realized the

---

*William J. Watkins Jr. is a research fellow at the Independent Institute and author of the book *Crossroads for Liberty: Recovering the Anti-Federalist Values of America's First Constitution*.

need to protect the individual against the will of the collective. He knew that "power must in fact always be exercised by a few" and believed that power was "less likely to be abused if the power entrusted to the few can always be revoked by those who have to submit to it."[7] In the American context, Thomas Jefferson postulated that in cases where the elected officials of the national government abuse power "a change by the people" at the ballot box is the rightful remedy.[8]

This remedy, however, does not exist when the few exercising power, for all practical purposes, are unaccountable to the people. Today, the United States Supreme Court has the final say on numerous policy issues such as abortion, capital punishment, affirmative action, and marriage. The Court acts as a continuing constitutional convention that makes policy under the guise of the law. The foundation for this activism is animated by a spirit of egalitarianism read into the Equal Protection and Due Process Clauses of the Fourteenth Amendment. The Supreme Court's 2015 opinion in *Obergefell v. Hodges*, which nationalized marriage law by holding the traditional definition of marriage as unconstitutional, is the most recent example of the Court's use of these two clauses to reach desired policy results.[9] Through interpretation of the Fourteenth Amendment, the Court has undermined legitimate state policy experimentation encouraged by our federal system.

The pedagogical elites, however, want to further enliven interpretation of these provisions. Robin West, associate dean at Georgetown University Law Center, urges that the Fourteenth Amendment be used "to wield collective action toward the end of ameliorating the suffering that is consequent to private maldistributions of wealth and security."[10] In other words, West protests that the Court's current jurisprudence targets only state action and she instead demands that private actors be brought within the Fourteenth Amendment's purview. This push for greater progressive equality, according to David Strauss of the University of Chicago School of Law, "requires substantial equalization of results" rather than just open entry to the field of play.[11]

Hayek saw the folly in such leveling schemes and noted that "[e]quality before the law and material equality are . . . not only different but are in conflict with each other; and we can achieve either the one or the other, but not both at the same time."[12]

This paper examines the effect of the egalitarian impulse on the Court's Fourteenth Amendment jurisprudence. The next section explores the origins of due process and equal protection and the evolution of the Court's handling of these provisions. Next, I provide a refresher on first principles of constitutional interpretation from St. George Tucker, an eighteenth-century legal giant. I conclude by using Tucker's wisdom and commonsensical legal reasoning of the mid-twentieth century jurists to offer a reasonable jurisprudence congruent with Hayek's understanding of equality under the law.

Section One of the Fourteenth Amendment

Due Process

The Due Process Clause of the Fourteenth Amendment provides that no state shall "deprive any person of life, liberty, or property without due process of law."[13] The idea of due process dates back to chapter 39 of Magna Carta, which provides that "[n]o freeman shall be taken, imprisoned, or disseized, or outlawed, or exiled, or in any way harmed—nor we will go upon or send upon him—save by the law of the land."[14] By the end of the fourteenth century, Englishmen viewed "due process of law" and "law of the land" as interchangeable phrases.[15] Sir Edward Coke, in his *Institutes*, unambiguously equated law of the land with "the due course and processe of Law."[16] By at least the 1600s, due process meant that before the government could punish a person for some act or omission, government had to resort to the courts and use established procedures under pre-existing laws. Alexander Hamilton was clear about the scope of due process when writing in the late 1780s: "The words 'due process' have a precise technical import, and are only applicable to the process and proceedings of courts of justice; they can never be referred to an act of the legislature."[17]

In the late 1800s, the Supreme Court abandoned the idea that due process concerned only procedures and latched onto the idea of substantive due process when reviewing state laws enacted to protect workers from the unpleasant side effects of the Industrial Revolution. Corporate lawyers, attempting to free their clients from state restrictions, argued that laws circumscribing business operations deprived corporations of due process because the laws were arbitrary.

The classic judicial statement accepting substantive due process is *Lochner v. New York*.[18] *Lochner* dealt with a New York statute prohibiting bakers from working more than 60 hours per week and/or 10 hours per day. The state argued that the statute was a simple exercise of the police power—the reserved power to pass general legislation for the health, safety, and welfare of the people. The High Court, however, held that the statute deprived bakers of liberty without due process of law. Asserting that bakers were not "wards of the state," the Court found "no reasonable ground for interfering with the liberty of person or the right of free contract by determining the hours of labor, in the occupation of baker."[19] The Court rejected the idea that reasonable legislators could conclude that working long hours near hot ovens was unhealthy and thus should be regulated. In short, the *Lochner* Court substituted its judgment for that of New York's elected representatives.

Although the policy result achieved in *Lochner* appeals to many libertarians and conservatives, the mechanism for achieving this result—raw power exerted by unelected judges—should frighten us. Policies set by legislatures can be changed through elections and vigorous debates protected by the First Amendment. Constitutionalized policy decisions cannot be so easily corrected or modified. We are far better off leaving policy decisions to elected and accountable bodies rather than black-robed Platonic Guardians who we hope share our same ideas and predilections. If they do not, then we have no recourse.

The use of substantive due process regarding economic legislation died in the late 1930s when President Franklin D. Roosevelt confronted the Court with his court-packing plan. FDR's efforts were a response to the Court striking down New Deal legislation as unconstitutional. The Court backed off from substantive due process for a short time but then resurrected its use on non-economic legislation. The Court has declared that certain unenumerated constitutional rights are so rooted in the traditions and history of our people that they cannot be infringed without a compelling justification. If they are improperly infringed, due process is violated. Examples of these implied fundamental rights include the right to interstate travel and the right to privacy.

Prior to *Obergefell*, the most familiar modern substantive due process case was *Roe v. Wade*, in which the Court struck down a Texas restriction on abortion as violative of due process of law.[20] The fundamental right involved was the right to privacy. The Court then crafted a trimester system governing abortion regulations. Put bluntly, the Court legislated on abortion for the entire nation.

Equal Protection

In addition to due process, most litigants in the constitutional arena also bring equal protection claims. We should note that almost every law creates classifications and imposes burdens and benefits on different groups. For example, a law prohibiting individuals who have felony convictions from possessing firearms distinguishes between felons and non-felons and imposes greater burdens on the former. Similarly, a law prohibiting individuals under the age of 16 from obtaining a driver's license distinguishes between those under 16 and those over this magic number. Children and adults over 16 enjoy the privilege of operating motor vehicles that persons under 16 do not enjoy.

While the two examples above seem mundane and beyond constitutional challenge, they run afoul of the letter of the Fourteenth Amendment, which in pertinent part declares that "[n]o State . . . shall . . . deny to any person within its jurisdiction equal protection of the laws."[21] At its most basic level, the Equal Protection Clause requires that state and local governments treat similarly situated individuals the same.

To make sense of the Fourteenth Amendment's command of equal protection, one must view it in context. After the end of the Civil War, many states adopted "Black Codes." Some of the stricter codes prevented blacks from owning property, required blacks to carry a pass or license when traveling, and declared any unemployed black man a vagabond. To counter the Black Codes, Congress passed the Civil Rights Act of 1866 over President Andrew Johnson's veto. In its essence, this Act provided that blacks and whites would enjoy the same governmental privileges and immunities. For example, the Act explicitly provided that blacks could make contracts, testify in court, hold and convey property, etc. Many in Congress questioned the constitutional authority for the Civil Rights Act and this led to the drafting and passage of the Fourteenth Amendment. Although the Amendment speaks in more sweeping terms, its parentage is closely connected with efforts to require the states to treat blacks and whites as equals under the law. At its core, the Fourteenth Amendment posits that skin color is not a constitutionally appropriate distinction to be used by government when imposing burdens on, or conferring benefits to, persons within its jurisdiction.

Until the second half of the twentieth century, the Equal Protection Clause was rarely invoked outside of racial discrimination cases. The Court tended to view equal protection claims in other cases, in the word of Justice Oliver Wendell Holmes, as "the usual last resort of constitutional arguments."[22]

A good example of the Court's traditional treatment of equal protection can be found in *Railway Express Agency, Inc. v. New York*.[23] This case concerned a New York City ordinance that prohibited vehicles from displaying advertising except when the vehicle was used in the usual business of the owner and was not used primarily for advertising. Thus, a tobacco company could advertise its cigars on the sides of its trucks, but would be prohibited from selling the same space to advertise another company's product. The City's stated end for enacting the ordinance was traffic safety. By prohibiting the sale of advertising space on trucks, the City reasoned that drivers and pedestrians would have fewer distractions. Opponents of the ordinance brought equal protection claims. They countered that advertising is no less distracting because it is the ad of the vehicle's owner or the message of a paying customer. If the City wanted to protect the public from advertising, they argued, it could eliminate all advertising or regulate the size, color, and content of all advertising.

The Court held that the classification "does not contain the kind of discrimination against which the Equal Protection Clause affords protection" (i.e., it does not use race to burden or benefit members of society).[24] In showing great deference to the lawmakers, the Court further averred that "[i]t is no requirement of equal protection that all evils of the same genus be eradicated or none at all." Absent a showing that the stated motives—traffic safety—for the ordinance were "palpably false," the Court would not second-guess the propriety of the law.[25]

In his concurring opinion, Justice Robert H. Jackson showed much more sympathy toward the equal protection challenge, but offered the following as a standard of equal protection review: "I regard it as a salutary doctrine that cities, states, and the Federal Government must exercise their powers so as not to discriminate between their inhabitants except upon some reasonable differentiation fairly related to the object of regulation."[26]

The beginning of modern equal protection theory is typically traced to a footnote penned by Chief Justice Harlan F. Stone in 1938. In *United States v. Carolene Products Co.*, the Court upheld the power of Congress under the Commerce Clause to prohibit the shipment of filled milk, that is, skimmed milk compounded with any fat or oil.[27] The opponents of the regulation also brought equal protection and due process challenges. The Court swiftly dealt with these by noting that removing filled milk from commerce furthered the goal of public health and thus Congress had a rational basis for passing the law.

In footnote four, Chief Justice Stone hinted that judicial review might be more exacting in cases involving "discrete and insular minorities" or certain fundamental rights.[28] Stone's thoughts on this matter were highly inchoate and were likely meant to spur a scholarly debate on the scope of equal protection. A debate did develop and ultimately led to a revolution in equal protection and due process jurisprudence.

Major changes in the Court's equal protection jurisprudence occurred during the last decade of the Warren Court. In the 1960s, the Court developed a two-tier approach to equal protection cases. In addition to the deferential standard of *Railway Express*, the justices created a new equal protection doctrine whereby they strictly construed certain classifications. This heightened scrutiny is also used when a fundamental right is in play. The use of strict scrutiny proved lethal to most laws under examination as the Court required a close fit between the classification and legislative end. In addition, states could not simply put forward broad legislative goals, but had to show the Court that the classification furthered a compelling state interest. The Warren Court applied strict scrutiny to racial classifications, but also suggested such matters as wealth and illegitimacy might also be subjected to heightened scrutiny.

A prime example of the new equal protection jurisprudence is *Shapiro v. Thompson*, in which the Court examined laws (from Pennsylvania, Connecticut, and the District of Columbia) imposing a one-year residency requirement on indigents who sought public assistance.[29] The governments justified their laws on grounds that the legislation protected the fiscal integrity of the public purse by deterring indigents from migrating solely to take advantage of welfare benefits. This, in turn, would ensure that long-term residents falling on hard times would have access adequate benefits.

The Court observed that the laws created a classification: residents who had resided in the jurisdictions for one year or more and residents who had resided there for less than one year. The Court then applied strict scrutiny because the legislation, in the Court's estimation, implicated the fundamental right to travel—a right nowhere enumerated in the Constitution. Although the laws denied no one entry to the jurisdictions in question, the Court reasoned that the limitation of welfare benefits served as a deterrent to interstate travel and thus infringed on the constitutional right of free movement among the states.

Justice John Marshall Harlan II dissented. Harlan protested that "[t]he 'compelling interest' doctrine [of strict scrutiny] constitutes an increasingly significant exception to the long-established rule that a statute does not deny equal protection if it is rationally related to a legitimate government objective."[30] He noted that strict scrutiny "had its genesis in cases involving racial classifications," but "apparently has been further enlarged to include classifications based upon recent interstate movement, and perhaps those based upon the exercise of any constitutional right."[31] Harlan complained that he could find no authority permitting the Court "to pick out particular human activities, characterize them as 'fundamental,' and give them added protection under an unusually stringent equal protection test."[32] In so acting, Justice Harlan accused the Court of assuming the mantle of a "super-legislature" possessing a peculiar wisdom capable of leading the nation into a better world.[33]

Despite Justice Harlan's protests, the Court persisted in the new equal protection jurisprudence. It also added another tier to the framework. Today, equal protection jurisprudence can be summarized as follows: The top tier, as in *Shapiro*, remains strict scrutiny. To survive judicial review, a classification must serve a compelling state interest and be narrowly tailored to accomplish the stated goal. The classifications subject to strict scrutiny are race, national origin, religion, and alienage. In addition, if a classification burdens a right that the Court deems fundamental, strict scrutiny will apply. The second tier is often referred to as intermediate scrutiny. In defending a classification under this standard, the government must show that the classification serves an important government interest and that the classification is substantially related to serving that interest. Gender—not on the minds of the drafters of the Fourteenth Amendment—is the most frequent classification subjected to intermediate scrutiny. The final tier is rational basis review. The classification is upheld so long as the government can show that the classification is rationally related to furthering a legitimate government interest.

The fate of state legislation challenged in the federal courts often depends on the level of scrutiny applied. Commentators quip that the highest level of scrutiny is strict in theory but fatal in fact. As for rational basis review, they note that so long as the state can proffer a plausible justification for the classification, it will typically pass muster. Of course, the liberality of the rational basis standard is not always honored by the judiciary. Justice Clarence Thomas has observed that the "label the Court affixes to its level of scrutiny in assessing whether government can restrict a given right—be it 'rational basis,' . . . or something else—is increasingly a meaningless formalism. As the Court applies whatever standard it likes to any given case, nothing but empty words separates our constitutional decisions from judicial fiat."[34]

Obergefell: Due Process and Equal Protection Converge

The Court's recent decision in *Obergefell* exemplifies how the Court uses due process and equal protection together to achieve desired egalitarian results. Although a union between a man and woman has been the common-law definition of marriage from colonial times, the petitioners argued that the traditional legal definition is "irrational" and thus counter to the Fourteenth Amendment. The state of Ohio and the other respondents contended that the traditional definition of marriage is rational and should be upheld. They linked the right to marry with potential procreative activity, explaining that society has chosen to channel such activity into a stable social and legal relationship: marriage.

The Supreme Court held that state restrictions of marriage to opposite-sex couples cannot stand under the 14th Amendment. "The Due Process Clause and the Equal Protection Clause are connected in a profound way," the Court explained, as it declared a union between willing persons to be a marriage and thus fundamental.[35] The Court further concluded that this fundamental right must be available to all regardless of the genders of the participants. Proffered reasons for the traditional definition of marriage were not rational, but rather the result of a desire to impose a "stigma and injury."[36]

As with *Lochner*, many libertarians have cheered *Obergefell* as an advancement of liberty. To applaud the decision requires the overcoming of several hurdles. First, same-sex marriage is not "deeply rooted in this nation's history and tradition" (the test used by the Court in recognizing fundamental rights) inasmuch as no state permitted same-sex marriage until a Massachusetts court held in 2003 that limiting marriage to opposite-sex couples violated the state constitution. Second, a state's decision to maintain the meaning of marriage that has been accepted in every culture throughout history can hardly be called irrational. Distinguishing between opposite-sex and same-sex couples is rationally related to a legitimate interest in preserving the traditional institution of marriage. If gender is not a reasonable criterion for marriage, one must wonder what is. Finally, until *Obergefell* the Constitution did not enact any one theory of marriage. The people were free to change or keep the definition of marriage. Indeed, prior to the decision voters and legislators in eleven states and the District of Columbia had changed their definitions of marriage to encompass same-sex couples. This liberty of action has been quashed. The more decisions that are taken away from the people, the less free we really are.

In summary, current judicial conceptions of due process and equal protection have strayed far from the purposes behind the Fourteenth Amendment and the deferential approach exemplified by *Railway Express*. Americans need to reevaluate the revolution launched by the *Lochner* and Warren Courts and continued by their successors. A good starting point would be the man who scholars refer to as the American Blackstone.

St. George Tucker

St. George Tucker was born in 1752 in Bermuda. In 1771, Tucker immigrated to Virginia and studied law under George Wythe. During the revolutionary war, Tucker led an expedition to Bermuda that captured a large quantity of military stores that would later be used by George Washington's army. Tucker distinguished himself in battle and was wounded during the Yorktown campaign. After the war, Tucker enjoyed a thriving law practice and was selected in 1790 to succeed George Wythe as professor of law at William and Mary. Tucker served as a Virginia state court judge and was appointed to the federal bench in 1813 by President James Madison.

Tucker's greatest work was his annotated edition of William Blackstone's *Commentaries on the Laws of England.* In the words of historian Clyde N. Wilson, Tucker sought "to republicanize Blackstone" via extensive essays and notes.[37] Tucker believed that the principles of popular sovereignty adopted during and after the revolution made much of English precedent inapplicable to the New World. Hence, Tucker worked to explain to his students the significance of the supplanting of parliamentary sovereignty and the adopting of other republican institutions. During the first half of the nineteenth century, Tucker's annotated *Commentaries* was the textbook of American legal education.

In his essay entitled "View of the Constitution of the United States," Tucker noted that with the American Revolution, enlightened thinkers drew a clear distinction between sovereignty and government. "[T]he former," Tucker wrote, "was found to reside in the people, and to be unalienable from them," whereas the latter was but an instrument for exercising authority delegated by the people.[38] The branches of government were simply "servants and agents" of the people. When referring to the people, Tucker did not have in mind the undifferentiated inhabitants of the 13 colonies. Instead, Tucker thought of the people of the states as sovereigns. "From the moment of the revolution," Tucker explained, "[the former colonies] became severally independent and sovereign states, possessing all the rights, jurisdiction, and authority, that other sovereign states . . . possess."[39] The Constitution of 1787, Tucker continued, was ratified by conventions of the people in each state. This mode of ratification featured the action of "the people of those states in their highest sovereign capacity."[40]

From this point, Tucker reasoned that the Constitution was "a federal compact" through which "several sovereign and independent states . . . unite[d] themselves together by a perpetual confederacy, without each ceasing to be a perfect state."[41] Absent a specific delegation of power to the general government, Tucker believed that the states retained every power and jurisdiction they possessed before ratification. "The powers delegated to the federal government being all positive, and enumerated," Tucker wrote, "whatever is not enumerated is retained."[42] It would violate accepted maxims of political law for a sovereign state to be deprived of any power by implication.

Tucker then offered his cardinal rule of constitutional interpretation: "Since each state in becoming a member of a federal republic retains uncontrolled jurisdiction over all cases of municipal law, every grant of jurisdiction to the confederacy, in any such case, is to be considered as special, in as much as it derogates from the antecedent rights of the state making the concession."[43] With the national government receiving special and definite powers, Tucker believed that courts should give much discretion to state legislative efforts.

The flip side of the coin was strict construction of federal powers: "The sum of all which appears to be," Tucker wrote, "that the powers delegated to the federal government, are, in all cases, to receive the most strict construction that the instrument will bear, where the rights of a state or of the people, either collectively, or individually, may be drawn into question."[44] Absent this rule of construction, Tucker feared that "the gradual and sometimes imperceptible usurpations of power, will end in the total disregard of all [the Constitution's] intended limitations."[45]

Because of his belief in popular sovereignty, Tucker was a proponent of judicial review, i.e., the power of the courts to review decisions of other departments of government. However, Tucker believed that judges should not strike a legislative enactment unless the measure was at an "irreconcilable variance" with a constitution.[46] If there was any doubt about the legitimacy of a statute, it should be resolved in favor of the people's elected representatives by permitting the law to stand. This was especially so with federal courts reviewing state laws and the broad gamut of state powers.

One might protest that Tucker's advice on constitutional construction was pre-Appomattox and thus inapplicable to the Fourteenth Amendment's Due Process and Equal Protection Clauses. Such an objection might be valid if an effort were made to render the amendment nugatory. However, so long as one keeps in mind the purpose of the Fourteenth Amendment, nothing in Tucker's formula of construction offends. The Supreme Court, when first considering the Civil War amendments in the early 1870s in the *Slaughter-*

house Cases, correctly noted that "one pervading purpose [was] found in all of them."[47] This was, according to the Court, "the freedom of the slave race, the security and firm establishment of that freedom, and the protection of the newly made freeman and citizen from the oppressions of those who had formerly exercised unlimited dominion over him."[48]

Thus, Tucker's wisdom holds true so long as we recognize that whatever authority the states possessed in 1787 to make distinctions based on skin color was circumscribed by the Fourteenth Amendment. Skin pigmentation is not a constitutionally appropriate characteristic to use when burdening or benefitting people through governmental action.

Moreover, nothing in the Fourteenth Amendment compels a substantive understanding of due process. Tucker examined the Fifth Amendment's Due Process Clause in his "View of the Constitution of the United States" and instructed that due process "is by indictment or presentment of good and lawful men, where such deeds be done in due manner, or by writ original of the common law."[49] Tucker further stated that due process "must then be had before a judicial court, or a judicial magistrate."[50] Due process is procedural and nothing more.

Applying Tucker's wisdom to equal protection analysis would end the judicially created three tiers of scrutiny. Courts would continue to closely review state laws that distinguish between citizens based on race. Any law reminiscent of the Black Codes or modern efforts at affirmative action would be presumptively unconstitutional absent some compelling state justification.

But for all other classifications something akin to the *Railway Express* analysis would be the norm. So long as the matter regulated is within the state's traditional authority (i.e., outside of those powers delegated to the federal government) and the classification rationally furthers in some manner the state's goal, then the federal courts must uphold the law.

In our examples dealing with firearm ownership and driving privileges, common sense and *Railway Express* reveal no constitutional infirmity. The classifications are not race based, reasonably differentiate between citizens, and bear a fair relation to the objects of public safety and highway safety. Arguments could be made that, say, only individuals convicted of violent crimes should be prohibited from possessing firearms. A tax cheat or counterfeiter, one might assert, does not represent the same danger to public safety as a burglar or arsonist and thus should not have their rights infringed upon. While this is a valid point, it is a point to be made and considered in a legislative rather than a judicial arena. In our republican form of government, we do not need nor should we desire the courts to dig any deeper than determining that (1) the classification is not racial, (2) there exists a plausible justification for the classification, and (3) the classification has some nexus with the state's declared legislative goal.

The nationalizing of marriage is but another step along the path of judicial monarchs ruling under the guise of due process and equal protection. There is much more to come. Some liberal scholars have long argued that broad societal groups, such as the poor and the homeless, should be viewed as a suspect class akin to race.[51] They would have the courts strictly scrutinize any law that might arguably disadvantage low-income individuals. For instance, a state budget law reducing funding for unemployment benefits, subsidized school lunches, or Head Start-type programs would require the state to show furtherance of a compelling interest with the budget cut narrowly tailored to support the interest.

Conclusion

Archibald Cox, writing in the mid-1960s, noted that "[o]nce loosed, the idea of Equality is not easily cabined."[52] This is especially concerning when we remember the admonition of Gottfried Dietze that "equality competes with freedom."[53] Through modern due process and equal protection jurisprudence, the Court has stretched the Fourteenth Amendment beyond the limited objectives of its framers and has made itself, in the words of Justice Harlan, a "super-legislature." We have what Hayek would recognize as a telocratic (purpose-driven) judicial system rather than a nomocratic (law-governed) one. The purpose, of course, is animated by a sense of egalitarianism incongruent with a Hayekian understanding of equality before the law.

For instructions in judicial modesty, we should turn to the American Blackstone. In Tucker's work we find constitutional first principles and proven rules of construction. In light of the broad powers remaining with the states (our laboratories of democracy), state laws should not be struck absent an "irreconcilable variance" with the Fourteenth Amendment's plain language and certain purpose. Applying Tucker's constitutional insights, jurists should humble themselves and abandon the making of policy. Constitutionalization of prevailing sentiments renders our system inflexible and precludes a vigorous democratic debate in which the people can be persuaded of the rightness of new ideas and the wrongness of old ones and make the necessary reforms in accordance with the rule of law.

PART III

Egalitarianism, Economic Performance, and the Laws of Economics

10

Classroom Egalitarianism

Stephen Shmanske*

MANY ECONOMICS COURSES start with definitions of economics, and there are several, not necessarily mutually exclusive, ones. This essay will focus on one of the more common definitions, which although useful, does have some subtle problems that can set students off on the wrong foot. The definition in question is that economics is the study of the allocation of scarce resources to the production of goods and services, and the distribution of the goods and services. Using this definition an immediate connection is made to students by simplifying the technical language to focus on three questions that must be answered by society and are, therefore, worthy of study. Namely, what do we make? How do we make it? And, who gets it? It is customary to follow this up immediately by introducing the concept of scarcity.[1] Without scarcity the answers to these questions are trivially easy. Indeed, we could make everything we want in any wasteful method for everybody. I suppose in this nirvana the issue of egalitarianism would be moot and economics would be useless. Unfortunately, scarcity is all around us and we must pay attention to these three basic questions.

This popular definition, however, has the potential of leading students and practitioners astray in a couple of ways. This definition focuses too much attention on things, scarce resources and final goods, where they come from and where they go, and not enough attention on people. Indeed, people are in the definition only in the collective sense of "we" or "society," thus hinting that the problems caused by scarcity are to be solved in a top-down manner.

*Stephen Shmanske is Professor Emeritus of Economics in the College of Business and Economics at California State University, East Bay.

In reality, it is individuals who must make the decisions in an economy and one can study these decisions only after studying what the individuals want and how they act. To counter the collectivist theme of how "society" solves problems, it is important to also include Alfred Marshall's definition of economics: "Economics is a study of mankind in the ordinary business of life."[2] By starting with the individual there is less temptation to adopt an elitist, collectivist, or top-down mindset with respect to any social policy.

Another related problem with the allocation/production/distribution definition will be the theme of this essay. This problem has the potential of leading students and practitioners seriously astray if it is not forcefully and immediately qualified. The problem is that although there are different sets of considerations in each of the basic questions and although they can be focused on separately, they cannot be answered in isolation of each other because of the linkages and feedbacks among them. In effect, it is like a three-equation system with three variables. Such equations can be considered individually but they can only be solved simultaneously. Unfortunately, most people untrained in economics (and even some who are and who should know better) do not recognize this fact. They propose nice-sounding solutions regarding what should be made, or how, or for whom without recognizing the implications for the two issues they ignore. Their utopian visions will be thwarted by the reality of scarcity and the reality of the interconnections among the issues. Even though this paper will primarily consider the distribution question, which seems the most relevant to egalitarianism, one must not forget the linkages among distribution, allocation, and production.

At the outset, it is worthy to note that there is a natural and coherent system that does address and answer each of the what, how, and for whom questions. A market system of private property and free exchange with market prices automatically and simultaneously solves society's problems.[3] Producers decide what to make by attempting to employ a low cost set of resources to make what they think they can sell at a profit. Individuals own the resources, most importantly their labor and ingenuity, and either produce with them or sell or rent them to other producers, thus earning income. The producers' profits and the individuals' incomes feed into the demands that guide producers' allocation decisions. The production decisions are simultaneously addressed as producers must conserve in their expenditure on scarce resources,

and the distribution question is answered as each individual resource sup-
plier and profit-stream residual claimant spends their income on what is
deemed desirable to them. With market prices providing the information,
decentralized agents make decisions, and allocation, production, and distribution are achieved.[4] It is also worthy to note that all this was basically set forth
in Adam Smith's invisible hand as early as 1776.[5] Additionally, Smith, a full
century before Marshall, also recognized the primacy of the individual and
the value of exchange, noting that people produce and give to others what the
others want in return for receiving what they want for themselves. Smith also
intuited the desirable properties of the equilibrium that occurs, properties only
formalized later in the idea of Pareto Optimality,[6] and only formally proved
almost two centuries later.[7]

1. Classroom consideration of the distribution question.

In an attempt to solicit student participation I use an in-class exercise that
shows the folly of the top-down mindset. I set forth a fictional society in which
a king owns a supply of tomatoes and has to establish a method of distribution.
I then ask students to come up with one. In no particular order students will
make suggestions, and I will help to refine and categorize them eventually
coming up with a list like table 10.1.

Table 10.1. Methods of Distribution

1. Price Exchange System

2. Queuing/First-Come, First-Served

3. Equal/Fair/Egalitarian

4. Random

5. Fiat/Personal Characteristics

6. Might Makes Right

For example, a student might simply say that the king could give them
away. This is not a complete answer, however, and needs to be fleshed out.
How is the give-away to be accomplished? Without scarcity the answer is easy,
just provide access to the tomatoes and everyone takes as many or as few as
they want. But we do have scarcity and, as a consequence, open access to the

tomatoes would not assure that each get the tomatoes they desire. So in reality, this might actually lead to a first-come, first-served method to distribute the tomatoes, enumerated as (2) in table 10.1. However, unless people are nice and queuing is orderly, an open-access system would devolve into a free-for-all with all the negative connotations attached. Perhaps this would be more like system (6) in which those most aggressive in queuing or in cutting or dodging the queue get the tomatoes.

Furthermore, even if the queuing is organized and orderly, one must still consider who would have whatever characteristics are most important in lining up. That is, simply saying first-come, first-served is not a full answer to the distribution question either until it is explained who is and who isn't able to queue up soon enough to get the tomatoes. Lest one mistakenly think that a waiting-in-line system is egalitarian, a little critical thinking indicates that this is not so. Quite obviously aged or infirm people will not be able to line up as early or as long as others. Furthermore, people have different amounts of time available to spend waiting in lines, or simply different levels of patience. Thus, aspects of (5) in which those with certain identifiable (or revealed by behavior) characteristics such as free time, stamina,[8] or patience are important in obtaining tomatoes.

There are still more issues with respect to the queuing protocol. How early can you line up? How many tomatoes can you take when it is your turn? Can you get back in line? Can you hold places in line for others? Can you sell your place in line? Can you pay someone to get in line for you?[9] All of these questions must be answered before the distribution question is fully resolved.

But the student might actually have something else in mind in the statement, "just give them away." The king could specify by his own fiat who is to receive the tomatoes and how many. But, such a king must have some way to decide, thus implying a choice based on some observable characteristics of the individuals (5). Within the monarchical analogy, the king's relatives, concubines, lords, knights, and bishops of the favored religion would fare well. The peasants, foreigners, or otherwise outcasts would not. In today's world, the political class would fare well if a central authority were to decide the distribution question.

At this point either this student or someone else in the class will conjure up a benevolent king who attempts to distribute the tomatoes equally or "fairly." Consideration of this possibility presents an opportunity to examine "equality" and "fairness." Perhaps the first thing that even a second grader would argue is that it is fair to give out the tomatoes equally. This, however, is too vague. Equal could mean equal per capita, equal per family, or equal per capita of at least a minimum age. Then, of course, some people might conveniently forget their basic second-grade wisdom and justify the fairness in giving more tomatoes to some rather than others.[10] To bring up a recurring modern analogy, try to discuss what is fair when considering tax cuts in a progressive tax system. There is unlikely to be agreement in this arena.

Getting back to the tomatoes, there is still an unresolved issue with the logistics of equal division outside the improbable (impossible?) chance that the number of exactly equal, plump tomatoes happens to be a nice multiple of the population. I like to make students think about fractions at this point. Suppose there are n citizens and n-1 tomatoes. How is equal distribution to be achieved? Everyone except one would get a tomato with a small slice taken out but the last person would end up with tomato puree. At the second-grade level it is easy to proclaim that equal distribution is desirable without any critical thinking about whether it is even possible. Because of shallow thinking, it is little understood that equal distribution is impossible. Tomatoes are one thing, how about sailboat rides on the king's yacht? About the best that equal division can achieve in this case is to take turns. But who goes first? We are back in a queuing scenario (2) or in some other rule (5) to decide the order. Perhaps priority tickets could be distributed randomly as in (4). Random distribution of priority tickets might be considered a subset of equal distribution (3) if each has an equal chance of getting the first ride. Hopefully you will make it to your turn before you die and that it won't rain on your day. It seems to me very naive to think that the politically well-connected will not be able to jump the queue when convenient for them.

In general, equal division is not possible. Furthermore, it is less efficacious than it first seems. Equal distribution is not even desirable. A quick show of students' raised hands will indicate those who don't even like tomatoes or those who get seasick. Neither should insulin be distributed equally, it is life saving for some and poison to others.

Students usually are too nice and have to be prodded to come up with (6) might makes right. It is possible that the king's subjects could be fed up with any of his systems and simply storm the palace and take the tomatoes. This method of distribution is not nice, but it is a method.

Somewhere along the line a student will suggest that the king sell the tomatoes. One of the beauties of this system is that it has the potential to solve the distribution question exactly once the equilibrium price is established. Presumably, at a zero price there will not be enough tomatoes. Also, as a thought experiment, at an infinite price there would be no quantity demanded. So as the price comes down from infinity, more and more tomatoes are demanded until the quantity demanded exactly equals the quantity supplied. There is no need for lines (2), lotteries (4), ad hoc discrimination based on personal characteristics (5), or uncivil behavior (6). Furthermore, even without the use of money, an exchange can take place in a barter system with the "price" quoted perhaps in the number of weeds the buyer is willing to pull from the tomato patch.

2. The link between distribution and production.

The last point provides the perfect segue into the link between how the goods get produced and who gets them, while at the same time illustrating another beauty of the price exchange system. In a quid pro quo or exchange system there are actually good incentives supplied to produce the goods in the first place. The incentives supplied in each of the other methods are either wasteful, perverse, or nonexistent.

In the exchange system (1) the incentive is to have what the king wants in order to trade for tomatoes. This might be the willingness to work in the tomato patch, directly leading to more tomatoes. It might instead be a barter for some other home-produced good, thus feeding into the production (and allocation) decisions for other goods. In a money economy it leads to the incentive to earn income. With a few exceptions such as theft and fraud, people earn money by doing something nice for someone else, be it chopping firewood, stacking lumber, balancing ledger accounts, painting portraits, slopping the pigs, baking pies, teaching students, or whatever. This is where production comes from in the first place. The price exchange system exactly solves the distribution question while providing nice incentives to produce goods and services in the first place. This cannot be said of any of the other systems considered in table 10.1.

In queuing (2), the incentive is to line up fast. The incentive is also to learn how to manipulate the queuing system to one's favor. Can I save my place in this line while I go over to get in that line? Can I spread my children out in separate lines to see which goes fastest? These are curious incentives indeed. It is not clear why the king or why most people in any society would favor an incentive system dedicated to getting everyone to line up fast. A small percentage of people, perhaps, would find it easier to wait in line than to pick weeds in the tomato patch. I suspect, however, that most people would find it damaging to one's psyche and feelings of achievement if waiting in line was the only opportunity to get the goods they wanted. Regardless, waiting in line does not get the tomatoes produced in the first place.

Systems (3) and (4) do not provide any incentives at all. Just sit back and get your share of the tomatoes or wait your turn for a sailboat ride. In this system, one must consider why any tomatoes get produced in the first place. The unavoidable truth is that not as many do get produced. An economy where all share equally in the output, will never be as productive as the market exchange system. Citizens will have to be cajoled (possibly enslaved) to do the work for the good of their country (or comrades) as in "from each according to his ability" and then shamed from wanting more of the short supply as in "to each according to his need." Working cannot be voluntary in such a system and, therefore, is pursued with neither joy nor efficiency. Work is a necessary evil to be put up with until the end of your shift at which time you get the equal privilege of standing in line for the short supply of goods. It may seem nice to get your equal share of the production, but there is nothing nice about it once you consider the ramifications of such a distribution system in regards to getting the goods produced.

Furthermore, even if the impossible system of equal distribution were possible, the system still would not be egalitarian with respect to production. Some jobs are better than others and there will be competition to get those jobs. Even in a Soviet-style system, those better in sports or academics will rise up further in the system to jobs with more perquisites. For example, the Russian national ice hockey team members obviously got better nutrition and travel opportunities than the average Russian factory worker (so much for equal distribution of the goods that do get produced). As a corollary result to this unequal sharing based on job type, it is understandable that voluntary effort would be supplied in the sporting industry to maintain one's position while voluntary effort would not be forthcoming in mundane industries such as manufacturing or agriculture where, consequently (and predictably), short supplies were legendary.

The previous point deserves to be hammered home more forcefully. It is not only that corruption seeps in to give some workers better conditions than others. Rather it is the unavoidable consequence of an equal distribution system in which effort or productivity is theoretically divorced from one's ability to consume. As long as some jobs are better or easier than others (an aspect of scarcity) and as long as effort is costly (more scarcity), people will work harder to get or keep the good jobs and others must be relatively enslaved to do the bad or distasteful jobs. So much for egalitarianism in production when equal distribution of goods and services is forced upon a society.

The incentives supplied in a fiat system (5) would depend on the characteristics being favored. In fairy tales, one would try to marry into the royal family, presumably to get a higher standard of living. Hopefully, the king would favor hard-working, productive people and reward them with more tomatoes. Of course, the easiest way to do this would be to resort to the quid pro quo system in method (1) in the first place. If the king is not careful, the incentives could even be perverse as would be the case if goods and services were distributed according to measures of poverty. Even in our society it is possible that attempting to earn more income can make one lose eligibility for benefits, thus supplying a disincentive to work. The phasing out of any poverty relief system as income grows is, unfortunately, subject to this problem.

The uncivil society that allows violence (6) to decide the distribution of goods and services obviously supplies incentives that are unproductive or counterproductive. If one's tomatoes can be stolen, one is probably not going to grow them in the first place. If farmers do grow tomatoes, they have to divert effort from this productive activity to the activity of protecting the tomato patch from thieves and marauders. The result is a lower supply of tomatoes.

The obvious conclusion from this section is that the price exchange system (1), and *only* the price exchange system, gives nice incentives for the production of goods and services. Voluntarily offering to do something nice for someone else in exchange for more goods and services, or the purchasing power to get them, comes about naturally in this system. The other systems either provide no incentives (3) and (4), silly, unproductive incentives like lining up (2) or courting favor with the rulers (5), or perverse incentives like attempting to be poor (5) or outright violence (6).

3. The inevitability of the price exchange system.

We have seen that a system of equal distribution of goods and services is impossible to actually achieve and not particularly desirable in the first place. There is still another aspect to consider that also favors the use of the price exchange system. Namely, the other systems are not robust with respect to voluntary exchange between the citizens after the goods are initially distributed. Simple thought experiments with respect to each of the other systems indicate the extent to which this already happens in our society.

For example, consider an instance in which queuing is used to distribute goods and services because the price is too low. It is often the case that a blockbuster event like a much anticipated opening night of a movie, a popular rock concert, or a mega-sporting event are sellouts at the stated ticket price. One must somehow negotiate a queue (perhaps even camping out overnight) to get tickets. No one who does that and gets to the front of the line, says, "I'll have one ticket." People will buy the maximum amount knowing that they can be resold. In many cases, in a type of barter system with friends, the tickets are already "resold" as when the person who waits in line gets his car washed or another favor from the others in his party in exchange for spending time in line. Perhaps others will directly pay people to wait in line for them. Enforcing the distribution that comes about in queuing would require criminalizing these voluntary exchanges between citizens.

What happens in the case of theft (6)? I simply point out that a thief who steals your car stereo system doesn't do it because he wants to listen to music. Fences pay for stolen items, which get redistributed in a price exchange system.

In the egalitarian system of equal division, those who don't like tomatoes can barter them with their neighbors for something they do want. This retrading or redistribution is beneficial to both parties, as is the general occurrence whenever individuals engage in voluntary exchange. One is led to ponder why society shouldn't rely on a voluntary exchange system in the first place if the final distribution of goods and services ends up being determined that way anyway.

4. Freedom or Fascism?

Despite the win-win situation that comes from voluntary exchange there are probably some who would argue that an egalitarianism that ensures that all get the same thing is preferential to individual decision-making that, invariably, leads to differences in outcomes. Some will work harder, longer, or smarter than others, and will consume different sets of goods and services. Elites, perhaps, would look down upon the choices that some individuals make and attempt to insert their preferences upon the population in general. This urge can explain restrictions on things as varied as smoking (marijuana or tobacco), sugary soft drinks, or watering your garden. After all, if you use less water, there is more for everyone else. If you spend (waste?) less on some goods you will buy more of the others. On the other side of the coin of forced restrictions is forced consumption. Things such as nuclear deterrence capabilities, required minimum coverages in health insurance policies, required access to family leave policies at work, required payments for public schools, and items required by building codes, are just some examples. Some people, perhaps disproportionately those with higher incomes, may think it wise to consume these items and cannot fathom why other people would choose to go without them. Consequently, in the name of egalitarianism they support policies that subsidize, freely provide, or force consumption of these and other items. As a purely logical consequence, forcing equal consumption of things that not everyone wants, coupled with scarcity, means people must get less of what they actually do want.

In another more advanced lecture I present an analysis of the egalitarian urge to enable all to be able to consume a good like gasoline. Supposedly to help those with lower incomes, a price control might be levied on gasoline. As is well known, this would cause a shortage. At first, gasoline stations would simply close when they ran out of fuel. As a response to this, lines would develop, which are wasteful and inconvenient at the least, and sometimes turn ugly. In an attempt to deal with this, some politicians have proposed a type of rationing system involving coupons, such as in the coupon-ration books used during World War II. While it is not certain how the coupons would have been distributed (registered vehicle, licensed driver, per capita, per family), it is likely that the mayor, police, volunteer firemen, and the military get all the coupons they "need." In specifying what they "need," they may even surreptitiously get extra coupons to distribute through back channels as a quid pro quo for poitical favors. Will you get all the coupons you need or want? Probably not. Once again, because of scarcity someone will have to cut back. The coupons, themselves, have to be relatively scarce or they won't do the job of rationing the scarce gasoline. As such, the coupons themselves will have a value equal to the difference between the controlled price of gasoline and the equilibrium price. This extra value of the coupons gets captured by the recipients of the coupons, the distribution of which is determined by the political class.

There are many steps in the argument of the preceding paragraph and it takes another whole lecture combined with intermediate-level diagrams to cover fully, but the essence of the argument is telling. Instead of allowing a market equilibrium price for gasoline with the revenues going to the producers, some would think it more egalitarian if the price per gallon were kept low. Then the rationing coupons, which actually have a value, would be distributed to ration the short supply. This also seems egalitarian because, as a first approximation at least, the rhetoric would be all about distributing the coupons equally, whether or not this actually would happen. Recipients of the coupons, especially those who get more than they can use (non-drivers perhaps, along with the mayor and the politically connected) would actually receive a windfall based on the value of the scarce coupons. What has actually happened? Some of the value that would otherwise go to the producers of gasoline to ease the shortage by increasing production is usurped by those receiving the coupons and those in charge of distributing the coupons. While this is absolutely not egalitarian, those on the receiving end of the usurped value might favor such a convoluted system while rhetorically claiming that it is socially just, fair, and/or egalitarian. In the end we are less free to consume the amount of gasoline we want, poorer, less mobile because of the under-production of gasoline, and unequally segmented into politically favored and disfavored classes.

Choices can also be circumscribed and standardized at the production level. The aforementioned family leave policies are one example. In other settings it is well known that some unions will enforce work rules that restrict working too hard and that will flatten pay scales. "All for one and one for all" is the appropriate egalitarian epithet in this instance. In my university the administration and the high-performing faculty would typically be in favor of merit pay to reward the best professors. Unfortunately, the union would usually succeed in eliminating such merit pay from the final contracts. In the name of egalitarianism, my choices to work harder in an attempt to earn more or to trade away potential family leave in exchange for higher pay are taken away from me. Once again, forcing everyone to be the same in some dimension or other invariably harms those whose preferences lean another way.

One final example involves urban-zoning and land-use policies. Some people might actually choose to voluntarily have a long commute as a trade-off for more acreage. Elites may think that this is a bad decision and want everyone to live within an urban boundary. So-called sustainable, egalitarian, urban living spaces along mass transit corridors will be lauded and excessive carbon footprints from private automobiles will be derided in the attempt to standardize the outcomes for everyone.[11] If you like this lifestyle, fine, but if you don't, the egalitarian urge ends up seeming far more fascist than fair.

Financial Egalitarianism in America

Robert E. Wright*

THE CAUSES OF the financial fiasco of 2008 were many and complex, but at the core of the crisis stood mortgages that would not have been made by prudent lenders or allowed by rational regulators. From humble origins in the 1990s, the subprime mortgage market had become by 2005 a grand social experiment, an attempt to render homogenous (equal) that which was inherently variegated (unequal)—creditworthiness. Specifically, the financial egalitarianism of the Clinton and Bush administrations sought to close the gap between "minority" and "white" homeownership rates by relaxing lending standards in response to perceptions of high levels of financial discrimination.[1] Those perceptions ultimately were rooted in hard data that showed that access to home mortgages varied considerably by race, ethnicity, and gender,[2] although the statistics never clearly revealed *why* mortgage approval and interest rates varied so widely.[3]

In any event, not all borrowers proved equally likely to service their mortgages. Relaxed lending standards exacerbated asymmetric information (adverse selection and moral hazard), which soon led to a higher than expected rate of defaults, the economic import of which was magnified by leverage and other institutional factors. In effect, financial reality killed financial egalitarianism, at least the type of "equal outcome" egalitarianism envisioned by Clinton-Bush regulators. Moreover, the social problem that started it all, the fact that blacks, Hispanics, and women find it more difficult and costly to obtain home mortgages than members of other groups do, looms as large as ever.[4]

---

*Robert E. Wright is the Nef Family Chair of Political Economy at Augustana University in Sioux Falls, South Dakota, and the author or coauthor of eighteen books, including *The Poverty of Slavery: How Unfree Labor Pollutes the Economy* (2017).

A more realistic financial egalitarianism that stresses equality of opportunity, however, remains a viable policy option and in the past has proven itself potent. Previous to the Clinton-Bush experiment in "equal outcome" financial egalitarianism, the United States improved access to financial markets by encouraging innovation and entry, or "equal opportunity" financial egalitarianism.[5]

The second section of this article reviews how US financial regulators (at first, state legislators and bureaucratic officials and later, federal agencies) successfully encouraged more equal access to the financial system by allowing members of aggrieved groups to start their own financial institutions, import new financial institutions and markets from abroad, and develop homegrown financial innovations. The third section shows that the Clinton and Bush administrations broke with that tradition by effectively mandating equal but extremely low mortgage lending standards. The fourth and final section concludes that America's traditional type of financial egalitarianism (equal opportunities) is empirically superior to the financial egalitarianism (equal outcomes) of the Clinton and Bush administrations because it works in conjunction with, rather than in opposition to, economic realities like competition and asymmetric information.

Financial Egalitarianism as Equal Opportunities

America's current financial system is the product of over two centuries of innovation, much of it driven by and for people previously excluded from specific sectors of the system. In fact, the history of the US financial system can be told from the perspective of "minorities" or "outsiders" forcing their way into the system via innovative new financial institutions or products. Even the nation's founding can be seen as a response to financial discrimination against all of the colonists. Several times late in the colonial era, British Imperial authorities blocked the formation of joint-stock commercial banks proposed by leading colonial merchants like Thomas Willing and Robert Morris. Unsurprisingly, one of the first acts of the new nation was the creation of a joint-stock commercial bank, the Bank of North America, led by those same merchants and based in Philadelphia. Soon after, merchants who found it difficult to borrow in Philadelphia formed several additional commercial banks in the new nation's major seaport cities. Soon after, elites excluded from access to existing banks for political reasons formed commercial banks of their own.[6]

After frontier farmers, urban artisans, mechanics, retailers, and other small businessmen complained that they found it difficult to obtain loans from the banking institutions formed in the 1790s and early 1800s, state legislators granted them permission to form their own commercial banks.[7] Erstwhile artisan Benjamin Franklin also pitched in by creating microfinance funds for artisans in Philadelphia and Boston.[8]

After impoverished Americans discovered that they could not make deposits in commercial banks, even those run by artisans or shopkeepers, they joined with philanthropists (mutual) or investors (joint-stock) to form savings banks. When working people of middling means discovered they could not borrow from commercial or savings banks, they teamed up to create building and loan societies that helped the less-than-wealthy to both save and to borrow to build new homes or improve existing structures. However, building and loan societies would not lend to those who wanted to borrow for other reasons, so early in the twentieth century consumers created credit unions, non profit depository institutions for everyday folks interested in affordable, plain vanilla banking.[9]

Many of the poor were locked out of early credit unions, however, so North Carolinian Arthur J. Morris created Morris Plan banks, for-profit companies that lent from $50 to $5,000 on the basis of character, income, and co-signers. Eventually, some 170 Morris Plan banks lent $90 billion to millions of the working poor.[10] The Russell Sage Foundation and other philanthropists also sought to keep the poor out of the clutches of loan sharks by forming nonprofit "remedial loan societies." They also successfully advocated raising state interest rate ceilings in order to increase competition in the small loan market by allowing lenders making small, short-term loans, which naturally have high fixed costs, to earn a profit.[11]

Fighting discrimination via entry was not limited to the poor. After Western borrowers discovered that Eastern lenders charged them even higher interest rates than higher default rates on Western mortgages warranted, they established their own mortgage companies.[12] Similarly, when Wall Street brokers found it difficult to join the "Old Board," the original New York Stock Exchange, they formed a "New Board" and encouraged wider membership.[13]

Major parts of the insurance sector were also transformed by innovation and new entry spurred by the perception of discrimination. Specialized insurers regularly arose to underwrite newly identified risks, like wind damage, old risks that incumbent insurers stopped covering, like specific fire hazards, or to insure new types of businesses, like factories. Almost every major ethnic and religious group formed their own life insurance companies, as well as their own commercial banks, mutual savings banks, building and loans, credit unions, and even investment banks. In some states, like Massachusetts and New York, savings banks also offered modest life insurance policies. The poorest of the poor purchased industrial life insurance or fraternal burial insurance.[14]

Fraternals, which also offered the poor no-frills sickness and medical insurance, were numerous and generally successful because their intimacy allowed them to mitigate asymmetric information at low cost. They faded only after governments began to regulate them closely during the Great Depression.[15] During World War I, governments also squelched so-called "bucket shops," businesses that allowed common folk, including African-Americans and women, to speculate in the stock market without actually owning any securities.[16]

Blacks, Hispanics, women, and members of other ostensibly oppressed groups also combated unequal access to the financial system by forming their own institutions. Women, for example, formed their own mining stock exchange in San Francisco in the late nineteenth century. Early in the twentieth century, African-American Maggie Walker established a bank that catered to African-Americans of both genders. "Let us put our moneys together; let us use our moneys; let us put our money out at usury among ourselves, and reap the benefit ourselves," she argued in an early speech. By 1919, her bank, by then called the St. Luke Bank and Trust Company, had almost $400,000 on deposit and loans spread throughout Richmond, Virginia's African-American community.[17]

The first state-chartered banks to specialize in lending to women formed in the 1910s in big cities like New York, Chicago, Kansas City, and Dallas, as well as in rural Wyoming, Colorado, Iowa, and Kansas.[18] One of those pioneers was the First Woman's Bank of Tennessee, established in 1919 by Brenda Runyon. Shortly after, a savings and loan run entirely by women and 90 percent female-owned was established in the Midwest.[19] Women also joined the credit union movement. By 1978, seventeen female-controlled credit unions were in operation, along with four savings and loans and seven commercial banks.[20] One of those commercial banks, the Women's Bank, had been established the year before by Mary Roebling, erstwhile head of Trenton Trust.[21]

Women have also actively fought discrimination in the securities sector by striking off on their own. In 1947, Wilma Soss founded the Federation of Women Shareholders in American Businesses, which accumulated the proxies of female shareholders into a block that Soss used at stockholder meetings to verbally bludgeon and publicly shame corporate executives who refused to appoint qualified female directors to their boards.[22] A decade later, pioneers like Muriel Siebert were just breaking into stock brokerage and finding Wall Street's culture virulently misogynistic. In 1967, Siebert concluded that existing firms would not allow any woman to rise through the ranks, so she purchased her own seat on the New York Stock Exchange. It took another decade, however, for other females to join her on the Big Board.[23] The exploits of numerous other female pioneers in the securities industry have been chronicled elsewhere.[24]

African-Americans also fought discriminatory practices by forming and running their own financial institutions. Free blacks in the antebellum North and South shut out of jobs and insurance formed numerous benevolent and beneficial societies. For a small weekly sum, free blacks received payments when they became unemployed or ill. Some societies also paid death benefits. About half the free black population in Philadelphia reported being a member of at least one of the societies by 1849.[25]

In the 1880s, African-Americans were pushed into the formal life insurance industry when some white-owned insurers started to charge blacks higher premiums or refused their business entirely. Wealthier African-Americans took umbrage and struck off on their own because they knew that only impoverished blacks suffered the high mortality rates that the incumbent life insurers so feared.[26]

Prior to World War II, numerous insurers and banks owned and operated by African-Americans were in operation but not enough of them to meet all of the demand.[27] Between 1947 and 1964, African-American-owned savings and loan associations tripled their assets while black-owned commercial bank assets increased from a total of $5 million in 1940 to $53 million in the mid-1960s. Between 1951 and 1964, the assets of African-American-controlled insurance companies doubled to $320 million. The largest African-American owned bank was Freedom National Bank in New York. At its height, it boasted deposits of $30 million, making it the 1,734th largest bank in a country with over 10,000 banks.[28] The wealthiest African-American in the US after World War II may have been the president of an insurance company in Durham, North Carolina.[29]

Most wealth owned by African-Americans, however, remained invested in white-controlled banks and insurers because most blacks believed that mainstream institutions would provide them with superior risk-adjusted returns due to ingrained institutional racism.[30] In Chicago in 1947, for example, 21 mortgage companies run by African-Americans found raising adequate capital "all but impossible" because "non-Negro institutions" would not buy, or lend on the collateral of, their mortgages.[31] Instead of helping minority-owned financial institutions to improve their offerings, however, regulators encouraged bigger, invariably white-controlled ones, to gobble them up during the great merger waves of the 1980s–2000s.[32] Maggie Walker's bank, for example, survived the Depression (though Walker herself died in December 1934) but its identity as a bank for African-Americans died in the merger craze of the late twentieth century.[33]

Financial Egalitarianism as Equal Outcomes

In an effort to ensure that everyone could achieve the "American Dream" without attempting politically fraught reforms to improve education, reduce unemployment, underemployment, and racial bigotry, or ameliorate the other root causes of income and credit disparities, policy makers in the 1990s and early 2000s opened up access to credit for people who traditionally, and for rational reasons, could only borrow small sums for short periods, if they could borrow at all.[34] To induce banks to lend to such borrowers, regulators threatened sanctions while simultaneously helping lenders to relax their credit standards and providing them with a government safety net.[35] Combined with the contemporaneous deterioration of corporate governance, the result was a dystopian disaster that almost brought down the global economy.[36]

The details of financial discrimination varied over time and place as well as did the specific attributes of the loan or insurance applicant. Wealthy, single white women, for example, long enjoyed access to the financial system almost on a par with white men while poor, married women of color sometimes found it difficult to pawn personal items because pawnbrokers presumed the items had been stolen. Both law and custom commanded those proscriptions, which changed only slowly until the 1960s and 1970s, when various pieces of civil rights legislation removed the legal basis for outright discrimination and exclusion. Financial institutions, however, initially remained the final arbiters of who they would, or would not, count as customers.

The Community Reinvestment Act of 1977 (CRA) mandated that government-insured banks provide mortgage loans throughout their respective areas of operation, even poor ones. Banks allowed CRA's passage because it was initially toothless. When William Clinton assumed the presidency in early 1993, however, most policy makers were convinced that African-Americans and other minorities, including women and the poor, still faced discrimination in the nation's financial markets and intermediaries, though many academics countered that discrimination had grown much more subtle, and hence difficult to detect, since the 1960s. Even direct tests of lender and insurer conduct towards legally protected groups proved inconclusive, as well as costly to conduct and difficult to interpret. Due to data limitations and the large number of variables used by bankers/insurers in loan/coverage decisions, statistical analysts could not reject the hypothesis that financial intermediaries turned away members of group X not out of bigotry but because the rejected applicants were objectively poor credit risks.[37]

For decades, uncertainty about the extent of financial discrimination handcuffed policy makers not eager to tamper with "market forces" or arouse the ire of Wall Street. The Clinton administration, which wanted to increase a home-ownership rate that had fallen a few points from its 1980 high of almost 66 percent, hit upon a compromise with devastating unintended consequences.[38] It gave the CRA teeth by preventing banks with low CRA compliance scores from merging. That was a major penalty by 1993 because deregulation of bank branching restrictions had set off a major merger wave. The change allowed community interest groups like ACORN (Association of Community Organizations for Reform Now) to pressure banks to increase lending in poorer areas. Starting in 1999, good CRA ratings were also necessary for banks that desired to form financial holding companies under the Gramm-Leach-Bliley Act, which many did in order to participate in a wider variety of financial markets.[39]

At the same time, however, the government undertook several policy reforms that made it easier for banks to lend to higher-risk borrowers. First, it pushed its government-sponsored enterprises (GSEs), Fannie Mae and Freddie Mac, to make housing more affordable. In March 1994, the GSEs responded by promising a trillion dollars to enable 10 million low-income earners and minorities to purchase their own homes. The GSEs borrowed the money for the risky endeavor under an implicit government guarantee of their debt. In 1995, the Department of Housing and Urban Development (HUD) mandated that 42 percent of all mortgages traded by Fannie and Freddie had to go to households with "low and moderate income" and 14 percent to families with "very low income." With the government footing the risk, Fannie and Freddie actually exceeded their quotas, which the government increased to 50 and 20 percent, respectively, in 1999. The following year, Fannie pledged $2 trillion to support low-income borrowers. At the same time, the Federal Housing Administration (FHA) also lowered its standards by reducing the minimum down payment to just 3 percent while raising the maximum loan to $235,000.[40]

To originate loans eligible for resale to the GSEs, however, mortgage companies like Countrywide had to stretch the rules. Many prudent bankers did not like the new order of things but they felt competitive pressures to conform. (Throughout the postwar period, conservative bankers complained that regulatory liberalization forced them to abandon prudent banking practices.[41]) When regulators like the Boston Fed signaled that lending guidelines should be loosened, however, originators became increasingly bold. Personal interviews of borrowers ceased, as did checks on property appraisals. Poor credit histories were just that, history, under new regulatory guidelines that demanded "flexibility." Subprime mortgages, as mortgage loans to high-risk borrowers came to be known, became increasingly easy to obtain. By the first decade of the new millennium, NINJA (no income, no job or assets) and liar's (no documentation) loans became commonplace.[42] In the end, the definition of financial discrimination devolved from banks rejecting loan applicants for *unwarranted* reasons into banks refusing to make loans to poor credit risks, the very definition of prudent banking.[43]

A similar process took place in consumer debt, with new computerized risk assessment technologies and less stringent regulations combining to render the issuance of credit cards to the working poor increasingly attractive. In 1989, 18 percent of families in the bottom quintile and 35 percent of families in the second lowest quintile of the national income distribution held at least one credit card. By finding ways to lend to those with thin or bad credit histories, card issuers by 2001 extended credit to 31 and 45 percent of families in the bottom two income quintiles, respectively.[44]

Along with the stick represented by the CRA, bankers also saw the carrot of more business and, eventually, the carrot cake of massive bonuses. Bankers know that more reward means more risk, but they convinced themselves that they could make many lucrative loans to shaky borrowers safely. The key was "securitization," the bundling of numerous risky mortgages into one ostensibly safe security. Some predictable, relatively low percentage of subprime mortgages would default but no one could predict which specific ones. By putting them all together (into mortgage-backed securities, or MBS, and collateralized debt obligations, or CDOs, and similar instruments), it was thought that the idiosyncratic risk inherent in each mortgage was essentially rubbed out by the law of large numbers and "diversification." For a fee, rating agencies happily granted AAA ratings to such securities, allowing them to be sold to even the most conservative institutional investors. When one of the rating agencies, Fitch, balked on an unusually risky type of security called a CPDO (constant proportion debt obligation), the issuers simply shopped it to Moody's and S&P instead.[45]

The lax mortgage system worked as long as housing prices stayed buoyant, as many assumed they would. Some people, however, both inside and outside of the industry, were not so sure. A few in academe knew that six previous mortgage securitization schemes had ended badly and many others were skeptical of the GSEs.[46] One member of the Bush administration, Armando Falcon Jr., raised alarms about the GSEs in 2003 but was immediately sacked by a new president who wanted to create an "ownership society."

Falcon was brought back after accounting scandals rocked the GSEs, but the mortgage giants used a small portion of their massive profits to successfully lobby against substantive reforms. The ensuing battle, however, left them beholden to Democratic congressmen who wanted even more loans for the poor, especially the poorest of the poor. Eager to make up for profits lost during their accounting scandals and with their implicit government subsidy fully intact, the GSEs were happy to comply. Fannie Mae's CEO Daniel Mudd told his employees to "get aggressive on risk-taking or get out of the company." Meanwhile, Freddie Mac's CEO Richard Syron in effect told his company's chief risk officer that Freddie "could no longer afford to say no to anybody."[47]

What Bush and other acolytes of the "ownership society" did not grasp was that government policies, particularly the mortgage interest deduction (especially after the deductibility of interest paid on other types of debt ceased in 1986) and low interest rates, encouraged Americans to borrow as much as possible rather than to accumulate equity in their homes. (Dickerson offers a stunning critique of the misnamed "ownership" ideology.[48]) So consumers had a big incentive to seek loans with minimal, or even negative, equity. Instead of having to invest 10 or 20 percent of the purchase price of a house, homeowners were allowed to borrow 10 or 20 percent more than the purchase price, which of course increased moral hazard to high levels.[49]

Critics of the new regime within the financial industry had incentives to keep their conclusions quiet so they could successfully short the market (profit from the impending bust). And nobody listened to professors, like New York University's Nouriel Roubini, who made it clear in a 2006 speech at the International Monetary Fund (IMF) that the fragile system was about to break down entirely.[50] The doomsayers were proven right in 2007–2009 as the housing market stalled, recession hit, unemployment increased, and defaults soared.

Big banks and the GSEs ignored all the warnings because of their implicit government guarantees and their inadequate corporate governance. The former was called "Too Big to Fail" (TBTF) policy and was basically a license to print profits because it encouraged the biggest banks to take big gambles without much risk of bankruptcy.[51] The latter was due to the erosion of almost all the checks against arbitrary CEO power.[52] Most recently, CEOs had developed "poison pills" that prevented corporate raiders like KKR from taking over poorly run companies.[53] Again, all-powerful CEOs and other top bank executives wrote themselves "heads I win, tails I win" contracts. If their banks performed well financially, on paper, they took home enormous bonuses. If their banks were headed for a crash, they could jump out wearing a "golden parachute" that gave them more money than most Americans make over their entire lifetimes.[54]

Because other factors, including low interest rates, securitization, and weak regulatory supervision, were present in earlier real estate bubbles of similar magnitude, including one in the 1920s that did not lead to financial or economic meltdown, it is clear that the main cause of the subprime crisis and subsequent global recession was the federal government's aggressive experiment in financial egalitarianism as equal outcomes.[55]

Conclusions

According to Princeton University sociologist Paul Starr, American liberalism, writ large, "asks to be judged by its real effects on human freedom and happiness."[56] If that is the case, liberals of all stripes should reject the type of egalitarianism that seeks equal outcomes because its record is one of unequivocal failure. Attempts to create equal outcomes eventually encounter reality and foment a crisis of some sort or another as natural processes work to restore inequality. In communist countries in the twentieth century, commitment to equal incomes for all made it difficult to incentivize innovation, which led to economic stagnation and eventual systemic collapse. In the early third millennium US mortgage market, commitment to equal access to mortgages for all increased asymmetric information to unsupportable levels, which led to high default rates and financial crisis.

The type of egalitarianism that seeks equal opportunities for all, by contrast, will often ameliorate perceived problems and will rarely lead to crisis because it is checked by market forces. In the financial system, equal opportunity means the ability to form new financial institutions and markets owned and controlled by members of any group who believe that they are being irrationally denied equal access to the financial system. If the discrimination is real, if members of the group are in fact being turned away for loans or insurance for any non-objective reason (e.g., racial bias), the new institution should thrive with ample support from those being discriminated against.[57] If the unequal access turns out to be justified by objective criteria, however, the new institution will suffer from higher default or claim rates and eventually exit. Thus the allegation of discrimination will be tested in the marketplace instead of merely being debated at academic conferences, in legislative sessions, or behind the closed doors of regulators.

For this second type of egalitarianism to work, however, regulators must allow *free* entry and *fair* competition. That means tolerating the potential failure of small insurers and de novo banks, an outcome regulators seem unwilling to countenance anymore. (Better the loss to competition of a 1,000 financial institutions with assets measured in the millions, however, than the failure of one LCFI [large complex financial institution] pushed into insolvency by regulators attempting to mandate equal outcomes for all.) In other words, regulators can reduce the impact of bigoted private institutions by being unbiased themselves and simply allowing aggrieved parties to put their money where their mouth is and form their own institutions. Regulators only need to ensure that the subsequent competition is fair by not providing incumbents with subsidies (like TBTF guarantees), encouraging reductions in minimum efficient scale (which is happening anyway due to technological improvements,[58] including new blockchain technologies[59]), and countenancing the formation of mutuals, co-operatives, fraternals, and other organizational forms that have proven their worth in the past.[60]

12

The End of Absolute Poverty

Art Carden, Sarah Estelle, and Anne R. Bradley*

THE POOR WE have always had with us. We worry about the fact that some people are *poor* in an absolute sense—lacking access to food, clothing, and shelter—far more than we worry that some people simply have *less* than others. Pick any point in history, and you will find unequal material standards of living. Pick a time in the past two or three centuries, though, and you will notice an important difference: where most inequality was before that point between people in the same society, an enormous gulf thereafter opened between members of different societies.[1] The gap between the rich and the poor in Europe and its overseas extensions narrowed as more and more people were able to enjoy what to their ancestors had been luxuries. The process was already evident when Adam Smith was writing of "the industrious and frugal peasant" in 1776:

> Compared, indeed, with the more extravagant luxury of the great, his accommodation must no doubt appear extremely simple and easy; and yet it may be true, perhaps, that the accommodation of an European prince does not always so much exceed that of an industrious and frugal peasant, as the accommodation of the latter exceeds that of many an African king, the absolute master of the lives and liberties of ten thousand naked savages.[2]

*Art Carden is an associate professor of economics at Samford University and a research fellow with the Independent Institute. Sarah Estelle is associate professor of economics and Ruch Faculty Fellow at Hope College. Anne R. Bradley is Academic Director at The Fund for American Studies.

We would obviously use different language today, but Smith points to a stubborn and persistent fact. Even the "poor" in wealthy countries are fantastically wealthy by global standards.

The differences in "accommodation" between rich-by-Western-standards and poor-by-Western-standards Westerners does not concern us nearly as much as the differences between rich-by-global-standards Westerners and their poor-by-any-standard brothers and sisters in different countries. Instead of asking, for example, "Why are some Americans richer than other Americans?" the question is, "Why are Europeans and Americans so much richer than almost everyone else?" The Great Fact discussed by Deirdre McCloskey is the enrichment of ordinary people in European societies and their overseas offshoots, with prosperity spreading, as evident in rising per capita income around the globe and the development of a global middle class.[3] The global middle class is growing; poverty in Africa is falling.[4] The Enrichment, emerging from the unevenly and imperfectly realized conviction that people are equal morally or politically, made us more equal materially.

The gap between very rich Americans and Americans who are poor relative to their own society's "haves" (but spectacularly wealthy relative to both the vast majority of those who came before them and most of the world's population today) is not, we think, as important as the gap between the average member of a wealthy society and the average member of a poor society. Given the choice between eliminating absolute poverty (holding inequality constant) and eliminating inequality (holding poverty constant), we would end poverty. If poverty, not inequality, is what stands between some people and the opportunity to flourish, the concern over income inequality per se is misplaced. If alleviating absolute poverty is our objective, the moral and legal equality that made the Enrichment possible should be our priority, not equalizing material standards of living.

Industrialization, Not Redistribution, Created First-World Problems

"We are converging on an enrichment of the poor."
—Deirdre McCloskey, *Bourgeois Equality*

There is no entry for *equality* in the *Syntopicon* of the Britannica series Great Books of the Western World, though it is said general editor Mortimer Adler later regretted it. This isn't to say the ancients weren't seriously concerned with equality. Plato understood that the distribution of material well-being is important to social stability, even going so far as to say in the *Laws* that funeral expenditures for the richest must be no more than five times what is spent on the poorest.[5] Aristotle took more of a justice approach and said that imposing equality upon that which is naturally unequal is unjust. However, a closer look at the *Politics* reveals that he also was concerned by the granting of unequal treatment to those that are equal.[6] That is, Aristotle was not an inequality skeptic. Although modern scholars have traditionally exercised great care in distinguishing between equality of opportunity, equality of consumption, and equality of outcome, most colloquial uses of the term *inequality* refer to unequal statistical distributions of income and wealth.

Inequality has always been an important topic in economics, and new data and methods are helping us fill in historical gaps in our understanding of it. Esteban Nicolini and Fernando Ramos Palencia, for example, assemble mid-eighteenth-century census data to estimate inequality for Spain; where previous approaches had used proxies, they are able to provide estimates using income data.[7] Metin Cosgel and Bogac Ergene construct estimates for the eighteenth-century Ottoman Empire using probate inventories.[8] There was rising inequality in Kastamonu, where they get their data, just as there was rising inequality in Europe. Relative decline in wages combined with capital concentration meant rising inequality in the Southern Low Countries in the lead-up to industrialization.[9] Religion and estate division practices influenced economic inequality in Canada at the beginning of the twentieth century.[10] These are just a few examples of how we are coming to better understand the causes and consequences of historical inequality.

Joseph Molitoris and Martin Dribe document persistent inequality in mortality outcomes in Stockholm in the late nineteenth and early twentieth centuries; however, they caution readers not to lose sight of the fact that there were still large absolute gains in absolute standards of living, such as child mortality, even though gaps persisted: "The working classes saw more of their children surviving beyond the first years of life, a three-fold increase in individual purchasing power and greater access to hygienic living conditions. Although they may have remained worse off than the upper classes in these regards, they certainly reaped the gains of Stockholm's industrialization."[11] These gains are especially illuminating when we consider this passage on inequality from Adam Smith: "No society can surely be flourishing and happy, of which the far greater part of the members are poor and miserable. It is but equity, besides, that they who feed, clothe, and lodge the whole body of the people, should have such a share of the produce of their own labour as to be themselves tolerably well fed, clothed, and lodged."[12] That a gap remained between rich and poor in industrializing Stockholm should not bother us that much. What is important is not a stubbornly persistent gap between the rich and the poor but the fact that the poor were enjoying higher incomes and burying fewer children.

Those children and their descendants have grown rich by making the rest of us richer, as anyone who has ever been in an IKEA store can readily see—or taste and smell in the case of IKEA's restaurant patrons. Now the first world suffers from having *too much* to eat. Cluttered closets and cluttered calendars are first-world problems, too. Cluttered closets are a product of material superabundance, and cluttered calendars are products of social superabundance. For many—the readers of *The Independent Review* and the students we teach—the time-use problem is not that we have too few opportunities to engage with great ideas and great people but that we have trouble saying "no" to an overabundance of social, intellectual, and professional opportunities.

In a well-known summary of what creative destruction has wrought, Joseph Schumpeter describes what he calls "the capitalist achievement":

> There are no doubt some things available to the modern workman that Louis XIV himself would have been delighted to have yet was unable to have—modern dentistry for instance. On the whole, however, a budget on that level had little that really mattered to gain from capitalist achievement. Even speed of traveling may be assumed to have been a minor consideration for so very dignified a gentleman. Electric lighting is no great boon to anyone who has money enough to buy a sufficient number of candles and to pay servants to attend to them. It is the cheap cloth, the cheap cotton and rayon fabric, boots,

motorcars, and so on that are the typical achievements of capitalist production, and not as a rule improvements that would mean much to the rich man. Queen Elizabeth owned silk stockings. The capitalist achievement does not typically consist in providing more silk stockings for queens but in bringing them within the reach of factory girls in return for steadily decreasing amounts of effort.[13]

Modern economic growth did not benefit kings and queens nearly as much as it benefited the rest of us. Henry VIII and his courtiers ate some forty-five hundred to five thousand calories per day, and the king eventually grew so fat that he could not move without help.[14] The beneficiaries of capitalist growth were not corpulent Henry and his courtiers. The beneficiaries have ultimately been the commoners and their descendants, who can today, for the price of half an hour or so of labor at average American wages, eat forty-five hundred to five thousand calories on *one* visit to a buffet restaurant or college dining hall—hence, new college campus arrivals' struggle to avoid putting on the "freshman fifteen."

The problem facing the world's poor is not that there are people who have more than they do. The problem is that they are absolutely poor in a meaningful sense, lacking the access to the food, clothing, and shelter that people in wealthy countries take for granted. McCloskey suggests that when we are assessing the well-being of our fellow human beings (not country versus country Gini scores), we are interested in real income levels, not in rankings.[15] Ranking matters in sports, but the income distribution is not a soccer game or a boxing match. What matters ultimately is what one's income will buy, not how that income compares to the income earned by the Joneses down the street. Jones eats and drinks better if he has a higher income, and perhaps he is able to take his family on a vacation to see *Starry Night* at the Museum of Modern Art. If those at the bottom of the income distribution can experience what are by historical and geographic standards extraordinary levels of well-being—levels that extend beyond food, shelter, medical care, and education to the leisure that allows us to read, knit, hike, or just watch TV—then in a meaningful sense they are able to exercise great autonomy over all their choices. This autonomy enables but does not guarantee flourishing. Wealthy Mr. Jones might buy $1,000 bottles of whiskey and smash them on the sidewalk just to show people how rich he is, or wealthy Mr. Burns might pay Homer to eat a copy of *Spider-Man* number 1 page by page just to be mean to the Comic Book Guy. Mr. Smith might spend his more modest (or meager) income in dissipation and drunkenness. Nevertheless, in the most practical terms we might choose to ignore the complexities of these conceptual differences between inequality and poverty, except for one significant rub: so many strategies proposed for ameliorating inequality have in practice detrimental consequences for equality of opportunity, absolute poverty, and the prospects of human flourishing.

Financial and Political Access to Positional Goods and High Status

What about positional goods and competition over status? Some inequality is positional and irreducible. There are only so many Picassos or originals of Van Gogh's *Starry Night* (one), and it has been reported that there were only twenty-four bottles of Springbank 1919 50 Year Old scotch ever produced, available for $78,000 each at the Whiskey Exchange. But this price seems a bargain compared to that of the Macallan M bottle, sold in a Hong Kong auction for $628,205 in 2014. The Macallan M is a work of art: *MoneyNation* reports that "17 craftsmen worked for 50 hours each just to make the whiskey's bottle. . . . The glass is hand blown, and 40 of the bottles were destroyed because of imperfections before perfection was attained," and "[t]he seven barrels that make up this whiskey were chosen from the master blender out of 200,000 barrels."[16]

You might feel much poorer than Bill Gates, who can have the best and rarest whiskey on command, but this comparison misses the larger point about advances in wealth that spread across the entire income distribution. It is the case that Bill Gates can have better whiskey than we, but it is not the case that the rest of us have no access to whiskey at all. In fact, the massive wealth generation of the past three centuries has given ordinary folks access to things unthinkable to kings and queens of the past. This is true because wealth is created in society when suppliers figure out, through the prudent application of their entrepreneurial energy, how to solve the problems that we all face—such as access to whiskey or stockings.

Fine art and elite whiskies are positional goods, with the most ambitious and most able effectively taxing themselves in order to be able to afford them.[17] Just as works by Picasso and Van Gogh helped redefine art, the most expensive whiskies in the world are the ultimate exemplars of the whiskey-making craft. The high prices call forth the kind of expertise that allows a master blender to select the best combination out of 200,000 casks of twenty-five- to seventy-five-year-old whiskey. The additional effort required to get to the top and therefore to have access to the *best* in a commercial society spills over into benefits for others who enjoy the new products or lower prices or greater output or better scholarship that people produce in order to get this kind of access. Should we be upset that wealthy connoisseurs can buy bottles of whiskey costing tens of thousands of dollars while the hoi polloi make do with Johnnie Walker Red Label or whiskey from the bottom shelf? Would we really prefer that access to these goods be distributed politically rather than financially?

It is true that the dollar votes of the rich "matter" more than the dollar votes of the poor in that the rich have more of them, but elite contempt for Walmart and McDonald's suggests a conviction that *the poor's* money speaks too loudly for some tastes. Furthermore, why shouldn't the rich be allowed to vote with their money for ultraelite education, ultraelite whiskey, and so on? People do not go into academia or the arts for the money, nor do we suspect that vintners and brewers and whiskey blenders get into their crafts for the money alone. By telling the rich, "You cannot buy a $600,000 bottle of whiskey," we are limiting the Macallan blenders' ability to excel at their crafts.

Moreover, taxing high-end consumption doesn't make us more equal. In fact, it puts out of business this niche-whiskey maker and his entrepreneurial efforts and thus by definition reduces his or her flourishing and the flourishing of those who would have purchased the designer whiskey. The undeniable truths of humanity are that each of us has unique and subjective preferences. What markets do best is cater to the hundreds of thousands of preferences around whiskey from the glass-blown bottle to the plastic jug. In this task, the market provides powerful incentives for suppliers not just to cater to the tastes of the rich (royals) but to cater to everyone, including ordinary people like you and me. The market does not exist to cater to the rich, quite the opposite. We all are richer because we have increasing access to whiskey, heart medication, cell phones, enormous televisions, great literature, and stockings for steadily decreasing amounts of effort. The nature of markets and the lure of potential profit ensure that status is not what drives innovation but rather the search to fulfill the demands of everyone—rich and poor alike.

Let's suppose for a moment that we can equalize material income and wealth. For better or for worse, status motivates people. If we equalize income and wealth, we can expect people to move toward other, perhaps more pernicious kinds of status competition, if not by money income. People can obtain status not by production, but by domination, earning income not by providing people with products they want at attractive prices but by gouging it out of the politically powerless. This brings us back to Henry VIII and his court or George Orwell's Napoleon and his coterie of animals who are "more equal than others." David Henderson, Robert McNab, and Tamas Rozsas discuss the privileges available to the political elites in socialist countries that might not show up in official statistics.[18] In aristocracies of pull, the politically connected enjoy privileged access to food, health care, and other goods and services that are unavailable to the masses. Meaningful inequality in socialist countries, they argue, is understated by official income measures.

In a world in which people value status heavily—as they presumably do in ours—working to eliminate status seeking on one margin will shift status seeking onto other margins. F. A. Hayek argued that money inheritances are, socially speaking, the least expensive way for people to provision their descendants because restricting inheritance given these preferences shifts the search for status and provision onto nonfinancial margins:

> It seems certain that among the many ways in which those who have gained power and influence might provide for their children, the bequest of a fortune is socially by far the cheapest. Without this outlet, these men would look for other ways of providing for their children, such as placing them in positions which might bring them the income and the prestige that a fortune would have done; and this would cause a waste of resources and an injustice much greater than is caused by the inheritance of property. Such is the case with all societies in which

inheritance of property does not exist, including the Communist. Those who dislike the inequalities caused by inheritance should, therefore, recognize that men being what they are, it is the least of evils, even from their point of view.[19]

High status correlated with great wealth and great money income is likely the cheapest way (from society's perspective) for people to indulge their elite pretensions. By restricting inheritances or status competition, we provide people with incentives to move these pursuits into other sectors. Instead of accumulating wealth, the status-hungry might accumulate power. Instead of passing along a great fortune, someone might spend a great deal of time and energy working to get his or her children into positions of power and advantage. These rational responses are not costless. The displacement itself is costly, as revealed by the fact that rational agents facing a broader set of options would have chosen otherwise. Still more, spillovers arise due to the politicization of everything, as zero-sum political games become relatively more attractive than positive-sum, or value-creating, commercial games.

Legal and Moral Equality

We think legal and moral equality are crucial. Consider this passage from the Italian Constitution of 1948: "All the citizens have equal social dignity and are equal before the law, without distinctions of sex, of race, of language, of religion, of political opinion, of personal and social position."[20] It recognizes an inherent dignity of each and every person that is obvious to us today but that wasn't obvious—and was explicitly and vigorously resisted—for the better part of history.

Equality before the law harnesses individual motives and knowledge to provide maximal relevant social knowledge to bear on individual choices and therefore on collective outcomes. Hayek, like Smith before him, made a persuasive case for classical liberal institutions as those that best make use of social knowledge. Voluntary interaction generally and market exchange specifically make it possible for people to use knowledge that only others have for purposes only they know. Attempting to engineer equal outcomes is fraught with problems for the very reasons that diverse tastes and talents make equality before the law a compelling institutional goal.

To rectify material inequality requires creating political inequality, a type of inequality that might in fact be more objectionable and that, as moral notions and ideas about justice evolve, might require future recompense. As Harry Frankfurt points out, the lines between desirable types of equality are not particularly clear, and to the extent that we are concerned with the moral quality of egalitarian endeavors, the precautionary principle suggests we should tread lightly with respect to egalitarian interventions lest these interventions result in other blameworthy types of inequality.[21] Consider Frankfurt's explanation:

> The disorientation and the anguish of a person who is treated arbitrarily, without the elemental respect that consists in recognizing him as what he actually is, has nothing much to do with comparing his own circumstances with the circumstances of others. Rather, it is rooted in a morally foundational need to affirm and to be confirmed in his own reality. This is profoundly different from the essentially comparative focus of egalitarian concerns.[22]

Inequality on some margins can be compensated for by inequality on others; moreover, intervening in order to fix inequality attempts to remedy an evil that is not a harm or injustice by introducing an evil that is both. Attempting to counteract, for example, income inequality harms the one who is taxed arbitrarily. If he is punished, in effect, not for a crime or an injustice but for an occasion of wise stewardship of uneven blessings, this inequality of treatment might be considered an injustice. Furthermore, it is by no means clear that replacing what *might be* an evil with what *is* a harm makes for a better society. This is doubly true when societies deviate from principle—the protection of private-property rights and enforcement of impersonal laws—to indulge what is politically expedient at a particular point in time because doing so weakens the rule of law and (almost certainly unintentionally) encourages people to seek to improve their lots via redistribution. In practical terms, punishing otherwise desirable behavior such as stewardship has disincentive effects with wide-ranging ramifications. Moreover, even if we decide we want to do this, we face knowledge constraints that make us unable to understand how to do it in a way that would not set in motion a tide of unintended consequences.

Conclusion

Societies should concern themselves with legal and moral equality of liberty and dignity rather than with superficial income and wealth equality at a specific point in time. The most effective way to ensure the equal dignity of each person is to ensure property rights enforced by the rule of law. Secure property rights, the rule of law, and a social conversation that tolerates and dignifies innovation and entrepreneurship encourage people to make the most of their talents in ways consistent with what people want and for which they are willing to pay. We are interdependent creatures who are able to thrive only because of the efforts of countless people we will never know, who, guided by their own goals, are working to help us achieve our own.

This is true of both the richest person and the poorest person. What bridges the wealth, income, and consumption gap is that market-based societies bring us together because of our differences through trade. Markets equalize in ways that no other mechanism can. Profits give us the best hope, which human history verifies, that on net people will use their talents to serve all of us rather than to plunder. This is the way that we all have become extraordinarily richer.

Poverty is a far bigger and far more important problem than inequality. A society in which people are equally poor has far less scope for flourishing than a society in which people are unequally rich. With enough force, we can equalize incomes and wealth, but we cannot get around the fact that many people are still motivated by the pursuit of status. Taxing income-generating production and utility-generating consumption will induce people to shift away from production and consumption and toward other ways of satisfying their wants. This shift might include even more status seeking. For a given set of preferences for status, closing off financial means to status will lead people to do their status seeking on other margins—margins that are not necessarily benign.

In fact, we might ask whether these attempts to equalize outcomes through creating political inequality are equivalent, in effect, to cutting off one's nose to spite one's face. We now are watching the largest migration of human beings out of absolute poverty in the history of the species. This has happened not because of redistribution from rich to poor but because of increased economic growth brought about by improved institutions and a new social esteem for innovation. On one hand, societies have loosened the shackles on the invisible hand. On the other, they have come to better tolerate and appreciate the "mere" merchant buying low and selling high.[23] The payoffs in the form of lower poverty and less worldwide inequality have been substantial.

13

The Unfair Cost of Reducing Inequality

Nikolai G. Wenzel*

INCOME INEQUALITY IS a contemporary hot-button issue. Of late, it has informed popular movements like Occupy Wall Street, and economists-turned-public-intellectuals like Joseph Stiglitz, Paul Krugman, or Thomas Piketty.[1] Beyond popular dissatisfaction, what does economics have to say about this question? Philosophy can sometimes tell us the "ought"[2]—but it is helpful to know means-ends relationships before we blithely pursue ends.

Alas, the problem of income inequality in the US is laced with sophistry.[3] Thus, while the question of egalitarianism is fundamentally philosophical, the discipline of economics can tell us if we are adopting the right solutions. After all, basic political economy tells us that there will likely be unintended consequences to government's action. We must thus tread cautiously in adopting policies, lest the proposed medicine be worse than the proverbial disease. In the words of economist Gene Callahan, "fantasy is not an adult policy option."[4]

This paper addresses the question of egalitarianism by looking at the economic cost of reducing income inequality. I begin by asking if inequality is a problem in the first place—then, in the style of Mises, look at the cost of fighting it, if we assume good intentions on the part of policy makers.[5] Then, I examine the cost of fighting inequality and show that the cost will be high for all—especially for the poorest. I conclude by arguing that egalitarianism is

*Nikolai G. Wenzel is the L.V. Hackley Chair for the Study of Capitalism and Free Enterprise, and Distinguished Professor of Economics at Fayetteville State University (Fayetteville, NC).

misguided. It is unfair to those whose income is coercively taken from them, it is unfair to the poorest, who are ultimately hurt by redistribution, and it erodes the liberties of all. Instead of equality of outcome, policy efforts should focus on equality of opportunity, especially economic freedom.

Is Inequality a Problem in the First Place?

Before I address the cost of fighting inequality, it bears pausing a moment to examine some of the rationales for fighting inequality in the first place—rather than merely asserting that inequality is bad.

First, there seems to be a visceral reaction against inequality. To many, it just doesn't seem right that some should have more than others. I'm no philosopher, but it is quite obvious that people have different abilities, and different levels of luck, and make different choices; inequality is thus inevitable. More important, relative standing is a distraction from the fundamental question of the absolute lot of the poorest.

Second, there are concerns about the health of the polity and social cohesion within a democracy with high levels of inequality. High disparities in income can lead to concentration of power at the top and social unrest at the bottom. But this is not a problem within a market system, where opportunity exists at the bottom, and the size and scope of the state are so limited as to obviate the problem of political power. In sum, political capture is a consequence of government expansion, not of inequality. The problem is that state efforts to redistribute wealth contribute to both poverty and to the increasing the power of the state.

Third, inequality can lead to envy, and thus greater demands for redistribution at the ballot box. This is problematic for two reasons. First, redistribution is bad for growth, and especially for the poorest, in a cycle of unintended consequences. Second, redistribution leads to an idea trap—bad ideas lead to bad policies; in turn, bad policies lead to bad outcomes; the wrong ideas are blamed, and more bad policies are adopted. Bad ideas, bad policies, and bad outcomes thus become mutually reinforcing.[6] In this case, the predatory state blocks growth and favors political activity over economic activity, thus concentrating wealth at the top. Voters blame markets and demand more government activity (redistribution); redistribution thwarts growth and increases inequality, but voters blame markets and demand more intervention. The cycle continues—and the only way to break it is to scale back government impediments to wealth creation and access to jobs.

Finally, there is a macroeconomic argument to be made. Top economic earners will tend to invest marginal dollars—at least at a higher rate than lower earners, who will tend to spend more (or all) of their marginal dollars.[7] Presumably, then, government redistribution of income from higher earners to low earners will increase aggregate consumption (and thus national output), if at the cost of decreased investment. There are three problems with this line of thinking. First, the cost of decreased investment cannot be neglected, as explained in the next section: decreased investment means decreased productivity, decreased capital accumulation, and decreased growth—all of which hurt the poorest disproportionately. Second, this reasoning is predicated on Keynesian thinking. It is beyond the scope of this paper to demonstrate "the failure of the new economics";[8] suffice it to say that there is plenty of such doubt. Third, this assumes that policy makers know more about creating economic growth than do entrepreneurs and the market process; this is unrealistic, at best.[9]

The Cost of Redistribution

Redistribution and Lost Growth

Consider table 13.1 as a thought exercise.[10] Let us assume that a more equal distribution of income is a national priority, to be pursued with eyes wide open and the sober recognition that there is no such thing as a free lunch. Redistribution of income will come at a cost. There will need to be a government bureaucracy assigned to redistributing the income, by taxing higher-income individuals, perhaps using a higher marginal tax rate on income or discriminating among sources of income (e.g., taxing dividends and capital gains at a higher rate than income). That bureaucracy will then redistribute the tax revenue to lower-income individuals. Perhaps the bureaucracy will get creative beyond simple redistribution, and extract resources from top income earners to invest in the human capital and job skills of low-income earners. Or perhaps some other scheme is employed. Regardless, there will necessarily be some expense for the government agency in charge of redistribution.

Table 13.1. A Tale of Two Countries: Growth versus Redistribution

Year	Years Elapsed	Growth 4% growth			Redistribution 2% growth		
		Poor	Middle	Rich	Poor	Middle	Rich
1910		1,000	2,000	4,000	1,500	2,000	3,500
1920	10	1,480	2,960	5,921	1,828	2,438	4,266
1930	20	2,191	4,382	8,764	2,229	2,972	5,201
1940	30	3,243	6,487	12,974	2,717	3,623	6,340
1950	40	4,801	9,602	19,204	3,312	4,416	7,728
1960	50	7,107	14,213	28,427	4,037	5,383	9,421
1970	60	10,520	21,039	42,079	4,922	6,562	11,484
1980	70	15,572	31,143	62,286	5,999	7,999	13,998
1990	80	23,050	46,100	92,199	7,313	9,751	17,064
2000	90	34,119	68,239	136,477	8,915	11,886	20,801
2010	100	50,505	101,010	202,020	10,867	14,489	25,356

Redistribution of income from top earners will cause disincentives to earn, whether through investment or labor, depending on the details of the tax and redistribution scheme.

Top earners will earn less not only because of the redistributive taxation itself, but also because of the lesser effort exerted in response to the lower marginal return to labor. Likewise, the diminished investment among the top tiers of earners will mean less national investment, and thus less capital growth and less productivity gain. Because of these effects, there will be less growth in the country that redistributes wealth. The details are subject, of course, to an empirical study, but the principle remains that every action, no matter how desirable, comes at a cost, including opportunity cost.[11] For the sake of argument, we can thus assume that our hypothetical growth society will grow at 4 percent per year, whereas redistribution society will grow at only 2 percent per year. On the face of it, there is not much of a difference.

But if we compound the growth over a century, we see that there will be large effects, especially for the poorest.

In our example, let us assume that in some arbitrary base year 1910, the richest third in growth society earn $4,000, the middle third $2,000, and the poorest $1,000. After a century of growth at 4 percent, the poorest will earn about $50,000 per year, about one quarter of the $200,000 earned by the most productive third.

Starting in 1910, redistribution society attempts to dampen inequality, by redistributing $500 from the richest third to the poorest third. Thus, we see incomes of $3,500 for the most productive third, $2,000 for the middle, and $1,500 for the least productive. Redistribution society grows at 2 percent per year, because of the cost of redistribution (especially in thwarted investment, capital growth, and productivity gains, as described above). At the end of the century, the lowest third is earning about $11,000, just slightly less than half of the $25,000 earned by the richest third.

We can now ask which society is more desirable. On the one hand, re-distribution society sees the lowest third earning about half of what the top third is earning, while growth society would have the poorest earning only about a quarter of what is earned by the richest third. On the other hand, if we examine the lot of the poorest income earners, in a cross-country, rather than inter-temporal analysis, the poorest income earners in growth society have an income that is almost five times higher than the income of the poorest in redistribution society.

To put this in contemporary context, 2015 GDP per capita for the US was roughly $50,000, while $11,000 approximates the GDP per capita of Egypt. In sum, we can ask in a hypothetical sense, who is better off? Somebody earn-ing the GDP per capita of contemporary Americans in an unequal society? Or somebody earning the GDP per capita of Egyptians in a more egalitarian society? In fact, the US has a higher variation of income (more inequality) than Egypt, so the example does mirror reality.[12]

Of course, this example is intentionally simplified. I intentionally side-stepped questions of inflation and purchasing power—which are compen-sated by questions of productivity gains. The point, for now, is simply to ask whether equality trumps growth, once we have accepted the assumption that redistribution (just as anything else in life) cannot come without a cost.

I now turn briefly to the insights of Austrian economics. Specifically, the knowledge problem tells us that policy makers lack the information to understand—let alone fix—the workings of a complex market economy.[13] In a market, entrepreneurs require information about the goods and services consumers wish them to produce. This information is generated and transmitted through the price mechanism.[14] Thus, even if policy makers have good intentions—which may, or may not, actually be the case[15]—we must be wary of the dynamics of intervention: intervention in one market distorts the epistemic function of prices[16] and blocks the knowledge-generating functions of the market.[17] This leads to a distortion in a related market . . . followed by calls for intervention to fix that market . . . and the cycle continues. As we will see, interventionism—even with the noble aspiration of reducing inequality—has a direct and visible cost, especially on the poorest.

The Regulatory State and Poverty

Moving from the basic theory to the problem of poverty, we can start by looking at regulations that have an impact on poverty.[18] Consider the following:

- The cost for Americans to comply with federal regulations exceeded 10 percent of GDP in 2015.[19] This represents resources that are diverted away from productive investments, job creation, and productivity gains.

- Approximately one-third of Americans today require occupational licenses, up from 5 percent in the 1950s.[20] It is immediately apparent that this kind of job licensing will be regressive, as those with higher incomes are more able to pay for the required courses, exams, and other licensing fees than will be those at the bottom end of income, and especially those who are attempting to enter the job market.

- Five-sixths of wealth transfers today in the US are not means-tested.[21] This means that these wealth transfers are not going from wealthier Americans to poorer Americans, as might be anticipated. Rather, these wealth transfers are going from the politically less organized and less visible to the politically more organized and more visible, in what public-choice economics calls the special-interest effect of concentrated benefits and diffuse costs. It is also quite obvious that these wealth transfers are regressive, as the politically well-connected tend also to be the wealthier (who can afford to buy political and regulatory favors).

- Crony capitalism—the use of public means to advance public interests, through government favoritism of politically connected industries— has a direct and visible cost, especially on the poorest.[22]

The Welfare State and Poverty

We have already seen that redistribution and the rise of the regulatory state impede growth and thus hurt the poorest, who need growth the most. The next problem is government attempts to reduce poverty. For these purposes, it is noteworthy to juxtapose figures 13.1 and 13.2.

Figure 13.1 includes the official poverty rate in the US since 1959. It is interesting to note that the rate of poverty, which was in the mid-20-percent range in 1959, was falling—significantly—before the US government took aim at poverty through President Lyndon Johnson's Great Society. By the

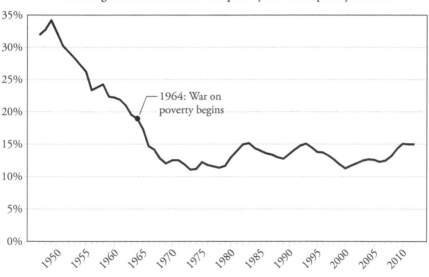

Percentage of individuals who were poor by the official poverty standard

Source: Data from The Heritage Foundation, *Poverty Rate, 1947–2012*, September 2014, https://web.archive.org/web/20161031111849/http:// www.heritage.org/ multimedia/infographic/2014/09/poverty-rate-1947-2012.

Figure 13.1. US Poverty Rates, 1947–2012

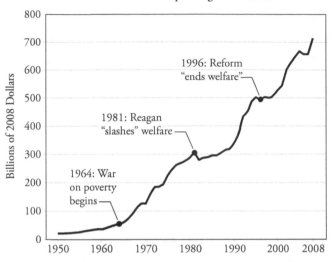

Total Welfare Spending Since 1950

1996: Reform
"ends welfare"

1981: Reagan
"slashes" welfare

1964: War
on poverty
begins

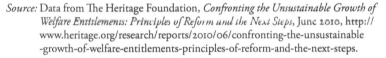

Source: Data from The Heritage Foundation, *Confronting the Unsustainable Growth of Welfare Entitlements: Principles of Reform and the Next Steps*, June 2010, http://www.heritage.org/research/reports/2010/06/confronting-the-unsustainable-growth-of-welfare-entitlements-principles-of-reform-and-the-next-steps.

Figure 13.2. Government Expenditures on Poverty, 1950–2008

mid-1960s, when the Great Society was launched, the poverty rate in the US had already fallen below 15 percent, thanks to strong economic growth. It is also interesting to note that despite 50 years of federal government involvement, the rate of poverty remains right about at 15 percent today, the point to which it had already fallen *before* the Great Society efforts. The ineffectiveness of the federal war on poverty is also highlighted by Figure 13.2, which shows total welfare spending since 1950. Over the half century in which the federal government has been actively fighting poverty, to the tune of more than $1 trillion in 2015,[23] the national poverty rates have not changed. Again, it is worth drawing the comparison between figures 13.1 and 13.2, which show exponential growth in federal welfare spending, alongside a flat national poverty rate.[24] Moving back to income inequality, Henry Hazlitt notes that income inequality was falling in the two decades before the Great Society, and has been rising since.[25] While the Great Society welfare programs may not be solely responsible for this, there is certainly a compelling pattern of government growth, lingering poverty, and *increasing* inequality.

Why would government efforts at fighting poverty be unsuccessful (or even detrimental)? Start with the simple example of price controls. Minimum wage laws cause unemployment, as basic economic theory can tell us. But the problem is especially prevalent when uneducated and unskilled workers are priced out of the market because they cannot provide as much value to employers as the law requires them to be paid. As Hazlitt explains, "We cannot make a man worth a given amount by making it illegal for anyone to offer him less. We merely deprive him of the right to earn the amount that his abilities and opportunities would permit him to earn, while we deprive the community of the moderate services he is capable of rendering."[26] Related to minimum wage, most households in the bottom quintile have nobody working.[27] While welfare policies in the US may arguably have some short-term palliative effect, they also typically do not invest in human capital, and thus do not do anything for the movement into higher income and self-sufficiency.[28] Returning to the arguments above, the government crowds out private enterprise and investment, and thus capital accumulation and growth. In the years "1995–2012, The Organization for Economic Cooperation and Development (OECD) member countries that increased government expenditures as a percentage of GDP grew 30 percent slower than member countries that trimmed government expenditures as a percentage of the economy over that span—average annual growth of 1.9 percent compared with 2.5 percent."[29] And as we have seen above, it is precisely the poorest who benefit the most from growth.

Fundamentally, though, the welfare state provides disincentives to work: "to the extent that the expanding welfare state allows more people to live without working—and therefore without earning income or developing their own human capital—supporters of the welfare state are contributing to the very income disparities they so much decry."[30] Moving from theory to practice, consider the following facts from Tanner and Hughes:[31]

- Welfare pays more than minimum wage in 35 states.
- In 13 states, welfare pays more than $15/hour.
- In 8 states, welfare pays more than the median income; in 40 states, welfare pays 80 percent or more of the median income.
- Less than 42 percent of adult welfare recipients are actually working (despite the 1996 welfare reforms).
- There are currently 126 federal anti-poverty programs.

These figures simply reflect the moral hazard of creating a dependent class of able-bodied adults, a problem long recognized by several thinkers.[32] I discuss alternative solutions to poverty in the conclusion.

Crushing Innovation: From Luxury to Banality

At best, the government is ineffective in its efforts. At worst, state efforts have caused the poorest of Americans to be largely excluded from national productivity gains. If government efforts at fighting poverty have been counterproductive, we can expect the same from government efforts to fight inequality—and that is the crux of the problem.

Hazlitt explains that the progressive taxes used to fight inequality seize mostly investment funds—thus ultimately hurting the poor more than the rich, because of diminished growth in productivity, capital accumulation, job creation, and dampened decreases in real prices.[33] He also reminds us,[34] with echoes of Bastiat,[35] that private property is already public wealth, in a sense, because it serves the public need for capital accumulation. F. A. Harper likewise argued that investment was the greatest form of charity.[36]

Beyond the consequences of disincentives to earn and invest inherent in any redistribution scheme, there is one more problem associated with attempts to reduce income inequality: consumption effects. Because top earners have more disposable income, they can purchase luxury goods, in addition to investing their marginal income. Thanks to these purchases, entrepreneurs can invest in production and bring those goods to the market at lower price, thus making them accessible to the middle class, and eventually to all. Take cars in the early twentieth century, or mobile phones in the 1990s, or smart-phones and car rearview cameras in the early 2010s—all of these started as luxuries, and eventually became everyday items. Imagine the consequences of attempting to level income disparity by imposing a progressive consumption tax. Imagine taxing cell phones in the early 1990s—the increased price would have discouraged many of the few consumers from purchasing a cell phone, and would have thwarted investment to lower the price of cell phones. Today's smartphone penetration rate approaches 80 percent[37]—that's not just 80 percent of Americans who can now look at pictures of cats on Facebook, instantly chat with friends, or enjoy other frivolities. It also represents cheap and easy access to the internet for school research, or job searches, or online banking (an especially important point, because high costs—largely driven by federal regulations—keep an estimated 10 percent of Americans out of the formal banking sector).[38] Hayek summarizes the point nicely: "A large part of the expenditures of the rich, though not intended for that end, thus serves to defray the cost of the experimentation with the new things that, as a result, can later be made available to the poor. . . . Even the poorest today owe their relative material well-being to the results of past inequality."[39]

Summary: Fighting Inequality Is Unfair

In sum—even if we assume that inequality is a problem—the cost of fighting inequality will be higher than the benefits to a society with less disparate incomes, because of the unintended consequences of interventionism.[40]

Fighting inequality is problematic for the following reasons:

First, it is a distraction from the real problem of poverty and detrimental to economic growth—and thus unfair to the poorest. In the words of development economist, Peter Bauer, "the promotion of economic equality and the alleviation of poverty are distinct and often conflicting."[41]

Second, redistribution of income comes at a cost, beyond the operating costs of the government bureaucracy tasked with reducing inequality: diminished incentives for top earners to create wealth, diminished investment, diminished capital accumulation, diminished productivity gains, and diminished overall economic growth. All of these things hurt the poorest disparately.

Third, redistribution, as part of an increased weight of the state, ultimately has a regressive effect on the poor. Just as the war on poverty, a war on inequality will ultimately be counterproductive and ineffective, even if it has immediate palliative effects. Hazlitt reminds us, once again, that the real solution is not government relief, but an increase in productivity: "One is ashamed to keep repeating anything so obvious, but the only real cure for poverty is the production of wealth."[42]

Fourth, fighting against inequality will thwart the development of new technologies and consumer goods that are available today only to the wealthiest, but become everyday items tomorrow. Thus, attempts to alleviate income inequality will not only end up increasing poverty and income disparity, but also the consumption gap.

Finally, a fight against inequality through interventionist efforts is a distraction from the wonders that markets have already performed. Hazlitt bluntly reminds us that "capitalism has already eliminated mass poverty."[43] Moving from poverty to inequality in consumption, Schumpeter elegantly reminds us that:

> The capitalist engine is first and last an engine of mass production which unavoidably also means production for the masses. . . . It is the cheap cloth, the cheap cotton and rayon fabric, boots, motorcars and so on that are the typical achievements of capitalist production, and not as a rule improvements that would mean much to the rich man. Queen Elizabeth owned silk stockings. The capitalist achievement does not typically consist in providing more silk stockings for queens but in bringing them within reach of factory girls.[44]

It is unfair to exclude the poorest from the bounty of capitalism—even if that exclusion originates in good intentions.

Conclusion

The purpose of this paper has not been to dismiss income inequality—but to question whether inequality is the real problem, and outline the costs of changing it. It is frustrating and morally reprehensible to see such lingering poverty in the midst of plenty—especially when that poverty is largely solved by markets and perpetuated by wasteful interventionism. As Richard Posner opines, "In a world of scarce resources waste should be regarded as immoral."[45] While the income gains to the poorest of Americans over the past 40 years are positive and non-negligible, they would also be much higher, had government expansion not crowded out growth.[46]

Income redistribution, which stifles growth, is not a solution, as we have seen from the abysmal US war on poverty. Any real solution to poverty must address the ability to earn, i.e., productivity. This means that as a starting point, government ought to step out of the way and stop favoring the politically well-connected at the expense of the poorest. It also means that any governments serious about addressing poverty must address economic freedom.[47] After all, the poorest are the most in need of economic liberty. The poorest are also those who are most hurt, in the long run, by the government's intervention. In the spirit of Bastiat, we must be careful to distinguish between what is seen and what is not seen.[48] In this case, we must not confuse the potential positive effects of palliative government handouts, with their lack of long-term positive effects on the accumulation of human capital and income among its poor recipients. The point here is not to abandon the poor. But, rather than engage in redistributive programs with unintended consequences, governments can do two things: first, get out of the way, and stop thwarting the market's wonderful process of growth; and second, let civil society handle those who fall through the cracks of the market.[49] In sum, markets create and distribute more wealth more evenly than government intervention. Markets are fair; interventionism is not.

Income inequality exists in the US, and it has clearly been increasing in the past 40 years.[50] However, it would be incomplete to look only at income inequality. The poorest of Americans are better off in the US than they were 40 years ago. Income has increased for all. But this is not enough. Too much poverty still remains—especially because the world has figured out how to feed the masses, simply by adopting the right institutions. There is no good reason for so much poverty to persist in the US. Alas, government efforts at fighting poverty do not work. They are even counterproductive. For the sake of the poorest of Americans, it is of vital importance that policy makers not make the same mistakes in addressing inequality as they have made in attempting to address poverty over the past half century. As Hazlitt foresaw, "any attempt to equalize wealth or income by forced redistribution must only tend to destroy wealth and income."[51]

I leave philosophy to the philosophers. In the meantime, economics tells us that egalitarianism is unfair and unequal.

14

Equality Comes from Economic Growth

Ben O'Neill*

IN MORAL AND political theory libertarians and classical liberals have favored a system of equal rights and "equality before the law." Acquisition of property is dependent on production, saving, and voluntary transfer from person to person, and the virtues and other casual factors that affect these actions. Since people differ in their productive capacities, personal attributes and virtues, and also benefit from voluntary gifts, the resultant ownership of wealth exhibits inequality. Proposals for redistributive egalitarianism object to inequality in the ownership of wealth and propose coercive redistribution to reduce or eliminate this inequality.

Hostility to unequal ownership can often be traced to hostility to the natural inequality in personal characteristics and virtues causing success in the production of wealth, or alternatively to familial relationships through which wealth is often transferred by gift. Some authors refer to the "moral irrelevance" of natural endowments, asserting that a product of "arbitrary" natural endowments is "unearned" or "unfair." Though this argument was popularized by John Rawls[1] it can be traced back to Karl Marx, and has probably existed for as long as humans have had the capacity to feel envy at the natural talents or familial circumstances of others. Marx recognizes that some individuals naturally possess more ability than others, which affects their contribution in the economy, and he sees this as a "defect" of any system of equal rights.[2] According to Marx, ". . . one man is superior to another physically, or mentally, and supplies more labor in the same time, or can labor for

---

*Ben O'Neill, Ph.D., is lecturer in Statistics at the University of New South Wales at ADFA in Canberra, Australia.

a longer time. . . . This *equal* right is an unequal right for unequal labor. . . . [I]t tacitly recognizes unequal individual endowment, and thus productive capacity, as a natural privilege. . . . To avoid all these defects, right, instead of being equal, would have to be unequal."[3]

This redistributive egalitarian view abolishes equal rights and liberties to act in ways that give rise to unequal outcomes, thereby punishing people to an extent proportional to their successes in using their talents and virtues. It has been critiqued at length by theorists such as Ayn Rand and Murray Rothbard—the former referred to it as "hatred of the good for being the good" while the latter characterized it as "a revolt against nature."[4] Aside from being hostile to virtue and merit on a fundamental level, such a system can only be maintained by abridging the liberties of people to use this income in ways that cause the distribution of wealth to become unequal.[5] Moreover, as Jan Narveson points out, "[i]f justice is served by depriving people of what they came by as the result of morally arbitrary processes [under this egalitarian viewpoint], then we must take *everything* from *everyone*—a kind of 'equality,' I suppose, but hardly what they had in mind."[6]

Key Assumptions of the Redistributive Argument

The proposal for redistribution of money is often augmented by an appeal to what economists call the "diminishing marginal value" of wealth, allowing this position to be presented as an exercise in utilitarianism. According to this argument, the marginal value of wealth is higher in the hands of those who are less wealthy, implying that redistribution to a more equal outcome causes an increase in some aggregated measure of human "utility" leading to a greater "social good."[7] In describing the academic literature on this argument, David Schmidtz observes that "[e]galitarian and utilitarian perspectives diverge in theory. As a practical matter though, they converge on similar implications in virtue of the phenomenon of diminishing marginal utility."[8] Based on this idea, redistributive proposals often argue that there is a trade-off between economic growth and economic equality.[9] Advocates of redistribution present these as countervailing objectives to be "balanced" and opponents often concede that these are opposing forces.

One aspect of criticisms of wealth inequality that is often quite superficial is concentration on the fact that the distribution of wealth is clearly "skewed" (in a statistical sense) to give a small proportion of high values that are orders of magnitude above the main body of the distribution. This fact is often presented as conclusive evidence of "excessive" inequality and a cause for outrage. However, the skewed distribution of monetary wealth and income is not at all aberrant as a statistical outcome: many measures of characteristic size and social outcomes for humans lead to statistical distributions that—like wealth and income—are "on a logarithmic scale."[10] This statistical property occurs with such human characteristics as numbers of sexual partners for people of the same age cohort,[11] the sizes of cities,[12] and many more variables pertaining to the outcomes of human behavior.

Many criticisms of inequality of wealth in the free market are also quite superficial, insofar as they often refer to wealth inequality in a mixed economy, with inequality being attributed to the presence of the free-market portion of the economy, rather than government privilege or intervention. It is of course very difficult to determine the aggregate effect of many government actions on overall inequality. Nevertheless, it is possible to get an indication of the efficacy of government in reducing inequality by looking at data for socialist systems that have an explicit commitment to equality of outcome. Studies comparing inequality of wealth in socialist and capitalist nations have found variable results, but many show broadly similar levels of wage inequality.[13] Examining wages in the former Soviet Union, Abram Bergson notes that "what emerges is a rather striking similarity in inequality between . . . the USSR and Western countries. Inequality in the USSR fluctuates in the course of time, but only rarely does any particular percentile ratio fall outside the range delineated by corresponding measures for Western countries."[14] Although Bergson refers to this result as "striking" it is not all that surprising given that the system of socialism grants special privileges to government functionaries, resulting in inequality of wealth. It is a notorious feature of socialist systems that members of the managerial class were granted enormous special privilege unobtainable for ordinary workers. Indeed, in an analysis of Soviet law, Feldbrugge et al. find that, "[f]or leading members . . . privileges [were] virtually unlimited."[15]

In view of the fact that capitalist and socialist systems differ little in wealth inequality, it is likely that any alleged gain in equality coming at the expense of the superior economic growth of capitalism will be illusory. Even if some reduction in inequality in the distribution of wealth is possible, a crucial point to consider is that *money* only represents a partial measure of the classes of available goods and so it gives an incomplete picture of the true relative economic position of human beings. Even when this partial class of goods is an appropriate focus of interest for inequality analysis, a meaningful analysis must take account of systematic changes in the relative value of this class of goods over the period of the analysis.

Measuring Inequality in the Distribution of Wealth

Inequality analysis usually focuses on investigating the shares of the total property or income in society. Monetary wealth or income is used as a proxy for a large class of goods of interest. (I use the term "monetary" to refer broadly to net wealth or income from all property that can be bought and sold with money.) The distribution of wealth in society is usually measured by recourse to the distribution of money, either by measuring income or wealth. Inequality is then measured by distributional properties like the Gini coefficient or other metrics that quantify the level of inequality in a statistical distribution.[16]

There are several important economic phenomena that must be incorporated into inequality analysis in order to account for artificial effects on the distribution of wealth. A proper analysis must incorporate all sources of wealth and must account for the trajectory of income or wealth over a lifetime of each person, rather than looking at the "raw" distribution and failing to filter out the effects of age. Unfortunately, it is often the case that identical wealth trajectories are measured (irrationally) as inequality, since people of different ages are compared at different stages of this wealth trajectory. This defect can be corrected by incorporating age into the analysis and looking at the trajectory of wealth over the lifetime of each person, and such a correction must certainly be made in any sensible measurement of wealth inequality. A proper analysis must also take account of price inflation and changes in purchasing power to give some measure of money adjusted to achieve "purchasing power parity." An important question may arise over whether it is appropriate to look at total monetary wealth or income, or only the portion that is "disposable" after payment for some baseline goods like a fixed quantity of food, health, or housing. *Ceteris paribus*, inequality in disposable income is increased when the cost of baseline goods increases and is reduced when the cost of baseline goods reduces, so this can be an important consideration if the costs of baseline goods change over the period of analysis. Mark Warshawsky points out that rising health insurance costs in the US impact negatively on disposable income and increase the level of inequality in post-health-insurance income.[17]

Even when all these important considerations are incorporated into the analysis (and frequently they are not), traditional analysis of inequality in the distribution of wealth does not account for diminishing marginal returns to wealth. From the fact that money is the *object of interest* in the inequality analysis, it is often (wrongly) concluded that money is also the appropriate *standard of measurement* for the analysis, and hence, the level of wealth or income of each person is measured in money (e.g., dollars, pounds, rubles, etc.). Unfortunately, this method of analysis is defective and leads to serious bias.

The main defect of looking at inequality in monetary wealth or income while also using money as the numéraire for analysis is that, by definition, the standard of measurement cannot take account of any relative change in the real value of the class of goods represented by money compared to other classes of goods. Money accounts only for the class of goods that people can buy and sell with money (which, admittedly, is a very broad class of goods), but it does not consider any goods that are either so abundant as to be free, or goods that are nonexchangeable. In cases where there is substantial economic growth over time, the real value of money is changing quite substantially over the period of the analysis and so the relative values of these different classes of goods also changes substantially. Focus on the distribution of monetary wealth, measured in money, involves a serious failure to measure in appropriate "real" terms, taking account of diminishing marginal returns on the class of goods represented by money as the level of overall wealth increases. This error is somewhat ironic, given that advocates of redistribution commonly invoke this principle as a justification for their proposed program.[18]

There is one other important aspect of monetary wealth that is not accounted for when money is used as the standard of measurement. This is the fact that the level of time and effort involved in monetary transactions can change systematically over long periods of time, and this changes the real cost of the class of goods represented by money. Since measurement of monetary wealth is used as a proxy for the class of goods that can be purchased with money, it must be borne in mind that there is also a time and effort cost in any transaction to acquire these goods, due to the time taken to search out an appropriate good and conduct the purchase. If the time and effort costs of these transactions are reduced over time (e.g., due to new technology) then this class of goods becomes cheaper in real term, but not in measurement by money.

To deal with diminishing marginal returns, we need to measure monetary wealth in real terms that account for long-term growth in wealth and reductions in time and effort costs of monetary transactions. We require a numéraire for analysis that is fixed over a long period, allowing comparison of real wealth over a period of economic and technological growth. The numéraire must account for changes in the relative value of all classes of goods over the period of analysis, and thereby incorporate the effect of diminishing marginal returns on the class of goods that can be bought with money. While there has been some call in the economic literature to take account of diminishing marginal returns to wealth, the proposal is in its infancy and has not been incorporated into analytical work.[19] Since the ultimate standard of value is the utility of the agents in the economy whose wealth is under consideration, the measure of wealth should be a Hicksian measure appealing to underlying utility (e.g., compensating variation).

Time is fixed over a fixed interval of time—by definition—and therefore serves as the ideal numéraire, being an inherent natural quantity that is the fundamental factor of production for all human activities. Monetary wealth can best be measured in real terms by looking at the "compensating variation" in time that is required to compensate a person for taking away all their property.[20] Economic growth over time affects the value of money, but does not change the number of hours in the day, so we can measure a person's wealth in real terms as the time taken to earn back their level of utility if their wealth is taken away. This yields a resultant time-value of wealth that converts the measurement of wealth from monetary terms to the underlying time that is the ultimate factor of production of all wealth. The result is an objective measurement of a person's wealth in real terms, conducted on a Hicksian basis that appeals directly to the utility of that wealth.

Economizing Exchangeable and Nonexchangeable Goods

The class of monetary wealth under consideration is actually only one of two broad classes of goods available to human beings. All goods of value to human beings can be demarcated into the class of "exchangeable" goods and the class of "nonexchangeable" goods, and thus, overall wealth consists of both these classes of goods. Those in the former class are goods that can be transferred (exchanged) from one person to another—goods like a car, house, or cup of tea. Those in the latter class are goods that cannot be transferred (exchanged) directly from one person to another—goods like intelligence, beauty, or a good sense of humor.[21] The analysis of wealth in monetary terms looks only at the command of the former class of goods and so it gives us a partial analysis of overall wealth. Indeed, even within this class, any goods that are sufficiently abundant to be free are not bought with money, and so they are outside the scope of the class of goods represented by money.

A person has a fixed amount of time to labor to acquire goods and so there is an economic trade-off in the time allocated between the acquisition of exchangeable goods (money, a car, a house) and nonexchangeable goods (a happy marriage, greater erudition, losing weight). Both exchangeable and nonexchangeable goods are subject to diminishing marginal returns and this means that as a person acquires more of one class of goods, the relative importance of the other class of goods increases. If there is aggregate economic growth in a society on a per-capita basis, then there are more exchangeable goods available and the time-price of these goods is reduced (i.e., it takes less labor time to earn these goods). This effect is compounded by the fact that economic growth is usually accompanied by technological improvement that reduces the search costs and time costs of monetary transactions, further reducing the time-price of this class of goods. All of these effects are historically evident. The amount of labor time required to purchase particular exchangeable goods has tended to reduce over time, and search costs and transaction time have been substantially reduced by systems of communication that allow rapid and wide search of items for purchase, and rapid banking and transaction facilities that allow quick and easy transactions.

Over time, as aggregate economic and technological growth occurs, the relative time-price of exchangeable goods compared to nonexchangeable goods is reduced, or in the parlance of economics, the "marginal rate of trans-formation" increasingly favors the class of exchangeable goods.[22] Under broad assumptions pertaining to production and utility—broadly requiring that the classes of both exchangeable and nonexchangeable goods are normal goods and not inferior goods—economic theory tells us that there will be a shift in time allocation to the allocation of nonexchangeable goods and an increase in the relative output of exchangeable goods (both of which are simultane-ously accomplished, since the acquisition of exchangeable goods has become relatively less time-consuming). Creation of new goods or creation of free goods further adds to the scope and relative importance of the class of goods that are not bought and sold with money. All of this means that, as people become richer, as a result of aggregate economic growth, there is a shift in time allocation towards greater effort in the acquisition of nonexchangeable goods, but there is also greater relative abundance of exchangeable goods.

These predictions are confirmed empirically by observing that, historically, work hours (i.e., time allocation to the acquisition of exchangeable goods) have tended to reduce as societies grow richer, and yet the abundance of exchange-able goods nonetheless grows relative to nonexchangeable goods.[23] Economic growth causes less "materialism" in wants; the society that is growing richer tends to put greater emphasis and time allocation on the acquisition of nonex-changeable goods. At the same time a huge class of additional goods is created that did not previously exist, and some goods become so abundant that they become effectively free and are taken outside the scope of monetary exchange.

Convergence to Equality of the Real Value of Wealth

The total "utility" of each person is derived from his command of both ex-changeable and nonexchangeable goods, which are complementary to one another. If exchangeable goods become relatively more abundant, the ef-fect of diminishing marginal returns means that inequalities in the scale of productivity of exchangeable goods (i.e., inequality in the amount that can be acquired in a fixed amount of time) will be diminished in their impact on the overall inequality of utility of the people in society. The result is that the distribution of the real time-value of wealth is narrower around its mean than the distribution of wealth measured in purely monetary terms. (This follows even when there is *no cost* to the redistribution, which is unrealistically favorable to the egalitarian case.) As economic growth occurs, and the relative productivity of exchangeable goods increases, this narrowing of the distribution of the real time-value of wealth continues, and there is an eventual convergence towards real equality. This means that economic growth—on its own—leads to a convergence to equality in the real value of wealth, *even when the distribution of monetary wealth remains unequal.*

Particularly striking in this process of wealth creation is the fact that entirely new goods and methods of transaction are created that have not previously existed, and so it is impossible to account for this new source of utility in analysis with money as the numéraire. Thirty years ago a person wishing to communicate with someone overseas would have to use physical mail, or a relatively expensive long-distance telephone call. To get information about a specialized subject they would most likely have to travel to a library, and then look through index cards to find an appropriate book, perhaps having to order the book they need. Even if they had money and wanted to purchase a particular kind of item, there would be substantial time costs to search out appropriate shops or printed mail catalogues to find and purchase the desired item. Only thirty years later and these desires are now facilitated by systems of rapid communication that allow effectively free and instantaneous satisfaction of these wants. The past thirty years has seen the construction and commercialization of the internet, email, social media, search engines, and repositories of online encyclopedias, books, articles, music, movies, etc. It is now possible to communicate instantaneously with people around the world, by voice or written message, find encyclopedic information on any subject in an instant, or find a song, movie, or television show you like in an instant and listen to it on your computer or phone. You can find enormous repositories of items for sale and rapidly find and purchase a desired item without leaving the comfort of your home. Beyond an initial cost to purchase a computer and internet connection, the marginal costs of all these resources is effectively zero. It is not merely that previous technologies have become cheaper (accounted for in monetary measures of purchasing parity), but that they are now available to everyone at a marginal cost that is effectively zero. This is an enormous real reduction in inequality that is completely ignored in traditional inequality analysis.

Of course, I hasten to add that this convergence to real equality is only a convergence in respect to wealth—i.e., exchangeable goods. People will still have all sorts of inequalities in their command of *nonexchangeable* goods and so overall inequality in utility will remain. Some people will have happy marriages, great friends, deep knowledge and wisdom, etc., and others will have disease, depression, no friends, bad relationships, ungrateful snotty kids, and other low-quality nonexchangeable goods (or even bads). This kind of inequality is beyond the scope of the delusions of even the most fervent egalitarian redistributionist.

The above argument alerts us to the fact that traditional inequality analysis systematically overstates the persistence of inequality in a society with long-run economic growth. Growth causes an increasing shift to relative abundance of exchangeable goods, and the diminishing marginal returns for this class of goods means that real inequality gets smaller and smaller. Most importantly, this equalizing phenomenon occurs *even when the distribution of monetary wealth remains unequal.* This finding has implications for the proposal for redistribution of wealth. Free-market capitalism, by virtue of its rapid economic growth, has a built-in but unseen byproduct, which is a rapid convergence to real wealth equality. A lasting free-market system would most likely entail massive growth in aggregate wealth and a shift of time and effort away from "materialistic" concerns. It would retain inequality in the distribution of wealth *measured in monetary terms*, but there would be an underlying convergence to equality in the distribution of the real value of wealth *measured by its time-value in utility terms.*

15

Taxes and the Myth of Egalitarianism

Brian J. Gaines*

AMERICANS UNDOUBTEDLY PRIZE equality as a fundamental value, but what kind of equality is prioritized: equality of opportunities and treatment by the state or equality in outcomes? These distinct applications of equality prove antithetical. In practice, the term *egalitarianism* now connotes favoring "a greater degree of equality of income and wealth across persons than currently exists."[1] Egalitarianism is thus a marker of modern, progressive liberalism rather than liberalism in its original sense of valuing liberty and aiming to limit coercion by government as much as practicable.[2] Do most Americans embrace coercive redistribution in the interest of reducing inequality?

Decades ago, F. A. Hayek was pessimistic, fearing that collectivism had displaced liberalism as the dominant doctrine of policy debate. Whether in the polemical mode of *The Road to Serfdom* (1944) or in the more analytical style of *The Constitution of Liberty* (1960), he observed that a state powerful enough to impose substantially equal outcomes would, by nature, not only prevent the benefits of competition but also demolish essential individual liberties.

Of course, Hayek did not merely lament the allures of socialism and its "fatal conceit" but also tirelessly argued against concentrating power in the state. Did his ideas take root? The huge growth in public-choice theory is but one sign that skepticism about statism has steadily grown. In a debate with Hayek in 1945, the renowned political scientist Charles Merriam was

---

*Brian J. Gaines is professor of political science in the Department of Political Science and the Institute of Government and Public Affairs at the University of Illinois.

apoplectic that Hayek could see in what Merriam called the "creative forces of government" a threat to freedom.[3] Thirty-six years later, in one of the most quoted lines from any presidential inaugural address, Ronald Reagan took Hayek's side: "Government is not the solution to our problem; government is the problem."[4]

Few ordinary Americans hold utterly consistent views on deep questions of political philosophy or all policy debates. They embrace, to some degree, conflicting values. Mining survey data identified not only a stable, widely held set of values that produce conservative attitudes toward policies aimed at reducing inequality but also a growing attraction to interventionist social liberalism, particularly among the young.[5] From a highly innovative attempt to conduct a laboratory test of John Rawls's theories[6] about how much inequality people see as tolerable, Norman Frolich and Joe Oppenheimer concluded that the desire to set a floor on poverty is almost universal. But they also found strong support for "letting people keep what they earn, without a ceiling, after providing for a floor."[7]

Fairness Rhetoric in Public Debate on Taxes

A thorough review of the landscape of empirical debates on the place of equality in the American mind is impossible in a short essay. My limited ambition here is to reconsider how Americans fare with competing demands for equality of treatment and equality of condition in regard to taxes. Survey firms routinely claim that Americans are anxious or angry about wealth inequality and eager for government remedies.[8]

There is it seems, at least according to these surveys, consensus that Americans support higher taxes for the wealthy. Following the presidential election of 2012, a conservative columnist conceded, "Yes, a solid majority favors higher taxes for the rich. That's been true since the dawn of man."[9] President Barack Obama, meanwhile, when asked about the wealthiest paying more, noted, "By the way, more voters agreed with me on this issue than voted for me." Many of Obama's campaign speeches featured a short description of the "Buffett rule," which says that "if you make a million dollars a year, then you shouldn't pay a lower tax rate than your secretary."[10] Obama nearly always asserted that Democrats had the public on their side in this debate: "And I intend to keep fighting for this kind of balance and fairness until the other side starts listening, because I believe this is what the American people want."[11]

Four years later, Donald Trump's victory over Hillary Clinton might be seen as a repudiation of that alleged consensus, given that he emphasized tax reduction, whereas she again promised to raise taxes on the wealthy. But it is not yet clear how important tax policy was to Trump's surprising win, and, of course, Clinton won the popular vote by about two percentage points. She constitutionally has no legitimate claim on the presidency, but her popular-vote win indicates that her policy stances commanded more support.

Survey Says . . .

Politicians routinely claim to be advocating positions preferred by majorities, but Obama and Clinton could in fact point to survey support. Consider a fairly representative study published by the Pew Research Center, "Tax System Seen as Unfair, in Need of Overhaul: Wealthy Not Paying Fair Share Top Complaint" (2011). The title belies the survey's finding that the most popular choice for describing the current system was "moderately fair" (40 percent), ahead of "not too fair" (31 percent) and "not fair at all" (24 percent). The subtitle, meanwhile, describes a question that offers respondents three statements and asks which one "bothers" them most about the tax system. Fifty-seven percent had "the feeling that some wealthy people get away not paying their fair share," far ahead of those who chose "the complexity of the tax system" (28 percent) and those who chose "the large amount you pay in taxes" (11 percent) as the thing that bothers them most. The percentage selecting that first answer also rose slightly from 2003, when it was 53 percent.

One wonders why a "feeling" was in competition with two less-fuzzy claims and how other complaints might have fared. In a survey I distributed in 2004, I gave respondents a similar list, with the addition of "Government wastes so much of the money collected in taxes," and allowed them to select as many responses as they liked. Almost 80 percent agreed with the government-waste claim, making it the most popular complaint.

Is there stronger evidence of American egalitarianism in other survey items? Every year from 2012 to 2016 in surveys timed to coincide with the April income-tax-filing deadline, at least 60 percent of Gallup respondents have said that upper-income people pay too little federal taxes. When I likewise asked respondents to assess the taxes paid by the rich in a study administered by YouGov in February 2012 to a representative sample of about 3,500 Americans, 64 percent of respondents said the rich paid too little, rather than the right amount or too much.[12] Although those responses seem to reveal broad support for increasing taxes on the rich, the questions, like Obama's campaign rhetoric, are regrettably vague.

What does the response tell us about the public's preferred tax system? Who is rich? What sorts of rates do respondents believe that the people they regard as rich are presently paying in income tax? If those rates (whether they are accurate or not) are too low, how much higher should they be in order to be fair? These points are critical to understanding exactly what sentiment is being expressed, and I take them up in sequence.

Do people agree on where to draw the lines between "poor," "middle class," and "rich"? I know of no survey on taxation that has explored this question, despite the preponderance of questions inquiring into whether these groups are taxed at appropriate levels. In the survey I conducted in 2012, I asked respondents to name the minimum annual income levels to qualify for "middle class" and "rich." About 88 percent of respondents were willing to pick threshold values, but there was a great deal of variation in where respondents drew their lines. Roughly one-third of the respondents thought that "rich" started at $100,000 per year; another third drew the line somewhere between $100,000 and $250,000; and the balance picked a higher value (with nearly 10 percent selecting a level of $500,000 or higher). About one-quarter of respondents thought that the line between poor and middle class should fall below $25,000 per year, but 35 percent picked a figure higher than $70,000.

Figure 15.1 shows the income thresholds that respondents chose, with middle-class zones shaded gray, ordered by the size of the middle-class-income range. Clearly, there is much variation, and there is no broad consensus on what the terms *rich* and *poor* mean. In turn, responses to questions using those terms are inherently ambiguous. Those whose responses fell on the left side of the figure and those who were placed on the right will generally mean very different sets of people when they discuss "the rich."

Second, asking if the rich or poor are paying about the right amount of taxes begs the question of how much tax these groups presently pay. Survey

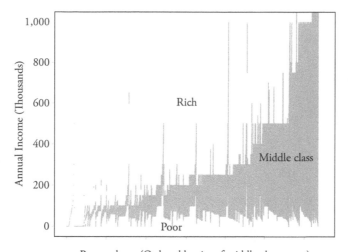

Figure 15.1. Many Definitions of Rich, Middle Class, and Poor

researchers implicitly assume either that respondents know what others pay in taxes or that accuracy is immaterial. Either assumption is problematic. If the point of a survey question is merely to assess subjective fairness, without regard for accuracy, the conclusion that the public wants higher taxes obviously does not follow. A widespread belief that the rich pay too little might rest on widespread underestimation of actual tax rates. In that case, conclusions of the form "Americans want the rich to pay more" could be more accurately rephrased as "Americans want the rich to pay about what they now pay, but they also mistakenly believe that the rich currently pay less."

Conventional wisdom holds that the general public is ill equipped to discuss tax codes because of the latter's complexity and the former's ignorance of key terminology. Public ignorance about important aspects of taxes is emphasized in a study done by the Kaiser Foundation, the Kennedy School, and National Public Radio in 2003,[13] in an influential book arguing that Americans are actually content to pay higher taxes that reduce inequality,[14] and in the Pew study done in 2011,[15] among others. It is thus ironic that so many questions about fairness rest on an unstated assumption that respondents actually know what various kinds of people presently pay.

Do many people have an accurate sense of what others pay in income taxes? I asked respondents how much federal income tax was owed in 2011 by hypothetical single taxpayers who had annual incomes of $60,000, $250,000, and $1 million and who took standard deductions rather than itemizing. Admittedly, very few who earn a quarter of a million or more fail to itemize, but the question allows comparison of responses to precise, correct answers. The correct answers were $8,750, $64,262, and $323,989. For the $60,000 earner, 52 percent of respondents guessed amounts that were more than 10 percent too low, 9 percent were within 10 percent on either side, and the remaining 39 percent were more than 10 percent too high. For the tax bill on $250,000, 73 percent were low, 11 percent about right, and 16 percent high. For the tax bill on $1 million, 75 percent were low, 20 percent about right, and only 5 percent too high.

Before I conclude that underestimation of the tax burdens of the comparatively wealthy is very common, one might wonder if respondents ignored the language about itemizing and perhaps gave estimates that are roughly in accord with what actual taxpayers, most of whom take advantage of a vast array of credits and deductions, really pay. Internal Revenue Service (IRS) data permit a second comparison. For 2011, the average percentage of adjusted gross income paid in taxes by earners in the $50,000–75,000 range was 8.6 percent. For a $60,000 earner, that rate implies a tax bill of $5,160. The rates for households in the $200,000–500,000 range and $1–1.5 million range were 19.7 percent and 24.9 percent, respectively. Applying those rates to my hypothetical incomes, I get lower estimates, to which I can again compare respondents' estimates. With this approach, the proportions of respondents whose guesses of tax owed were more than 10 percent too low, within 10 percent, and more than 10 percent too high to match these new estimated true tax bills were 31 percent, 8 percent, and 61 percent, respectively, for $60,000; 59 percent, 13 percent, and 29 percent for $250,000; and 66 percent, 7 percent, and 27 percent for $1 million. Underestimation of wealthy Americans' tax bills is indeed common.

If people agreeing that the rich pay too little tax not only disagree on who is rich but also underestimate how much tax such people pay, the modal survey finding is hopelessly ambiguous.

Better Measurement

Since 2004, I have periodically presented survey respondents with specific vignettes to generate more precise measurement of what constitutes a fair level of taxation. For example: "What do you think is a fair amount of federal income tax for a family of 4 to pay? For each of the income levels listed below, please enter the amount of federal income tax in dollars that you think should be paid by a couple, one of whom works outside the home, who have two children under age 18."

The actual income levels specified were randomly generated from a small set of increasing, round numbers. So a respondent might have been asked about families with incomes of $35,000, $70,000, $120,000, $300,000, and $500,000. One can also, of course, vary the taxpayer's other traits, prominently whether the subject is a married couple with one or two incomes or a single individual as well as how many dependent children the taxpayer has. Hereafter, for simplicity, I focus only on the fair taxes selected by respondents for hypothetical families of four with one income. But the main patterns described subsequently hold generally.

Figure 15.2 shows in two panels respondents' estimates of mean fair-tax rates for families of four with various incomes in 2012. The top panel shows the full range of incomes, with smooth curves to emphasize the patterns. For comparison, I also draw in the well-known flat tax described by Robert Hall and Alvin Rabushka,[16] based on a 19 percent tax rate with personal allowances of $16,500 and $4,500 child credits.[17] The crosses mark average rates of adjusted gross income reported by the IRS, drawn at the midpoint of the income ranges (e.g., for $50,000–75,000, I plot 8.6 percent at $62,500). The bottom panel shows only annual incomes of $200,000 or less to clarify how the three series compare in the income region inhabited by most Americans.

In brief, up to about $150,000 in income per year, there is little difference between what people regard as fair and the average tax rates presently paid, though the latter are sometimes a little lower. Those making about $40,000 or less and $200,000 or more are paying more than they would under Hall–Rabushka, whereas those in between pay less. If a 19 percent flat tax would lower the tax bills of those who make more than $200,000 per year, it is more striking that the public's view of what is a fair income tax is even lower. In

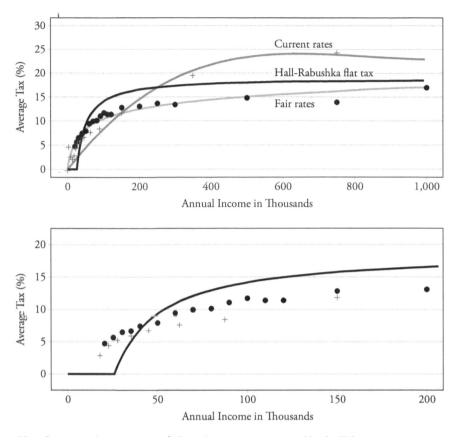

Note: Crosses mark average rates of adjusted gross income reported by the IRS, drawn at the midpoint of the income ranges.

Figure 15.2. Mean Fair Income Tax Rates Compared to Hall-Rabushka Flat Tax

the upper-income ranges, subjectively fair rates resemble a 17–18 percent flat tax, whereas the current system looks more like a 25 percent version (but with high variance around the means).

The data presented in figure 15.2 puncture the simple story told by most other public-opinion researchers: that most Americans are eager to make the rich pay more. Tax rates regarded as fair are lower than current rates for large incomes but about the same for low and moderate incomes. Insofar as these vignettes tap into true beliefs better than do the far more common but deeply vague questions, the default view should be that Americans like fairly low taxes, not just for themselves but for others, too, including the wealthy.

In the aftermath of the election of 2016, misforecast by most poll-based models, skepticism about the scientific value of surveys is running high. Could it be that these respondents who seem to defy the common wisdom that ordinary people want the rich to pay more were a strange draw? It is wise never to forget that survey results are merely estimates with inherent uncertainty. But several points reassure me that the conclusion that Americans think of quite low levels of taxation as fair is robust. First, I have employed related but distinct vignettes five times across about ten years and have consistently found that the rates chosen as fair map into relatively flat schedules more or less like those pictured in figure 15.2. Second, none of the surveys seemed badly skewed in terms of respondents' self-reported ideology or partisanship or in terms of respondents' self-reported incomes.[18] I next consider three other potential objections.

What If the Revenue Is Too Low?

The respondents whose answers are shown in figure 15.2 were free to select any rates of income tax as fair, without regard for revenue implications. How would they react in the event that the tax rates they regard to be fair generated less revenue than the present system? To find out, I calculated a conservative estimate of how much income tax revenue would be produced by the rates each of our respondents provided and then asked those whose preferred tax rates translated into reduced total revenue (which was about 90 percent of the respondents) how they would deal with the shortfall. I allowed them to choose as many of the following four options as they liked: cut government spending; raise the rates on all taxpayers; raise the rates on the more wealthy only; and/or let the deficit and debt grow.

The most popular response, from about 44 percent of respondents, was to endorse only the option of cutting government spending. About 22 percent endorsed both cutting spending and taxing the wealthy, and another 19 percent endorsed only taxing the wealthy. About 5 percent said they would favor raising all tax rates, and 4 percent said that they would both raise all tax rates and cut spending. The remaining responses were dispersed across other combinations in small numbers. In light of the explosive growth of government debt in recent years, it is noteworthy that only about 3 percent of respondents chose any set of options that included allowing the deficit and debt to grow, and a mere 2 percent chose that option alone.

In a survey conducted in 2015, I asked respondents to select tax rates for 1,000 hypothetical taxpayers falling into eight income groups, roughly mirroring the actual US distribution (i.e., 350 taxpayers with $15,000 earnings each; 240 with $30,000 earnings each; and so on up to only 2 with incomes of $2 million each).[19] Randomly half of the respondents were required to reach a revenue target, scaled roughly to correspond to actual federal spending, whereas the others were only instructed to choose only fair-tax rates. The revenue constraint did raise the rates selected as fair, particularly for conservative respondents, whose unconstrained rates fell well below the target. But the effect was not concentrated on the highest incomes ($2 million, $800,000, and $350,000). The proportional increase was about the same for the taxes chosen for the top six groups; only the $30,000 and $15,000 earners, usually assigned 0–5 percent tax rates, did not get elevated fair-tax rates when explicit revenue floors were set.

So there is some sign that some respondents can be talked into bending up their fair-tax curves, but cutting spending is much more popular.

What about the Superwealthy?

The penultimate paragraph of Warren Buffett's much-discussed *New York Times* op-ed in 2011 read: "But for those making more than $1 million—there were 236,883 such households in 2009—I would raise rates immediately on taxable income in excess of $1 million, including, of course, dividends and capital gains. And for those who make $10 million or more—there were 8,274 in 2009—I would suggest an additional increase in rate."[20]

Exactly what rates the Sage of Omaha wanted was left for the reader to guess. My fair-income-tax scenarios did not feature any incomes higher than $1 million, but the survey did include another item asking respondents to identify a fair-tax level for some very large incomes. I asked, "What is a fair amount of tax to pay on lottery winnings of . . . ?" and randomly assigned each respondent a prize level of $1 million, $2 million, $5 million, $10 million, $20 million, $50 million, or $100 million as the prize to be taxed. Respondents gave their answers in dollars, which I converted to percentages. This question did not explicitly distinguish between federal and state income taxes, but I intended for them to name a fair total tax bill. For winnings that large, winners presently pay very nearly the top rate in federal income tax (35 percent for 2011, which reverted to 39.6 percent in 2012, when the survey was conducted) and in most states 5 percent or more in state and local income taxes.

I found no evidence that the American public wants the (suddenly) very rich to shoulder a high tax burden or even to pay current rates. Figure 15.3 shows the mean rates selected by respondents for each prize level according to their self-identified party identification. Only about one-quarter of respondents chose a fair lottery tax of 30 percent or higher; for the vast majority, the Obama–Buffet rates were too high. Indeed, the average fair tax proposed by respondents was only 15 percent. Variation across prize levels was mildly sporadic, and, perhaps surprisingly, most differences across prize amounts were too small to be regarded as statistically significant. Whether taxing $1 million or $100 million in prizes, most respondents chose rates of 10 percent or less. On this question, moreover, Democrats, Republicans, and independents

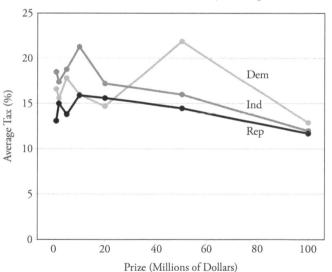

What is a fair tax on lottery winnings?

Figure 15.3. Mean Fair Income Tax Rates for (Large) Lottery Prize, by Partisanship

differed only a little. Republicans chose an average lottery tax of a little more than 14 percent, while Democrats and independents set it around 17 percent.

These rates are broadly similar to those shown in figure 15.2, and it thus seems unlikely that they are so low only because the hypothetical income was obtained in an unusual manner. Although hardly anyone ever accrues any significant lottery income, millions of Americans buy tickets and dream about the ultraslim possibility of a giant windfall. So a preference for low rates is probably not a function of lotteries being too strange or inaccessible for respondents ever to have given any thought to what level of taxation is fair for the winners.

What about Contrary Evidence?

I also asked a question about a specific instance of the Buffett rule: "Would you favor or oppose a law requiring millionaires to pay at least 30 percent of their income in taxes?" The responses were similar to those reported by others: 62 percent said they favored the tax, only 24 percent were opposed, and 14 percent said that they were unsure. Because the question is fairly specific, how can one reconcile this finding with the strikingly low fair-tax responses?

One conjecture is that people strongly associate high incomes with shelters and tricks that protect much of this money from taxes. In turn, one might endorse a 30 percent rate with the idea that only such a high rate can actually achieve effective rates in the range of, say, the 17 percent that is roughly the mean fair-tax answer for very large incomes. Of course, the whole point of the Buffett rule is to establish a fixed average rate for total income, and my wording was meant to convey as much. But to the extent that Buffett's argument has been widely aired, it has surely reinforced the view that people whose income has six or seven digits not only escape high tax *rates* but also accrue a great deal of wealth that is simply not taxed. It is difficult to write survey questions that successfully induce respondents to set aside their existing beliefs and to answer only for the hypothetical worlds as described by the survey researcher.

Arguably, asking about fair taxes for lottery income is useful precisely because lottery income is so unlikely to be shielded from taxation. One interpretation of the discrepancy between support for a Buffett rule and the low preferred lottery taxes is that people will embrace a 30 percent rate when they suspect that much of the income in question is sheltered but like low rates when they expect the whole income to be taxed. If so, even those who seem on board with Buffett might have in mind a fair-tax bill that is lower than 30 percent.

When asked to provide best guesses for current tax rates, those who said that they favor the Buffett rule gave answers that averaged out to 12 percent taxes on a $1 million income. Opponents' answers averaged about 21 percent. Both values are too low to be regarded as accurate, given the stated premise of the question, and respondents may have had in mind capital-gains rates (after having heard Buffett say, repeatedly, that his own effective tax rate is lower than 20 percent). But the difference points yet again to the importance of inaccurate beliefs about the status quo in regard to support for raising rates.

Indeed, although those who said that they favor a 30 percent tax on millionaires did tend to select higher fair-tax rates, only a minority of them actually picked an amount that converts into a 30 percent rate, whether answering for a $1 million income or a $1 million lottery prize.

In support of the conjecture that horizontal rather than vertical comparisons preoccupy Americans, I can point to one other item. The survey gauged preferences for revenue-neutral tax reform with this question: "Some tax reform plans being discussed would change the tax code without aiming to change the total amount of tax revenue collected. Which of the following alternatives would you prefer?" Thirty-six percent said they were "not sure," but the remainder broke strongly in favor of "Decrease tax rates, but eliminate some deductions" (43 percent) over "Increase tax rates, but increase deductions" (10 percent) or "Keep rates at current levels and keep current deductions" (10 percent). Many Americans, it seems, see unfairness less in low rates than in the myriad complexities in the current code.

Shallow Roots of Egalitarianism

Doubtless, many Americans hold not entirely consistent beliefs about what is fair in the realm of taxes. There is scope for talking them into and out of higher rates on fairness grounds. There is a visceral appeal to the main argument heard from the Left that the rich are not pulling their weight. Others have shown that tax support can be conditional on expectations about how the revenue is spent.[21]

Just the same, the difference between the portrait sketched in this essay and the portraits painted in most headlines about American attitudes toward wealth inequality and taxes is striking. When asked what is fair, Americans name fairly low and flat tax rates. Most support very low (even zero) rates for the poorest and only modest increases in rates across the range from median to high incomes. I did not ask for philosophical justifications in any of these surveys, but for the aggregate data recall Hayek:

> It is the great merit of proportional taxation that it provides a rule which is likely to be agreed upon by those who will pay absolutely more and those who will pay absolutely less and which, once accepted, raises no problem of a separate rule applying only to a minority. . . . In no sense can a progressive scale of taxation be regarded as a general rule applicable equally to all. . . . Progression provides no criterion whatever of what is and what is not to be regarded as just.[22]

Acknowledgments: My work on public opinion about fair taxation began long ago in collaboration with Doug Rivers and Lynn Vavreck, both of whom are, of course, blameless for this article. I am also grateful to the Hoover Institution and in particular to David Brady for strong support of this project. Too many audiences have heard some version of a talk on my fair-tax findings for a full listing here, but I am thankful for copious feedback from many along the way. In 1988, the late George Feaver first introduced me to the writings of F. A. Hayek in a dazzling, year-long tutorial.

16

Pushing for More Equality of Income and Wealth

Edward P. Stringham*

IS INEQUALITY IN income or wealth something society should attempt to reduce, or is inequality something individuals just have to live with? In America, the top 1.0 percent owns 42 percent of the wealth, and the top 0.1 percent owns as much as the bottom 90 percent.[1] It is easy to see why someone in the 1.0 percent would be okay with having a disproportionately high share of a pie, but what about others? A *New York Times* poll found that two-thirds of Americans believe that "wealth in this country should be more evenly distributed among more people."[2] When artist Steve Lambert stationed a large "Capitalism works for me" sign in Times Square and asked people to select true or false, the majority selected false. John Rawls famously asked people to think about what type of society they would like to live in, assuming they would find themselves the least well-off.[3] Let us continue with a thought experiment in the spirit of Rawls, and ask: Supposing you knew your income or wealth percentile, what type of society would you choose?

Consider choosing between the following two actual countries, supposing you knew you would be in the lowest, second-lowest, middle, second-highest, or highest 20 percent. Country B has much more inequality than Country A. On the Gini measure of inequality (where 0 indicates perfect equality and 100 perfect inequality), Country A has a Gini coefficient of 26, among the top-ten most equal countries, and Country B has a Gini coefficient of 45,

*Edward P. Stringham is the Davis Professor of Economic Innovation at Trinity College, Hartford, President and Director of Research and Education at the American Institute for Economic Research, and author of *Private Governance: Creating Order in Economic and Social Life* (2015).

Table 16.1. Disparities of Income in Two Countries

Suppose you were in the following quintile . . .	If you were in Country A, your quintile's share of society's income would be . . .	If you were in Country B, your quintile's share of society's income would be . . .	Choose where you would rather live.
Lowest	10%	5%	□ A □ B
Second lowest	14%	10%	□ A □ B
Middle	18%	15%	□ A □ B
Upper middle	22%	23%	□ A □ B
Highest	36%	46%	□ A □ B
If you had equal chances of landing in each quintile			□ A □ B

Source: Data from Barrientos and Soria 2016.

the 103rd least-equal country. Table 16.1 indicates the share of income by quintile in the two countries. The top and bottom rows show that in Country A the bottom quintile gets 10 percent of income, and the top quintile gets 36, whereas in Country B the bottom quintile only gets 5 percent of income, and the top quintile gets 46 percent. In other words, the people in the bottom quintile make less than one-ninth of what those in the top quintile in Country B make. Choose between the two countries in each of the five cases. Finally, choose where you would rather live if you had an equal chance of ending up in each income quintile.

Now let us consider an example that looks at wealth rather than at income. When income inequality is high, the rich have the opportunity to amass more and more wealth over time, increasing inequality even more. Assume home values measure wealth. Table 16.2 indicates how much each quintile's homes are worth as a percentage of total wealth in two neighborhoods. The top and bottom rows show that in the much more equal Neighborhood X, the bottom quintile's homes are worth 61 percent as much as the richest quintile's homes,

Table 16.2. Disparities of Wealth in Two Neighborhoods

Suppose you were in the following quintile . . .	If you were in Neighborhood X, your quintile's share of home value would be . . .	If you were in Neighborhood Y, your quintile's share of home value would be . . .	Choose where you would rather live.
Lowest	16%	8%	☐ A ☐ B
Second lowest	18%	10%	☐ A ☐ B
Middle	19%	11%	☐ A ☐ B
Upper middle	20%	16%	☐ A ☐ B
Highest	26%	54%	☐ A ☐ B
If you had equal chances of landing in each quintile			☐ A ☐ B

Source: Data from Zillow 2016.

whereas in the much more unequal Neighborhood Y the poorest quintile's homes are worth a mere 15 percent as much as the richest quintile's homes.[4] In neighborhood Y, the top 20 percent own more than everyone else combined. Again, you must choose between the two neighborhoods in each of the five cases. Finally, choose where you would rather live if you had an equal chance of ending up in each wealth quintile.

At this point, all your answers are final. Country B describes the United States, and Country A describes the far more equal former Soviet state of Belarus. Figure 16.1 displays average income per quintile in America, where gross domestic product (GDP) per capita is $62,000, and in Belarus, where GDP per capita is $5,700. In America, income in the highest quintile averages $143,000 and in the lowest quintile $15,500. In Belarus, income in the highest quintile averages $10,300 and in the lowest quintile $2,900. For the lowest quintiles, 5 percent of the very large American economic pie is much bigger than 10 percent of the very small economic pie in Belarus. If you chose to live in Country A, be sure to send postcards.

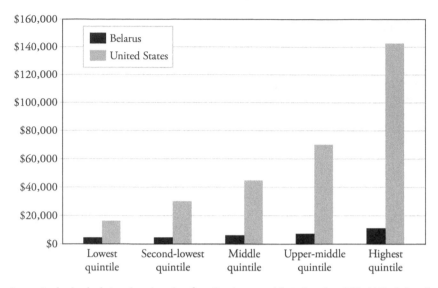

Source: Author's calculations based on data from Barrientos and Soria (2016) and World Bank (2016).

Figure 16.1. Income per Quintile in the United States and Belarus

Neighborhood Y describes a street in Holmby Hills, Los Angeles (next to Beverly Hills and Bel Air), whose residents have included Humphrey Bogart, Bing Crosby, Neil Diamond, Hugh Hefner, Casey Kasem, and Aaron Spelling. Homes on that street are, according to the online real estate database company Zillow, worth $8.9, $10.4, $10.6, $10.8, $10.9, $11.1, $11.8, $12.7, $12.9, $13.0, $14.0, $14.6, $16.1, $19.9, $26.5, $26.6, $58.0, and $68.1 million.[5] One for sale is described this way:

> 125 rooms. Exquisite 2 Acre Country English Holmby Hills Manor. Adjacent to Los Angeles Country Club. This magnificent walled estate includes remarkable grounds and privacy. 2 story entry, spacious living room w/ fireplace and beautiful garden vistas, large family room adjoins the dining room and eat-in gourmet kitchen opening to charming outdoor terrace. Enormous motor court. Rolling lawns, mature trees and wonderful private pool area.[6]

Neighborhood X describes a not-so-hot neighborhood a couple miles from where I live in Hartford. The somewhat-rundown homes cost $84,000, $85,000, $88,000, $89,000, $95,000, $97,000, $97,000, $101,000, $102,000,

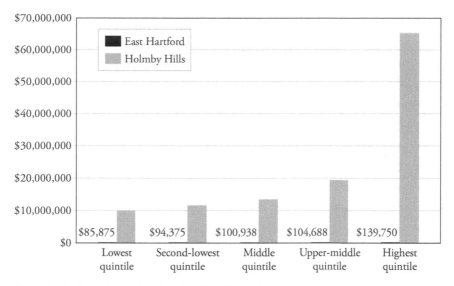

$85,875 $94,375 $100,938 $104,688 $139,750

Lowest quintile   Second-lowest quintile   Middle quintile   Upper-middle quintile   Highest quintile

Source: Author's calculations based on data from Zillow (2016).

Figure 16.2. Average Home Value per Quintile in Holmby Hills (Los Angeles) and East Hartford, Connecticut

$102,000, $103,000, $104,000, $105,000, $106,000, $127,000, $143,000, and $156,000. Figure 16.2 shows home value by quintile in the two neighborhoods. I don't know about you, but I'd rather be the poorest person on Aaron Spelling's street than the richest person in East Hartford.[7] It would be quite easy to make Holmby Hills like East Hartford—any tornado could do the trick. But should we bring all wealth down for the sake of equalizing it?

The fundamental problem with calls to make income and wealth equal or more equal is that they make judgments based on relative income or wealth (i.e., what people have compared to others), not on what people have in their own right (i.e., absolute income or wealth). In its strictest incarnations, egalitarianism considers it negative if everyone starts poor, and then everyone becomes rich, but some richer than others. In its strictest incarnations, egalitarianism endorses keeping or making everyone poor as long as it reduces differences in income or wealth. Increasing work skills, working more, working in jobs in higher demand, and saving and investing increase inequality compared to a society where everyone remains poor.

Egalitarianism takes different forms and different degrees. Its goal can range from "everyone should have equal income and wealth" to the milder calls that "we should push society to have more-equal income and wealth." Some egalitarians, deontological egalitarians, support equality as an end in itself, and others, instrumentalist egalitarians, support it because it advances other social goals such as helping the poor. Although many simply ignore the incentive problems that arise when monetary rewards are eliminated, others engage in ideal theorizing about how people will be motivated in their preferred egalitarian world. This essay argues that even if the standard incentive problem is solved, pushing for equal income or wealth for its own sake is deeply flawed, and egalitarianism as a means to other ends such as maximizing advantages for society's least well-off fails. Moreover, egalitarianism can encourage envy, pit the poor against the rich, and ignore how the nexus of market exchange is mutually beneficial even if people end up with different amounts.

Rejecting income or wealth egalitarianism does not imply rejecting equal rights, equal treatment, or equal access to opportunity, and it does not imply that some people are judged as morally inferior. C. S. Lewis argues that even if individuals are different, God has equal love for everyone,[8] and both F. A. Hayek[9] and Ludwig von Mises[10] argue that the law should treat everyone equally. Society need not attempt to mandate that everyone have equal height, weight, eye color, hair color, or religion, and society need not mandate that everyone make the same economic choices or be in the same economic situation. Even if society were to comprise otherwise-identical people who simply have different goals, we should not expect all people to have the same amount of income or wealth at all times. A tolerant and liberal society should respect not only equality of rights but also the different choices that people make. A tolerant and liberal society should recognize diversity among members of society and, rather than forcing people into the same economic outcomes, let people make their own choices to shape their lives.

How Egalitarianism Judges Enrichment of All but at Different Rates as a Negative

The net worth of the Forbes 400 richest Americans is now $2.4 trillion,[11] up from $400 billion in 1994.[12] Nobel laureate Muhammad Yunus says that the increasing concentration of wealth is "a ticking time bomb and a great danger to the world,"[13] and filmmaker Michael Moore has harsher words for the Forbes 400, stating that "four hundred obscenely wealthy individuals . . . now have more cash, stock and property than the assets of 155 million Americans combined" and referring to these individuals as "400 little Mubaraks" (denoting the former president of Egypt).[14] But provided that the rich get richer by serving others in the marketplace and not by expropriating income as did Mubarak, why are such increases in wealth bad?

One of the biggest problems with egalitarianism is it negatively judges people getting richer at different rates, even if everyone in society is getting richer in the process. Consider the plight of Warren Buffett, who was the richest person in America in 1993 but was surpassed by Bill Gates and now has 20 percent *less* money than Gates. Yet aside from potential jealousy for no longer being on the top of the list, Buffett has 7.9 times more money now than he had 1993.[15] Buffett has gotten a great deal richer, just not as rich as Gates. To put these numbers into perspective, construction of the new One World Trade Center cost $3.9 billion. Adjusting for inflation, in 1994 Gates or Buffett could have personally financed four of these 1,776-foot towers. Today Gates could finance twenty and Buffett sixteen of these towers. Should Buffett be sad that he has become poorer relative to Gates?

The same is true of my wealth and likely your wealth, which has increased in absolute terms but declined relative to that of Buffett, Gates, and all the newly minted decabillionaires from the past two decades. In 1994, nobody in America had a net worth of $10 billion, around $15 billion in 2016 dollars, whereas today forty-five people have a net wealth of more than $10 billion, and twenty-seven have a net wealth of more than $15 billion. That means we now have dozens who are richer than Gates and Buffett were in 1994. But even though the richest Americans' net worth has gone up by billions more than mine, I am not worse off because their fortunes rose. If I want to evaluate my financial situation, I should look at my income and wealth, not at theirs. Basing one's personal assessment on a comparison to what the richest people have is a recipe for disappointment.

Suppose we discovered that the Greek god of riches, Plutus, existed and had the same amount of material riches as all humans combined. That would not decrease what humans already have because the amount of wealth or the size of the economic pie is not fixed. Simply learning about Plutus's previously

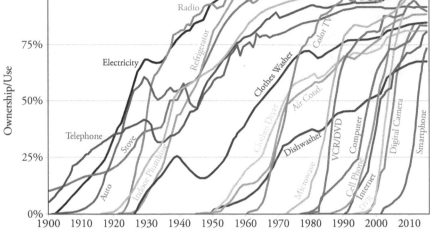

Source: Cox and Alm (2016, 13).

Figure 16.3. Spread of Products in American Households

unknown wealth would mean that wealth was twice the previous estimate. In the past two decades, humans have not discovered Plutus, but world GDP has doubled, and the proportion of people living in extreme poverty has fallen from 30 percent to 10 percent.[16] In America, one of the biggest problems afflicting lower-income people is obesity, indicating that even poor Americans can put lots of food on their table.

Figure 16.3, from Michael Cox and Richard Alm, shows that as recently as one hundred years ago the majority of American households lacked electricity, indoor plumbing, a stove, or a refrigerator, whereas today pretty much everyone has all of these amenities.[17] If one measures equality as access to these particular technologies, then we have much more equality than ever, even if relative income or wealth has diverged greatly. At present, two-thirds of Americans have smartphones, each of which has more processing power than a $9 million Cray computer from the 1970s. All of this is made possible because the economic pie is getting bigger through markets. Even though some have gotten richer at faster rates than others, this does not mean they are getting rich at others' expense. Enrichment of all, even at different rates, is a positive, but egalitarianism misses that point.

How Egalitarianism Judges Everyone's Enriching Themselves over Their Lifetimes as a Negative

Egalitarianism not only negatively judges everyone's getting richer but at different rates, but also negatively judges everyone's starting with less and becoming richer throughout their lives. Although certain scholars writing about the topic recognize the importance of lifetime income or wealth,[18] most measures of inequality, such as the Gini coefficient, are snapshots of what people in society have in any given year and do not track what individuals have over their lives. Most of the talk about the top one percent implies that the people in the top one percent remain there. This may have been true in feudalism, where one's title determined income, but in a market economy most people's income and wealth change, typically moving upward, over their lifetimes.

Figure 16.4 shows the present income distributions of Americans in their late teens and early twenties versus those in their late fifties. Younger workers

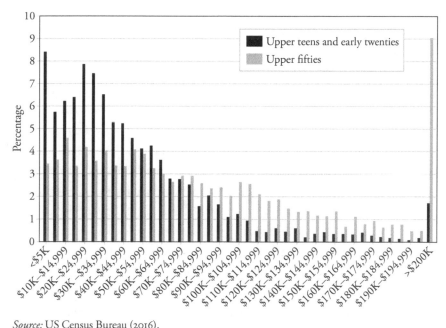

Source: US Census Bureau (2016).

Figure 16.4. Income Distrbutions for two age groups
　　　　　　　(percentage of age group in each income category)

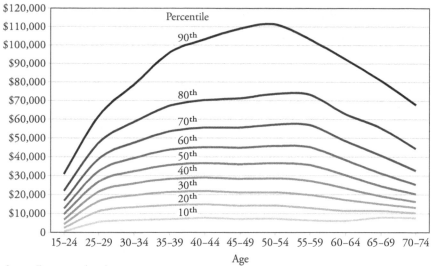

Source: Eyermann (2013).

Figure 16.5. Income Distributions by Age in the US

earn less and have a much tighter distribution than workers in their late fifties. Such patterns do not represent injustice in society and instead are explained by the simple fact that building up skills and experience takes time. A twenty-year-old future surgeon does not expect as much as he will make at age fifty-five, and predictably the percentage of young people who make more than $200,000 is much lower than the percentage of people in their late fifties who make that amount. Figure 16.5 displays what one has to earn at different ages to be in the different percentiles. A person who remains at the fiftieth percentile for his entire life would see rising income in his twenties and thirties, a peak and plateau in his forties and fifties, and subsequent decreases as he retires. Although the advocate of common sense would view improvements over time as a positive, those concerned with decreasing variance in income—that is, inequality—would view it as a negative.

It should be even less surprising that wealth also varies with age. Figure 16.6 shows average American household net worth by age. Average assets start close to zero in one's twenties; increase in one's thirties, forties, and fifties; peak before retirement; and start to decrease thereafter. Here, too, such changes do not represent injustice in society and instead simply indicate prudent saving and spending patterns. Figure 16.7 shows what one would have

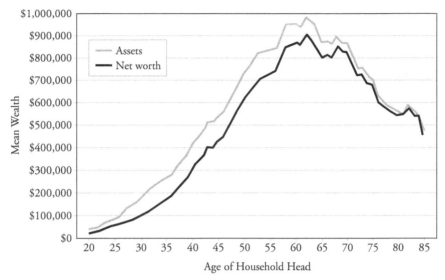

Source: US Federal Reserve (2015, 37).

Figure 16.6. Average Household Net Worth by Age in the US

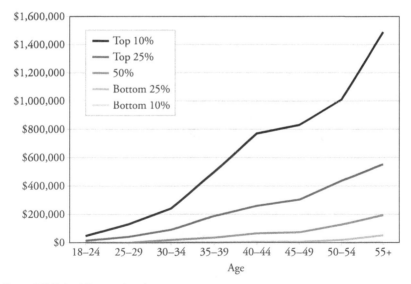

Source: US Federal Reserve (2013).

Figure 16.7. Wealth Distribution by Age

to own at any given age to be in any given wealth percentile. Among people fifty-five and older, the top 10 percent has compiled quite a bit more wealth than the bottom 10 percent, whereas among people eighteen to twenty-four years old the top 10 percent are not much richer than the bottom 10 percent. A policy to keep people such as the eighteen- to twenty-four-year-olds or to prevent anyone from building wealth would increase equality, but should we pursue the egalitarian policy to keep everyone poor?

Although any policy marketed as "we want to keep everyone more equal and poor" sounds absurd, many policies do just that. Consider Social Security, which Franklin Roosevelt promised would be actuarially sound and similar to an annuity. The reality is quite different because Social Security prevents wealth accumulation for both rich and poor. Consider anyone making the maximum taxable amount of $118,500 or more who, along with his or her employer, has to pay nearly $15,000 in Social Security taxes per year. The person who expects the current maximum payout of $32,000 per year upon retirement and expects to live to the average age of seventy-eight can look forward to a $384,000 lifetime payout. Yet without Social Security, if one invested $15,000 per year in a stock-market index fund that ended up earning 8 percent per year, one would have $1 million after twenty-five years or $4 million after forty years. Upon retirement (assuming a 5 percent payout and zero drawdown of principal), the person with $1 million would have $50,000 per year in perpetuity, and the person with $4 million would have $200,000 per year. One could also pass on the entire principal to one's loved ones upon death. I don't know about you, but I would much rather invest that $15,000 on my own, even though it would vastly increase inequality of wealth over the course of my life.

Social Security also prevents accumulation of wealth for those making much less. Those earning $28,000 per year, along with their employers, have to pay about $3,500 in Social Security taxes per year. Yet saving just $3,500 per year ($10 per day) for one's entire career and investing that amount in the stock market to earn average returns of 8 percent per year means one will become a millionaire after forty-two years. Think about that for a minute. Everyone who saves $10 per day and sees such compound growth can be a millionaire. Social Security instead gives those earning $28,000 and retiring at age sixty-six $14,000 per year upon retirement, which for those living to age seventy-eight amounts to a $168,000 lifetime payout. Among African-American males, life expectancy is around seventy-two years, so those contributing $3,500 for fifty years can expect a measly $94,000 lifetime payout, or less than 10 percent of the $1 million they could have had by saving and investing on their own. Social Security makes wealth over one's lifetime and wealth between people much more equal; as a result, it makes people much poorer.

Is Income and Wealth Egalitarianism Immoral?

Egalitarianism may be bad economics, but should one support it for moral reasons? Egalitarianism makes judgments about what people have compared to others, which can lead to many morally problematic positions. Consider how the Mahayana tradition of Buddhism lists *irshya* (envy) as one of the *pañca kleśaviṣa* (five poisons), defining it as "being unable to bear the accomplishments or good fortune of others," or how the Ten Commandments state, "Thou shalt not covet thy neighbor's house, thou shalt not covet thy neighbor's wife, nor his manservant, nor his maidservant, nor his ox, nor his ass, nor any thing that *is* thy neighbor's," or how the Quran warns against *hasad,* or envy. Yet one of the fundamental goals of egalitarian movements such as Occupy Wall Street is to get people to compare themselves to the one percent. Hayek's description of egalitarianism seems apt here: "Most of the strictly egalitarian demands are based on nothing better than envy."[19]

Instead of encouraging people to be grateful for what they have or encouraging people to strive to have more, egalitarianism pits people against each other. As Mises states, "Whoever stirs up the resentment of the poor against the rich can count on securing a big audience."[20] Egalitarianism rejects the much more sound dictum "Mind your own business," which can imply either "Don't worry about what others have" or "Pay attention to improving your own lot." As happy as I would be to have Bill Gates's home, I am totally okay with not having his home, and I am happy for him that he has what he has. If I want to increase my income or wealth, I think about what steps I should take rather than worrying about what Bill Gates has done.

Egalitarianism also encourages people to treat others' property as if it is not theirs. This can be summed by the "You didn't build that" mentality of the forty-fourth president of the United States. Many egalitarians don't like the term *redistribution* because they believe the distribution of income or wealth is entirely a governmental question, not one that government should change after the market determines it.

Egalitarianism also downplays the role of individual initiative for making money, and it discourages people from looking for ways to work for others' benefit. In contrast to the market, which tells the underemployed performance artist that others in society are willing to pay more for work elsewhere, strict egalitarianism says everyone is entitled to same amount of money regardless of effort or benefits to others. Consider the great personal effort given by and associated rewards given to foreign-born Silicon Valley workers. Markets have built-in signals and rewards (i.e., wages) for those who move from areas that others value less to areas that others value more. Strict egalitarianism, however, would have that person—who would invest in education, move halfway around the world, and work long hours—get paid the exact same amount as the drug-using performance artist. Why think about the future or work for the benefit of others when the costs of making difficult choices must be fully internalized but don't come with any compensation? Because egalitarianism prevents people from making more than others, it actually would prevent people from recouping those costs. I have nothing against drug-using performance artists, but I doubt we would have a single computer or hospital if the economy were organized like the model attendee of Burning Man.

Are Milder Forms of Income and Wealth Egalitarianism Less Bad Than the Strictest Forms?

In an episode of *The Twilight Zone* broadcast in 1985, children must take an IQ test on their twelfth birthday, and after one boy tells his parents that he thinks he did well, they get nervous, and soon after that the government informs him that he exceeded the legal intelligence limit and must be executed. Although policies targeting successful people sound like science fiction, just four decades ago Communists in Cambodia "singled out doctors, teachers, monks, journalists, the rich, artists, anyone with an education,"[21] and the country remains set back by the 2 million killed in this Communist "experiment." One can also observe scapegoating, expropriation, or targeted killing of rich people in many other Communist regimes or of Jewish bankers in Nazi Germany. After the French Revolution, many of the forty thousand victims of the guillotine were not aristocrats but merchants. In addition to targeting the rich, targeting below-average people can reduce variances of outcomes in society. Among the 5 million non-Jews killed by the Nazis were those with "mental deficiencies,"[22] and in the United States many founders of the American Economic Association advocated eugenics and forced-sterilization programs.[23] Policies that chop off either the upper or the lower end of a distribution will lead to lower variance in income and wealth.

Compared to more extreme manifestations of egalitarianism, milder forms of egalitarianism are infinitely more reasonable and humane. Thomas Piketty, for example, does not advocate abolishing private property, private enterprise, or accumulation of wealth.[24] Other less-extreme advocates of egalitarianism such as Rawls also believe that even if government should redistribute income, it must respect certain rights. Those who support egalitarianism because they believe it would bring about other desirable social goals such as helping the poor would be less likely to support punishing successful people for the sake of it. Compared to Cambodia's Pol Pot, all of these people deserve a Nobel Prize in economics or peace.

Despite the superiority of mild egalitarianism to the economics-be-damned or human-rights-be-damned forms of strict egalitarianism, mild egalitarianism still retains many of strict egalitarianism's flaws and is still harmful at the margin. Rather than advocating 100 percent tax rates, Piketty advocates progressive taxation that goes up to 80 percent for the rich, which is not nearly as bad as 100 percent but still would discourage work and the accumulation of wealth. Imagine the prospect of bearing 100 percent of losses if an enterprise performs poorly and earning only 20 percent if things go well. The expected value calculations of becoming an entrepreneur totally change. PayPal co-founder Elon Musk would not have invested his proceeds in the early-stage Tesla or dipped into his savings when his auto company was on the verge of bankruptcy. With an 80 percent tax rate, people would still work and found businesses, but not as often or as many. That helps explain why few Tesla Motors are founded in Cuba, where tax rates max out at 50 percent, or in Piketty's land of *égalité* and *fraternité,* where government spends more than half of GDP. Reducing rewards for increasing skills, working, or investing does not bring about the fully disastrous results of pure egalitarianism, but in milder doses egalitarianism is still mildly disastrous and inhumane.

Conclusion

By focusing on relative rather than absolute levels of income or wealth, egalitarianism mandates policies that can make everyone poorer as a result. A world where everyone drives 1971 Ford Pintos would be much more egalitarian but much less safe than the modern world. Likewise, a world where nobody saves or invests and nobody builds up skills over their lives would be much more egalitarian but much less developed than the modern world. Egalitarianism also ignores the fact that people want to make different choices and shape their own lives. Even if the world were composed of 7 billion clones, we should not expect people at different stages of their lives or with different experiences and different preferences to be in the same economic situation at any given time. The person who chooses to consume more leisure or the profligate who chooses not to save and invest should not expect to have the exact same monetary rewards as those who work long hours and save over a sustained period. Neither choice is necessarily better, but markets have monetary rewards for people who provide value to others.

By focusing on relative rather than absolute income or wealth, egalitarianism almost always ignores how people getting richer, even at different rates, can be good for everyone. We all can sit at home and be spiteful at Bill Gates's success, documenting our lamentation on Microsoft Word, or we can be thankful for what Gates and other titans of industry have provided for us. We are lucky that the market has invented an easy-to-send, quasi-anonymous thank-you note called money. Each year I and millions of others coordinate to send billions of these thank-you notes to America's richest to show our appreciation for providing Microsoft, Amazon, Georgia Pacific, and Google. Rather than looking down on increases in income and wealth in differing amounts, we should celebrate and be grateful for the efforts of those who work for the benefit of all.

17

Good and Bad Inequality

Vincent Geloso and Steven G. Horwitz*

ONE ASPECT OF the debate surrounding inequality is how problematic inequality really is. Inequality per se is presumably not a problem;
rather, inequality is bad because of the problems critics claim it produces. For
example, numerous authors[1] claim that inequality negatively affects economic
growth, a claim disputed by others.[2] Some scholars argue that inequality has
negative externalities that degrade social capital and health indicators.[3] Here,
too, this claim is disputed by other authors.[4]

Whatever the merits of the various positions, the participants in this debate have not made important distinctions among how individuals perceive
different forms of inequality. For example, we might be more concerned about
forms of inequality that prevent people from satisfying their preferences and
less concerned about forms of inequality that result from people actually
satisfying those preferences. Although some philosophers[5] and economists[6]
have attempted to make such distinctions, we hope to decompose inequalities
more carefully into those that are socially beneficial (or at least neutral) and
those that are socially harmful, especially to the least well-off.

Socially beneficial inequalities (what we call "good" inequalities) result
from the satisfaction of individual economic preferences or demographic
changes and have no perverse impact on economic growth. We argue that
using policy to attempt to reduce such inequalities would produce a great

*Vincent Geloso is a postdoctoral fellow at the Free Market Institute at Texas Tech Univer-
sity and obtained his Ph.D. in economic history from the London School of Economics.
Steven Horwitz is the Schnatter Distinguished Professor of Free Enterprise at Ball State
University.

deal of positive harm because they are desirable unintended consequences of economic progress that also improve the well-being of the least well-off or are neutral changes resulting from changes in family size, demography, and marriage patterns. Because the results of these inequalities are either good or neutral, and because they are unintended consequences of individual choice, they should at least get a prima facie assumption of not being policy relevant. By contrast, what we call "socially harmful" or "bad" inequalities are problematic because they result from limiting individual choice in ways that expand inequality by limiting overall growth and harming the least well-off. In this way, our criteria of social desirability are broadly Rawlsian in that one key concern is whether inequalities benefit the least well-off.[7] Our argument also parallels that of Tomasi and other recent literature arguing that inequalities created in largely free markets should be held to the Rawlsian difference principle and that they can meet that test.[8]

We start our analysis by reviewing the extent of the rise in inequality since the 1970s and argue that although inequality has increased, various problems with measurement indicate that the extent of the growth in inequality is overestimated. If overall inequality is actually less than believed, we should be even more hesitant to adopt costly policies that are claimed to reduce inequality. Next we point out that a substantial share of the increase of inequality is explained by "good" inequalities. Then we explore the "bad" inequalities and how they result from government interventions that push down the lower end of the income distribution while pulling up the higher end. Although there are inequalities of birth or family upbringing, we argue that they are much costlier to combat than inequalities resulting from misguided government intervention and thus are far less policy relevant. Rather than combatting inequality per se, we should be looking to address the sources of inequality that generate undesirable unintended consequences. More specifically, we should focus on inequality growth that results from limiting the options of the least well-off and thereby hampering their ability to move up the income ladder. That is, inequality policy should first attempt to do no harm by removing policies that exacerbate inequality by harming the poor and not by penalizing rising inequality that contributes to economic growth and improves the condition of the least well-off.

Measuring Inequality

Indicators of inequality generally show a consistent upward trend starting in the 1970s.[9] The increase seems consistent across the Western countries, even though inequalities worldwide have been decreasing.[10] The Organization for Economic Cooperation and Development (OECD) reported that inequality (measured by the Gini coefficient for after-tax income) increased by 24 percent from 1980 to 2008 in the United States.[11] In fact, the same report shows that, with a few minor exceptions, inequality in all OECD countries has increased since the mid-1980s.[12]

Yet those claims are plagued with measurement problems with regard to *(a)* the price indices used to deflate real incomes and *(b)* the measurement of income. The problem of prices is probably larger because it involves issues across both time and space such that we *overestimate* inflation and fail to account for regional price disparities. Let us start with the latter. Our point here, we must emphasize, is not to review the entire literature and arrive at a conclusion about the "actual level" of inequality. Rather, our contention is merely that the increase in inequality has been more modest than generally believed.

Economic theory suggests that incomes tend to equalize in real terms across regions as factors of production move around. Part of this equalization will occur in noninflation-adjusted wages, but another part will occur through price changes. For example, a greater population moving into New York City from Iowa to take advantage of higher urban wages will increase land prices in New York, and lowered demand in Iowa will reduce land prices there. The result will be a convergence of real wages. That said, one has to be very careful with regional price indices because of endogeneity issues between incomes and baskets of measured prices, including the way income determines the basket of goods demanded by consumers and thereby determines the basket that government agencies construct to measure the cost of living. However, it is still relevant to see how important price disparities are across the United States (see figure 17.1), as one can see with prices in New York being 15 percent higher than the national price level and prices in South Dakota being close to 13 percent lower than the national price level. There are huge gaps between

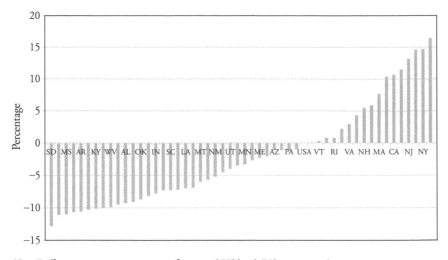

Note: Difference in percentage points from total US level (US average = 0).
Source: Aten, Figueroa, and Martin (2013).

Figure 17.1. Regional price disparities across the United States, 2011

metropolitan and nonmetropolitan areas *within* states. For example, a report from the Bureau of Economic Analysis using data from 2006 indicated that prices in metropolitan areas of New York and California stood at 35.9 percent and 29.8 percent higher than the national price level, whereas prices in nonmetropolitan areas in those same states stood at 20.8 percent and 9 percent lower than the national price level.[13] These gaps tell us that aggregating individuals together might lead to overestimating the inequalities among Americans. This is because deflating wages and incomes from cities such as New York and San Francisco by a national average or even a state average means that we are deflating their income by a lesser measure than we ought to and deflating the income of nonmetropolitan Americans by a larger measure than we ought to. Given that a large share of inequality in the United States is driven by a few key areas where prices are well higher than the national average, this point is crucial.[14]

The argument about regional disparities in prices is an argument about the price level, not about price trends. However, there are also problems with how to estimate changes in the cost of living in the United States. Since the 1990s, we have been aware that the Consumer Price Index (CPI) overstates annual inflation by roughly 1.1 percentage points.[15] Other authors have offered a wide range of other estimates of CPI biases, but all are positive. One bias is a substitution bias, which means that the CPI does not properly capture changes in relative prices that induce households to shift their consumption to different outlets or substitute goods. The other significant biases are ones linked to quality. Increases in prices linked with increases in quality should not be considered an increase in the cost of living, and treating them as such biases the CPI upward. Significant efforts have been made to estimate biases from quality and substitution and their impact on estimates of inequality.[16] According to this work, the use of the CPI for all urban consumers indicates no real wage growth for workers at the tenth percentile from 1979 to 2005, whereas a correction for the substitution bias shows growth of 13 percent in the same period.

Such biases mean that we likely underestimate the level of real income and wage growth at the bottom of the income distribution. Christian Broda and David Weinstein found such a problem in the case of the United States whereby corrections to the prices actually paid by both rich and poor reduce the ratio of the income of the ninetieth percentile to income of the tenth percentile from 4.49 to 4.26 (for 2006).[17] This amounts to roughly 5 percent less inequality. Bruce Meyer and James Sullivan have also found that corrections for the biases within the CPI imply that we are underestimating the true level of real income growth at the bottom of the income distribution.[18] We are therefore also likely overestimating both the level and the trend in inequality.

There are also problems with the measurement of income per se. Although prices are the denominators of real incomes, the numerator is subject to disagreement over definitions. One part of the disagreement stems from which source to use. Thomas Piketty and Emmanuel Saez believe that using the tax unit better incorporates the top incomes of the distribution.[19] However, Richard Burkhauser, Jeff Larrimore, and Kosali Simon point out that there is a difference between households and tax units and that the latter tends to underestimate actual incomes.[20] It is well known that household expenditures are not linearly related to the number of individuals in each household. If one household's size increases from two members to four members, this doubling will not result in a doubling of expenditures due to economies of scale. If the size of the average household were not changing over time and all households were relatively similar, the doubling's lack of effect on expenditures would not be a concern. However, household size has grown increasingly heterogeneous. One can correct for such a problem while using tax units only under the assumption that tax units and households overlap, but this is not the case.

If one uses the size-adjusted tax units to measure income growth prior to taxes and transfers from 1979 to 2007, one finds a 14.5 percent increase for the middle class. However, if one switches to size-adjusted households rather than tax units, the increase grows to 20.6 percent. Moreover, Burkhauser, Larrimore, and Simon point out that once one accounts for transfers, a harder task with the tax units, one finds that the household-size-adjusted income after taxes and transfers of the bottom quintile increased by 15 percent from 1979 to 2007.[21] This increase is less than the increase for the top quintile but more than the tax units data suggest. In fact, in the period from 1989 to 2000 the use of household-size-adjusted income after taxes and transfers suggests a decline in inequality. Although there are relative merits to the two types of units,[22] the shift made by Burkhauser, Larrimore, and Simon suggests that it is likely that the overall trend in income inequality is both lower in absolute amount and increasing at a slower pace than commonly portrayed.

An additional problem with income measurements is probably as large as the issue with the selection of households—namely, how we can best account for nonmonetary compensation. As Martin Feldstein notes, wages are a declining share of total compensation.[23] One reason for this trend is that the tax treatment given to health premiums provided by US employers tends to encourage more remuneration in the form of health benefits, at least on the margin. Although one can (and should) question whether individuals would prefer the health benefits provided by employers to the equivalent monetary sum, it would be incorrect to discard the value of health insurance completely from remuneration. Once one adjusts for such a value, one finds that inequality not only is at a much lower level but has also increased more slowly than seen by looking at wage data only. This result is found in numerous studies.[24]

In addition, we should ask whether income is the only or the best measure of inequality. Consumption is believed to be a more stable measure of well-being and hence a better measure of inequality. Individuals tend to smooth their consumption over time even though their incomes are more volatile, so consumption inequality will be lower than income inequality. The data collected by Meyer and Sullivan show that consumption inequality is less than income inequality and has increased much more slowly.[25] Krishna Pendakur found this same result in Canada,[26] and Matthew Brzozowski and his colleagues later confirmed it with updated data.[27]

This point is important because we have seen an appreciable increase in the share of the bottom quintile of the population that owns refrigerators, computers, cellphones, automobiles, microwaves, dishwashers, modems, cable TV, and air conditioning. This increase is well documented for the United States[28] and for Canada.[29] This trend is also indicative of a decline in inequality of well-being especially because many of these goods would initially have been present only in richer households, and data from the past decade or two show a continued decline in the gap in ownership rates between the rich and poor. Orazio Attanasio and Luigi Pistaferri's recent survey of the literature emphasizes the importance of accounting for the role of utility as well as for increasing hours of leisure in accurately assessing the effects of consumption inequality.[30]

One should be careful with these numbers. The corrections needed are important and complex, but precisely determining overestimation of inequality remains difficult. However, we will rest on the more modest claim that inequality has indeed increased since the 1970s but at a slower pace than the standard narrative suggests.

The Decomposition of Inequality: "Good" Inequality

Our decomposition begins by examining what we call "good" inequality. By this, we mean increases in inequality that derive from demographic changes, the value of the services provided by innovators, and structural changes to the economy. We see the effects of inequality resulting from these causes as either neutral or good.

Demographic changes are probably the easiest to understand. For example, it is fully possible that inequality in the society as a whole increases even while the inequality between different groups does not change. For such a case, consider the role of immigration. An increase of immigration that adds a greater proportion of unskilled laborers to the economy might generate an increase in inequality if it increases the quantity of "poorer" individuals. In Canada, once you exclude recent immigrants from censuses between 1981 and 1996, inequality increased at a slower rate.[31] In the United States, 5 percent of the rise in inequality was explained by immigration.[32] If immigration allows those moving into a country to improve their lifetime prospects and incomes while also enriching the host economy by increasing output and (in some instances) productivity,[33] it is hard to see this increase in inequality as socially problematic because it is emblematic of upward social mobility and generalized enrichment. The increase in income to the immigrant also represents a decline in global inequality. For these reasons, we see any increase in domestic inequality created by such processes as being part of the larger desirable process of economic growth and therefore not policy relevant.

Another desirable cause of inequality comes from the aging of the population. Thomas Lemieux best summarizes this approach. What we call "residual wage inequality," or inequality within groups of workers who have the same education and experience, "is generally believed to account for most of the growth in overall wage inequality."[34] This being the case, Lemieux points out that there are always unobserved skills when we estimate the determination of individual wages. If the dispersion of these unobserved variables were even across age groups, then the issue would be moot. However, Lemieux indicates that unobserved skills are more likely to be found among older and more educated workers. Hence, a composition effect is concentrated in one group. Moreover, this measurement error may be growing over time as the relative size of the group that is being mismeasured increases. Lemieux argues, as a consequence, that population aging explains roughly 75 percent of the increase in inequality. Recent research by Ingvild Almås and Magne Mogstad confirms that a substantial share of the increase in economic inequality might simply be the result of population aging and has little to do with unequal gains.[35] It is not clear why this source of rising inequality is problematic, especially if we think longer, healthier lives are a social good. We also label inequality resulting from this demographic change as "good" and question its policy relevance.

Another cause of measured inequality that is not problematic is innovation. Inventors who bring new goods to the market that allow them to amass large fortunes have not made anyone, except their competitors, worse off.

These inventors have provided the market with goods and services that are more valuable to consumers than the price. The general public does not see the innovations by Bill Gates and Steve Jobs, for example, as socially destructive. In fact, it may even be argued that these innovations tend to flatten inequalities of well-being. If we were to ask smartphone users how much it would take for them to give up their connectivity, it is quite likely that the price they ask would be many magnitudes greater than the monthly rate they pay for the service. This response is reflective of William Nordhaus's point that only about 2.2 percent of the total surplus from innovation is captured by the innovators.[36] The rest of the utility is shared among the greater public, such that the utility from this innovation acts as an equalizer in well-being that is not reflected in differences in incomes. If so, this increase in measured income inequality is also socially desirable, and we can label it as "good" and be skeptical of its policy relevance other than in the sense that we might like to see more of it.

The idea that differences in income might not be reflective of differences in well-being is harder to understand than the impact of demographic changes. However, it is more important. The proposition behind this point is simple: the monetary amount we earn (in real terms) is an inferior good for numerous individuals. More precisely, there is a point where the additional income earned provides less and less satisfaction to individuals, and that point is becoming more and more heterogeneous across the population. At low levels of development, when physical survival is an issue, preferences are relatively homogeneous: individuals will roughly want the same things as others in their group because obtaining the utility of meeting basic needs is interpersonally equal. However, once basic needs are met, individuals will start to have objectives that may not be well measured with dollar signs. Some individuals might work very few hours a week and prefer to enjoy leisure at many times the wage rate they would have been offered to sacrifice their leisure. Other individuals might be more financially ambitious and attribute a much lower value to their leisure. It would be hard to qualify this form of inequality as problematic because the two groups of individuals find higher utility in their choices than the monetary signs attached to the income earned would suggest.

By definition, rich societies will tend to be more unequal on an income basis because wealth provides such a range of choices that individuals will find it easier to increase their well-being in ways that income does not fully capture. As long as some individuals will be more financially ambitious than others and value their leisure less than others, income inequality will rise, but this does not imply any undesirable increase in inequality because the measured rise in income inequality cannot be equated with an increase in inequality of utility or well-being. In fact, there is evidence of such a divorce between income and well-being. Although income inequality has increased in the United States, inequality of "happiness" has actually declined.[37] A similar decline in the inequality of happiness has also been observed across ethnic groups.[38] Another relevant observation is that performance pay also allows workers to self-select according to their preferences over work and leisure. Thanks to the accelerating trend toward performance pay, workers who are more financially ambitious (and hence attribute a lower value to leisure) have tended to head to areas where their ambitions can be more easily met.[39] Individuals being able to better select the manner in which they want to maximize their well-being is not a bad form of income inequality.

The Decomposition of Inequality: Bad Inequality

It takes considerable effort to identify the inequalities caused by innate factors, and it also takes considerable effort to correct such inequalities. Some would then argue that it is necessary to provide some public services such as education or health care to offset innate differences. There remains much debate over whether such policies would be helpful. However, the benefits of addressing these innate inequalities might be considerable. They may also be high-hanging fruit in the sense that the initial costs are high and the fruit tend to take a long time to fully grow. And this possibility assumes that the policy will be implemented as planned, which public-choice theory gives us reason to doubt.

By contrast, a government policy that first does no harm may allow us to pursue more effective low-hanging policy fruit. That is, we must ask: Are existing policies exacerbating inequality in ways that are problematic, and if so, what would be the consequences of eliminating these policies? At the very least, we might agree that government should not make inequality worse, especially because such existing policies might exacerbate innate inequalities. Numerous government policies act to limit upward mobility and increase inequality and should be carefully assessed. Some of them push poor individuals down (through agricultural tariffs, zoning laws, the war on drugs), whereas others pull up the richest individuals (through bank bailouts, subsidies, regulated industry access).

Policies that would push the poorest down are those that distort prices in ways that disproportionately burden the poor. A prime example of this type of policy is agricultural tariffs. The bulk of trade distortions caused by governmental duties and regulations in international trade are concentrated in the agricultural sector. The result is that prices are higher than they would be if trade were liberalized, and the poorest are hurt disproportionately by those higher prices because of the large share of their expenditures that goes to food. Kym Anderson, John Cockburn, and Will Martin conclude that if international agricultural trade were liberalized, the number of poor individuals worldwide would drop by 3 percent, thereby reducing the global level of inequality.[40] Although that study is concerned with the world economy, Kristian Niemietz in Great Britain points out that the Common Agricultural Policy of the European Union hiked prices by roughly 25 percent.[41]

Niemietz also considers the impact of zoning laws that restrained the housing supply in Britain, resulting in a housing price increase of 40 percent. This increase is also a greater burden for poorer households. Christian Hilber and Wouter Vermeulen (2016) found that for England housing prices would have been 25 percent to 30 percent lower even in areas outside London.[42] Combining the effect of zoning restrictions and agricultural tariffs and comparing them with Niemietz's figures for household expenditures in Britain suggest that liberalization of both sectors would increase the income of the bottom decile of the population by 13.5 percent. That is an appreciable increase in real income.

Peter Ganong and Daniel Shoag show how land-use restrictions can increase inequality by restricting the mobility of low-skilled workers.[43] High housing costs in high-productivity areas are affordable only to high-skilled workers, so low-skilled workers move out of high-productivity areas. Poor workers' limited mobility is sufficient to explain 10 percent of the increase in inequality from

1980 to 2010. A recent study by Dustin Chambers and Courtney A. Collins combined data from the Consumer Expenditure Survey, the CPI, and a data set of the regulatory burden (RegData) and found that these sorts of regulations have highly regressive effects.[44] These regulations tend to increase both the volatility and the level of prices for goods that represent a larger share of total income for poor households than for rich households. Thus, this argument offers support to the idea that scaling back such policies might reduce inequality.

In addition to the expenditure side, various labor-market regulations reduce the income-earning options and therefore the upward mobility of the poor. Economists have long debated the precise effects of minimum-wage laws, but to the extent that such laws do cause unemployment among the least-skilled workers, they serve as an impediment to upward mobility. There is more agreement about the effects of occupational licensure. Laws that force new entrants to an industry to spend large amounts of time and money to obtain a license make it especially difficult for those of limited means to enter those industries, and they keep prices of the goods and services these individuals provide higher than they would be otherwise. Estimates of the burden suggest that licensing requires an average fee of $209 across all occupations and an average of nine months of training.[45] Zoning restrictions and general business licenses make it hard for poorer people to open businesses, especially ones based in their own homes.

Among the policies that harm the poorest, the war on drugs probably has the largest effect. As Pettit points out, the vast majority of America's growing penal population is composed of younger members of ethnic minorities.[46] These ethnic groups already exhibit lower-than-average earnings. However, because the majority of these individuals are young, prison time impairs them considerably on the labor market in the long run. The wage penalty is considerable relative to both preincarceration income and potential earnings had incarceration not occurred.[47] The result is that, as Bruce Western and Becky Pettit point out, the apparent narrowing of the wage gap between whites and blacks in America is largely an artefact caused by the facts that a larger share of the black population ends up in prison and that this share is concentrated among low-wage earners and young individuals, who are then not part of the wage-earning labor force.[48] When these individuals exit prisons, they are more likely to be unemployed and unmarried and therefore to live in single-person households, where the likelihood of poverty is greater.[49] As a consequence, the rate of wage growth for former inmates is slower. To the degree that those prison sentences are due to victimless drug crimes (as opposed to acts of violence), the increased inequality this factor generates is another example of bad inequality. Repealing drug prohibition would reduce the incarceration of many currently poor Americans, increase the income they earn, and thereby reduce inequality, with no harm to others and with positive effects on economic growth.

The other inequality-enhancing effect of some government policies is that they increase the income of the rich. A good case in point is the aforementioned agricultural tariffs. By limiting market access to foreign competitors in developed countries, the government is pushing up agricultural incomes. Farmers who benefit from agricultural protection are not in the middle of the income distribution. In Canada, annual farm household income was higher than CAD$100,000 (US$75,000), compared with CAD$72,000 (US$54,000) for the average Canadian.[50] These statistics place farm households well above the average standard of living, and a part of this relative position stems from higher prices caused by limitations on competition. A recent paper found that the burden of production quotas in Canada represented 2.3 percent of the income of the poorest 20 percent of households, compared with 0.5 percent for the richest 20 percent,[51] and another found that the quotas were responsible for at least 3 percent of Canada's poverty rate.[52]

Policies that serve these rent-seeking interests are by their very nature conceived to create inequalities. Their aim is to restrict competition from lowering prices and increasing quality so that there is a redistribution of the gains of exchange to the producer rather than the consumer. Think here of taxicab companies lobbying to raise Uber's costs or to block Uber entirely. Bailouts and subsidies have similar effects. If a bank is bailed out at taxpayer expense after having taken risks that its shareholders should have assumed, a wealth transfer from the overall population to individuals in the banking industry (who tend to be richer) increases inequality. The same applies to corporate welfare in the form of government subsidies to business: they redistribute wealth regressively. Ending policies whose net effect is a regressive transfer up the income ladder would end a bad form of inequality and thereby not only reduce inequality but also enhance economic efficiency and growth.

Conclusion

Measured inequality has increased in recent decades. However, we have argued that some portion of this increase actually stems from mismeasurement. With respect to what remains, we believe that it is necessary to distinguish socially beneficial or neutral from socially problematic causes of inequality. Attacking what we have called the "bad" inequalities generated by government policy has two major advantages over other strategies for fighting inequality. First, it avoids attacking forms of inequality that are either desirable or neutral and thereby destroying those benefits. Second, the explicit costs of reducing the policy-driven bad forms of inequality are, we believe, far less than trying to reduce inequalities of birth or environment. Admittedly, it is difficult to get the political process to roll back its power even when the fruit hangs low. However, if such interventions are exacerbating inequality while also either harming economic growth or worsening the condition of the least well-off or both, attempting to remove them seems a less risky and less damaging way to address inequality than by expanding high-cost policies that are unlikely to work as planned. Those who believe that market economies are to be preferred can both acknowledge the existence of some degree of increasing inequality and argue that some of the causes are policy relevant. Careful examination of the issue of inequality should not force defenders of markets to the sidelines. We have important insights and policy recommendations to offer as ways to reduce problematic forms of growing inequality.

Conclusion

Final Thoughts on Egalitarianism

Michael C. Munger*

THE CHAPTERS IN this book have considered a variety of perspectives on egalitarianism. As our authors have pointed out, for some supporters of egalitarian "social justice" there is an essential deontic unity between equality and equity. Egalitarians privilege equality as the ideal of justice, and then require anyone who would disagree to supply an argument that can overcome this presumption. This "I'm right unless you can decisively show I'm wrong" approach to argument is rhetorically effective, but it's not very good philosophy or social science.

For other egalitarians, the central argument is crudely utilitarian, though it is often dressed in various frilly disguises. The only assumptions necessary for the utilitarian approach are (1) interpersonally comparable welfare of individuals, and (2) diminishing marginal utility of income. Granted these premises, it follows immediately that "If we take a dollar from [some rich person, maybe Bill Gates] and give it to [hypothetical poor person, some guy living under a bridge], then the entire society is better off." It is obvious, to the utilitarian, that the loss of a dollar (or thousands of dollars) for the wealthy "hurts" less than the benefit to the recipients the egalitarian advocate has in mind.

One of the contributions this book has made has been to point out that the analytic divide between deontic and utilitarian logics is not always clean. It is common for deontic egalitarians to advance apparently moral arguments for an imperative of equality as an *end*, but then abruptly switch over to baldly utilitarian *means* as a way of accomplishing that goal. As the authors in the current volume have argued, any conception of equality that *starts* with outcomes and then compares the observed distribution with an "ideal" of perfect equality is morally and logically incoherent.

There are two kinds of problems with the "start with current outcomes" approach: (1) It ignores the origins of the current distribution and (2) it misses the (arguably) unintended consequences of the political apparatus required for coercive redistribution. I will consider each at some length here.

Origins: Why is Wealth Unequally Distributed?

A naive initial focus on outcomes cannot distinguish *earned* wealth or income from income that is the product of accident or theft. While one might grant that not all wealth was acquired by morally admirable means, any reasonable opponent would be obliged likewise to grant that *some* wealth was earned or worked for. William Graham Sumner, in his famous essay, "The Forgotten Man," highlights the problem succinctly:

> It is when we come to the proposed [measures of redistribution] that we reach the real subject which deserves our attention. As soon as A observes something which seems to him to be wrong, from which X is suffering, A talks it over with B, and A and B then propose to get a law passed to remedy the evil and help X. Their law always proposes to determine what C shall do for X or, in the better case, what A, B and C shall do for X. As for A and B, who get a law to make themselves do for X what they are willing to do for him, we have nothing to say except that they might better have done it without any law, but what I want to do is to look up C. I want to show you what manner of man he is. I call him the Forgotten Man. Perhaps the appellation is not strictly correct. He is the man who never is thought of. He is the victim of the reformer, social speculator and philanthropist, and I hope to show you before I get through that he deserves your notice both for his character and for the many burdens which are laid upon him.[1]

For Sumner, "C" is the person who played by the rules, started a business or saved money to make investments, and accumulated wealth through thrift, industry, and prudence. "C" is counting on a chance to live a comfortable life and perhaps be able to leave some bequest to benefit his children or grandchildren. The social schemers, the reformers, and the egalitarian zealots either forget or simply don't care that the schemes, reforms, and redistributive policies impose both suffering and worry on the "C"s of the world.

As Amity Shlaes pointed out, in her book *The Forgotten Man*, it is the signal achievement of the political left to have coopted the figure of sympathy in Sumner's formulation.[2] The "Forgotten Man" is not "C;" it's "X"! If the society does nothing for "X," then "X" is aggrieved, neglected, and deserving of immediate redress of the offense committed . . . by "C"! And "C's" offense? It is simply to be wealthy, and to want to keep control of the wealth that one has obtained within the rules and by creating value for society by investing and working hard.

Achieving equality through redistribution conceives of some members of society purely as ends, as sources of wealth that can be expropriated without any need to offer a justification. The fact of inequality allows the collective to take ownership of the assets of certain individuals. Even if one grants that individuals may not fully "deserve" their wealth, it hardly follows that the collective therefore deserves that wealth by default. One would have to work out who is entitled to the wealth, given the rules under which it was acquired and developed.

The incoherence of the utilitarian view that "the end justifies the means" is inherent in the aim of equal outcomes because whatever objective moral standard applies to ends also must apply to every means. Hence, people cannot ethically be treated unequally *as means* if equality is the only standard, because every means is an end. Yet egalitarianism requires such inequality of treatment. As a result, the only objectively tenable moral standard for "Equality" must instead be a "Law of Equal Liberty," but that principle will almost certainly result in unequal end-state patterns of distribution. Insisting on equality of ends forces substantial inequalities in the treatment of citizens as means, contradicting the claim egalitarians make to have a coherent moral basis for their arguments.

Unintended Consequences: Unchained Leviathan

The second category of difficulty would not deny the first type of problem. But even if one had better justifications than have to date been advanced for wealth equality achieved through coercive redistribution, there would be what some have called the "public choice" problem in implementation. The papers in this volume address a wide variety of different projects of achieving equality, focusing on taxes, income redistribution, welfare policies, the regulation of industries and professions, and education. But many of our authors have also noted some variety of unintended collateral problems created by establishing a government apparatus capable of carrying out such coercive schemes. Even if one doubts the substantive counterarguments that have been advanced here against the morality of redistribution, one would still have to solve the problem of chaining the expansive Leviathan powers any effective egalitarian scheme would require. Power doesn't stay where you put it. It expands, and corrupts, other activities and other government officials.

The problem was famously diagnosed in an essay by William Marina, who saw the problem of government expansion as a stage of post-colonial degeneration.

> As Western Civilization retreats from imperialism, it is confronted in
> its maturity, as have been civilizations such as Rome and China, with
> the dilemma of *empire* as a stifling, centralized, bureaucratic statism,
> which threatens, despite considerable material abundance and leisure,
> to rob life of freedom, creativity, and ultimately, of meaning itself.[3]

Later, Robert Higgs noted the tendency of the coercive mechanisms used by government always to "ratchet" upward toward greater size and power.[4] A skeptical observer might even claim that the expansion of government power and intrusiveness is the real, though unacknowledged, object of redistributionist ideology, but this is often not the case. The misuse of police powers, elective wars, and intrusive "surveillance state" activities are honestly regretted by many on the Left. What many Leftists fail to recognize is the painful paradox at the heart of the redistributionist project: the very centralized power granted to the state, in what Higgs describes as "crises," that seemed prudent in the short run as a means of solving social problems, that ultimately conflict with the left-liberal desire to achieve an egalitarian utopia. There is, after all, no relationship more abjectly inegalitarian than the gulf between ruled and ruler.

The two difficulties I have mentioned, problems with "the problem" as a moral diagnosis and problems with "the solution" as a practical matter of implementation, are all too rarely recognized or even discussed. That is the justification for the volume presented here, to consider the negative synergies created by the interactions of these two problems. In the rest of this concluding essay, I will take up two topics: the problem of "desert" and distribution of the social pie, and then a larger consideration of just what kind of inequality is being considered.

The Pie: J.S. Mill and A. de Jasay

One of the ur-texts of the redistributionist canon is John Stuart Mill's famous distinction between production, and—"the things once there"—distribution.

> The laws and conditions of the Production of wealth partake of the character of physical truths. There is nothing optional or arbitrary in them. Whatever mankind produce, must be produced in the modes, and under the conditions, imposed by the constitution of external things, and by the inherent properties of their own bodily and mental structure. Whether they like it or not, their productions will be limited by the amount of their previous accumulation, and, that being given, it will be proportional to their energy, their skill, the perfection of their machinery, and their judicious use of the advantages of combined labour. . . .
>
> It is not so with the Distribution of wealth. That is a matter of human institution solely. *The things once there*, mankind, individually or collectively, can do with them as they like. They can place them at the disposal of whomsoever they please, and on whatever terms. ... Even what a person has produced by his individual toil, unaided by any one, he cannot keep, unless by the permission of society.[5]

This logic seems attractive. Of *course* we need markets to produce things efficiently, says Mill; only a socialist heretic could doubt *that*. Production is scientific, and the province of economists. But distribution? That is the province of morality, because it is *ethical*, and therefore should be left to philosophers and devotees of social justice.

Nonetheless, as we have seen from the papers in this volume, this standard (and often uncritically accepted) argument has profound flaws. Competitive market systems have their own logic of justice and entitlement, based on voluntary exchange. Market processes based on prices treat likes alike and unlikes differently, precisely in proportion to the differences in their productive capacities and subjective values to participants. It is the essential nature of market function that inputs are paid the value of their marginal products.

Each input owner will be able to negotiate in a competitive setting to obtain his or her share of the value of physical output, expressed as the increment to production multiplied by the price that output commands in the downstream market. This process cannot be stopped, or even manipulated, in a pure market setting; the "value of marginal product" shares are the essence of justice: each input gets the share of the pie that it creates. Some contracts may vary slightly above or below this amount, because of costly information and stickiness in price adjustments, but these variations will be short-lived, unless of course the distortions result from state-imposed regulations that prevent price adjustment. Because the economy is dynamic, it makes little sense to use static conceptions of equilibrium, but market processes, in de Jasay's view, always at least tend toward justice because prices move in the direction of value-of-marginal-product shares.

Second, and more fundamentally, market systems both result *from* inequality, and *cause* inequality, in the distribution of talent and wealth. Markets come about in the first place because of the differences created by division of labor. Exchange and the benefits of production result from *differences*, from heterogeneity in ability, effort, location, and circumstance. Knowledge is dispersed across many different people, and some people are better able to take advantage of the opportunities for trading and creating wealth.

Thus, Mill's separation of production and distribution is simply untenable, and in fact absurd. The shares in the value created at the end of the process were divided at the outset in the process of contracting for the voluntary and cooperative activities from which production results. Any attempt to eliminate inequality at the "distribution" stage would prevent prosperity at the production stage, and would isolate society from the benefits of prosperity.

This problem was summarized most insightfully by Anthony de Jasay, who takes up the challenge of the division of the social "cake" explicitly. As de Jasay sees it,[6] the cake is not baked first and then independently bargained over to determine who gets how big a slice of this "cake that was baked for no reason." Mill's "the things once there" misses the real point: Production and distribution are never distinct phases of contracting in market processes. In a market for inputs, the width of the cake slices get determined by inputs' marginal contributions to the cake. The size of the cake itself is determined by how much society values the combined result, which could not have been produced without the initial agreements. All the important negotiations take place before the fact of production. Each input gets the share it was promised; there are no accidental cakes and no unearned increments.

De Jasay summarizes the argument this way, after punning on his view of cake as "just deserts":

> [In a market setting] output is distributed while it is produced. Wage earners get some of it as wages in exchange for the effort; owners of capital get some of it as interest and rent in exchange for past saving. Entrepreneurs get the residual as profit in exchange organization and risk bearing. By the time the cake is "baked," it is also sliced and those who played a part in baking it have all got their slices. No distributive decision is missing, left over for "society" to take.[7]

I turn now to a broader consideration, taking a step back from problems of implementation and considering some problems of definition and conception.

Equality of What?

In 1979, economic Nobelist Amartya K. Sen delivered a "Tanner Lecture" at Stanford University.[8] His subject was "Equality of What?" and his approach was to try to ground the disparate theories of egalitarianism on a common foundation. He reviewed what he saw as the standard categories—"equality of what?"—and found them wanting. The "whats"—utilitarian equality, total utility equality, and Rawlsian "social primary goods" equality—each had a limitation that made Sen reject them as a useful basis for an egalitarianism that could be both ethically coherent and practically useful.

Sen's critique of the standard categories rested on the notion that even if we grant the (dubious) premise of cardinal interpersonal utility comparison, there is the problem of the cripple and the "pleasure-wizard." The cripple has physical or mental burdens and handicaps that make the translation of resources into utility problematic, while the pleasure-wizard has a much higher marginal productivity of utility, and this difference in marginal productivity persists across the entire range of possible resource allocations. The last dollar spent by the cripple might not match even the first dollar spent by the pleasure-wizard, in terms of marginal utility. Any utilitarian standard would give the pleasure-wizard more resources. According to Sen:

> The cripple would then be doubly worse off: both since he gets less utility from the same level of income, *and* since he will also get less income. Utilitarianism must lead to this thanks to its single-minded concern with maximizing the utility sum. The pleasure-wizard's superior efficiency in producing utility would pull income away from the less efficient cripple.[9]

Sen proposes an alternative, the "basic capabilities" metric.

> The ability to move about is the relevant one here, but one can consider others, e.g., the ability to meet one's nutritional requirements, the wherewithal to be clothed and sheltered, the power to participate in the social life of the community. The notion of urgency related to this is not fully captured by either utility or primary goods, or any combination of the two. Primary goods suffers from fetishist handicap in being concerned with goods, and even though the list of goods is specified in a broad and inclusive way, encompassing rights, liberties, opportunities, income, wealth, and the social basis of self-respect, it still is concerned with good things rather than with what these good things do to human beings. Utility, on the other hand, is concerned with what these things do to human beings, but uses a metric that focuses not on the person's capabilities but on his mental reaction. . . . I believe what is at issue is the interpretation of needs in the form of basic capabilities. This interpretation of needs and interests is often implicit in the demand for equality. This type of equality I shall call "basic capability equality."[10]

To be fair to Sen, his point is not that the social goal "should" be equality of capabilities. Rather, his argument is that it is the equality of capabilities, broadly conceived, that should be the benchmark against which actual distributions in the world are compared.

Of course, as several of our authors have argued, in this volume and elsewhere, any conception of equality that starts with outcomes ignores the possibility that some rewards may be earned, and some denial of access to resources is deserved. Sen's notion of capabilities, abstracting to some point when our deeds have not yet been done and our abilities not yet developed, is a useful corrective to the outcomes equality fetish that plagues much of our politics.

Still, it is important to balance abstract concerns with the considerations that economists often bring to the table. Rather than saying "there's a rich person and a poor person" and deploying a static theory of justice based on a snapshot, it is useful to ask "why?" Why is the rich person rich, and why is the poor person poor? Those kinds of considerations are usefully matched up with other concerns, concerns that rarely interest economists. To their credit, Carden, Estelle, and Bradley (Chapter 12) in this volume do raise these considerations, and they do it in the right way, by invoking Aristotle.

Aristotle's notion of justice not only countenances, but requires, inequality. Some differences are earned, by virtue. Others are deserved, as punishment for a life not lived in accordance with moral values. Simply put, Aristotle's notion of justice requires that the equal all be treated alike, where "equal" means the sharing of certain morally and socially significant qualities. But justice also requires that the unequal be treated differently, in proportion that their differences are morally significant.

Thus, no one would complain that a law-abiding and productive worker earns a good living, while a violent thief is jailed and his stolen property confiscated. Of course, even if we accept the notion that earned wealth and deserved punishment might be exempt from static egalitarian impulses, there remains the problem of identifying which differences are "morally significant." Both Martin (Chapter 1) and Otteson (Chapter 2) take up this issue. Differences based on luck, perhaps even extending to intelligence (inherited) or character (inculcated by parents, or society), are not "deserved," and are therefore not morally significant. This notion of desert, Martin and Otteson each rightly conclude, is so extreme as to impoverish the very idea of the possibility of human virtue.

On the other hand, perhaps "earned" and "deserved" are impossibly high standards. After all, it's not clear why the state or other collective entity is the residual deserver of all things. What I mean is, suppose that one accepts that luck, good or bad, determines most of the differences in wealth and privilege we observe. It does not follow that therefore the state "deserves" wealth or power either. The state cannot legitimately take and redistribute wealth, if the only basis for claiming wealth is desert. In a world where luck is to be credited with everything, no one—including the state—deserves anything.

As many of the papers in this volume then conclude, a more plausible standard might be entitlement, rather than desert. That is, we might recognize, following David Hume, that a presumption in favor of private property has both excellent consequences and conforms with our moral intuitions. Thus, the convention of respecting private property, even if it enables and perpetuates inequality, is required for a society to be prosperous and (importantly) just. As Hume put it, property is a convention, endorsed and secured by the state.

> For when men, from their early education in society, have become sensible of the infinite advantages that result from it (property), and have besides acquir'd a new affection to company and conversation; and when they have observ'd, that the principal disturbance in society arises from those goods, which we call external, and from their looseness and easy transition from one person to another; they must seek for a remedy, by putting these goods, as far as possible, on the same footing with the fix'd and constant advantages of the mind and body. This can be done after no other manner, than by a convention enter'd into by all the members of the society to bestow stability on the possession of those external goods, and leave every one in the peaceable enjoyment of what he may acquire by his fortune and industry.[11]

As a number of the authors in this volume have observed, the notion that the redistribution of property through political rent-seeking contests is not only allowed but morally obliged simply returns us to the chaos of the commons. Where there is no reliable convention of private property, the "looseness and easy transition from one person to another" requires almost all our attention and creative energy.

There is also a dynamic element to the "problem" of inequality, one that is elaborated in this volume by Geloso and Horwitz (Chapter 17).[12] If the "1 percent" is fluid, and membership in the elite is evanescent because there is constant churn in the combination of luck and hard work that creates great fortunes, we might be much less concerned about static inequality. At the limit, the concern for equality at every point, and every moment in time, can be extremely destructive. Imagine that we were able to use some universal data source, perhaps Google Maps but on steroids, to envision all the traffic in the world, captured in one snapshot.

Imagine the gross inequality we would see in this one instant of time! On this street, at this intersection, the light is green. Those cars are being allowed to "go," while others must "stop" and watch as the privileged class parades arrogantly past. This is unjust! These stop lights must be eradicated, because they perpetuate injustice.

That's obviously nonsense, but you wouldn't be able to tell that it's nonsense from a snapshot. Stop lights are in some sense very egalitarian over time, though they are inegalitarian at any point in time. A dynamic capitalist economy bears much in common with stop lights, then, because inequalities at a point in time are constantly being eroded and reduced by change and innovation. The winners may not "deserve" all their spoils, and the losers may not deserve all their harms, but soon enough the current hierarchy will be destroyed in its turn.

Stop lights are egalitarian and also are important in another way, relying on the social convention of the justice of "stop" and "go." We take turns in a way that takes no account of the urgency of our trip or the costs of delay. Sometimes you get to "go," and sometimes you must "stop." But we call them stoplights, not go lights, because we all recognize that sometimes you must stop. If a snapshot of income distribution reveals, at this moment, profound inequality, we would need to ask if this inequality is persistent in the face of changes in luck or efforts to invest and accumulate wealth. Redistribution may worsen, rather than improve, social mobility by attenuating the incentives for hard work.

Of course, we could apply the theory of desert, and need, to this situation. That is, instead of the egalitarian notion of taking turns, where sometimes

I get to "go" and sometimes someone else moves up in the social hierarchy, we could examine need or some other conception of desert. David Schmidtz uses a parable as an illustration. His parable is the best way I can think of to close this discussion. It goes like this:

> I pulled over. The cop pulled in behind. Walked to my window, peered inside, asked for my license and registration.
>
> "New in town?"
>
> "Yes," I said. "Got in five minutes ago."
>
> "Know what you did wrong?"
>
> "Sorry. There was no stop sign or stop light. The cars on the cross street were stopped, so I kept going."
>
> The cop shook his head. "In this town, sir, we distribute according to desert. Therefore, when motorists meet at an intersection, they stop to compare destinations and ascertain which of them is more worthy of having the right of way. If you attend our high school track meet tomorrow night, you'll see it's the same thing. Instead of awarding gold medals for running the fastest, we award them for giving the greatest effort. Anyway, that's why the other cars honked, because you didn't stop to compare destinations."
>
> The cop paused, stared, silently.
>
> "I'm sorry, Officer," I said at last. "I know you must be joking, but I'm afraid I don't get it."
>
> "Justice isn't a joke, sir. I was going to let you off with a warning. Until you said that."[13]

The reason this anecdote is interesting is that it suggests a division of labor in the imposition of egalitarian obligations. Whatever its flaws in terms of implementation, our "Desert Town" at least has the advantage of elevating a bottom-up, consensus-based conception of who deserves what. If I need to get my daughter to the hospital, it may be that everyone will allow me preference, at every intersection. The poor person who is late for work may get to pass through before the wealthy person who owns the bank and therefore can't be fired. A conception of need, rather than opportunity cost of time, *might* be agreed on by all.

Or, it might not. But at least people in Desert Town stop and talk about it, as equals. Most of the essays in this volume, in addition to the particular problems they identify, also highlight an overarching difficulty, one that simply cannot be overcome. No matter how desirable a particular realized pattern of just distribution might be in the *abstract*, it would function practically through the creation of a monopoly agency possessed of great coercive power. The means chosen by egalitarians, then, can never achieve the object of their desires, because equality cannot be the result of creating great and irreducible disparities in control of the means of coercion.

Notes

Foreword, Epstein

1. See Mancur Olson, *The Logic of Collective Action: Public Goods and the Theory of Groups*, second edition (Cambridge, MA: Harvard University Press, 1971).

2. Johan Norberg, *Progress: Ten Reasons to Look Forward to the Future* (London: 2017).

Introduction, Whaples

1. Quoting McIntosh (1989, 4).

2. One might argue that zero shoes is perfectly adequate in some cases as well.

3. Peltzman, "Mortality Inequality," 175–90.

4. Gans, "The Positive Functions of Poverty," 278.

5. An economist might also note that "dirty work" will usually generate a *positive* compensating wage differential.

6. Sacks, *The Dignity of Difference*, 22.

7. His argument, my colleague explained, is a summing up of Thomas Aquinas: "Worth noting: in that passage, St. Thomas does not say that the purpose of inequality is to show forth the Glory of God. That's my gloss. St. Thomas doesn't address that specific question there. Nor can I think offhand of where he does address that specific question, but I do think it follows from his views on the point of Creation in the first place. He argues that God creates solely in order to communicate his goodness (to share his goodness with something)." For Thomas's views, see: Aquinas, *Summa Theologiae, First Part*. At http://www.newadvent.org/summa/1044.htm and http://www.newadvent.org/summa/1047.htm#article2.

8. Philosopher Nicholas Rescher (2002, 1) notes that "It is sometimes said that 'what is bad about inequality is its unfairness.' But this pious sentiment is very much of an exaggeration that needs to be carefully qualified. For only when there is a preexistence of equality of valid claims is an inequality of distribution bad, unreasonable, or unfair. . . . There is nothing unfair about it if the worker gets a wage and the onlooker gets nothing."

9. Lewis, "Screwtape Proposes a Toast," *Saturday Evening Post,* December 19, 1959.

Chapter 1, Martin

1. Hayek, *The Fatal Conceit*.

2. Rizzo, "The Problem of Moral Dirigisme," 781–835.

3. See Marcuse (1965, 83), and Bonilla-Silva (2013).

4. James Bohman (2016) provides a sympathetic view of critical theory. Kim Holmes (2016) is more critical, and Roger Scruton (2015) is extremely so.

5. Elster, "Hard and Soft Obscurantism," 162.

6. Hayek, *The Road to Serfdom*.

7. Blum, "Racism: What It Is and What It Isn't," 203–18.

8. McIntosh, "White Privilege: Unpacking the Invisible Knapsack."

9. McIntosh, "White Privilege."

10. Hayek, "Scientism and the Study of Society."

11. Haslanger, Tuana, and O'Connor, "Topics in Feminism."

12. Scruton discusses the importance of new terminology for the intellectual traditions that feed into New Egalitarianism (2015, 8).

13. See, for example, Greenberg (n.d.).

14. This concept of epistocracy may sound similar to ancient Gnosticism, on the one hand, or to Leninist vanguard, on the other, probably depending on whether one agrees with the core tenets of New Egalitarianism. I use the term *epistocracy* to remain neutral here.

15. Elster, "Hard and Soft Obscurantism," 159–70.

16. This is not to say that only criticisms of New Egalitarianism elicit such responses; these obscurantist responses can also be used preemptively against individuals whose ideas *could* act as criticisms or that New Egalitarians see as perpetuating oppressive structures. See Holmes, *The Closing of the Liberal Mind*.

17. Willett, Anderson, and Meyers, "Feminist Perspectives on the Self."

18. Marcuse, "Repressive Tolerance," 81–123.

19. Spivak, "Can the Subaltern Speak?" 271–313.

20. Spivak, "Subaltern," 280.

21. Lilla, "The End of Identity Liberalism," *New York Times,* November 18, 2016.

22. Franke, "Making White Supremacy Respectable Again."

23. See Marcuse, "Repressive Tolerance," 85. Conservative critics are not innocent of making these sorts of arguments. They often treat patriotism as a precondition for a functional social order, so, according to this view, anything that just sounds like a critique of one's own country—even if it is true—is harmful to the social fabric that secures other values. See Nowrasteh (2016).

24. Frankfurt, *On Bullshit*.

25. Frankfurt, *On Bullshit*, 63.

26. Hayek, *The Road to Serfdom*.

27. A corollary is the idea that it is impossible to be racist against whites, who are not situated in such structures.

Chapter 2, Otteson

1. Hayek, "The Use of Knowledge in Society," 519–30.

2. See, for example, Van Parijs (1991); Nagel (1995); Anderson (1999); Arneson (2000), (2004), (2012); Vallentyne (2002); Barry (2006); Voigt (2007); Cohen (2009); and Knight (2013).

3. See Anderson (1999) for a review of positions.

4. We must beware the Great Mind Fallacy, which proposes policies that can be effectively administered only by a Great Mind possessed of knowledge and motivations no actual human being possesses. For discussion of this fallacy, see Otteson (2010).

5. See Rakowski (1991) and Otteson (2006).

6. See Anderson (1999, 109) and Dworkin (1981, 283–345).

7. Anderson, "What Is the Point of Equality?" 290.

8. Anderson, "What is the Point of Equality?" 291.

9. Both of those elements of the position are necessary. If there is no differential in relative success owing to luck, then there is nothing to correct; and if differentials in relative success are not at least in part due to differing luck, then there is nothing for the luck egalitarian to correct. (There may yet be reasons to seek to minimize differences, but in the latter case there would be no *luck-egalitarian* reasons to do so.)

10. More particularized laws or regulations require more levels of administrative adjudication. Kristin Wilson and Stan Veuger find in the context of bank regulations that more such levels introduce "exogenous information frictions" in "the form of costly investments in expertise or direct engagement" with beneficiaries; they conclude, "This raises concerns of fairness and . . . may hinder the efficient allocation of capital" (2016, 209). The fairness concern arises in part because of the necessarily large amount of discretion granted to the program administrators, and the reduced inefficiency results in part from the uncertainty to which this discretion leads. These problems are generalized, however, and not restricted to banking regulation.

11. Frankfurt, "Equality as a Moral Ideal," 21–43.

12. Anderson, "What Is the Point of Equality?" 289.

13. On the incompleteness of knowledge, see Hayek (1945) and Otteson (2014, chaps. 2 and 3); on administrators' mixed motives, see Buchanan and Tullock (1962).

14. Arneson, "Rethinking Luck Egalitarianism and Unacceptable Inequalities," 158.

15. It should be noted that making one party better off at the expense of others violates the economic concept of Pareto optimality, although not everyone accepts it as a criterion.

16. Arneson, "Rethinking Luck Egalitarianism and Unacceptable Inequalities," 159. Arneson takes his argument to surprising lengths: "Suppose that we are not able to transfer resources from rich to poor and can compress the distribution of income and wealth only by leveling down. Maybe the only thing we can do is burn down the mansions of rich people, with no gains in the income or wealth of anyone else. So be it. Burning down the mansions of rich people is then morally required" (2012, 167).

17. G. A. Cohen suggests community (2009, 34–45); Arneson suggests social justice and happiness (2012, 167).

18. Anderson, "What Is the Point of Equality?" 314.

19. Piketty, *Capital in the Twenty-First Century.*

20. See Nussbaum (2011) and Sen (1992).

21. Fleurbaey, "Equal Opportunity or Equal Social Outcome?" 25–55.

22. I defend and elaborate on this principle and its application to policy in Otteson (2006).

23. Anderson, "What Is the Point of Equality?" 315.

24. Smith, *The Theory of Moral Sentiments.*

Chapter 3, Munger

1. Rawls, *A Theory of Justice*, 60.

2. Rawls, *Theory*, 14–15.

3. Rawls, *Theory*, 302.

4. Rawls, *Theory*, 303, italics in original.

5. See Caldwell (2010), Flew (2001), and Wilkinson (2004).

6. See Hayek (1976, 100, quoting Rawls 1963, italics added).

7. Hayek, *The Road to Serfdom*, 126, emphasis added.

8. Nozick, *Anarchy, State, and Utopia.*

9. One might object if the transactions were coerced or fraudulent, of course. But the force of Nozick's objection is that Rawls would redistribute even if none of the transactions were coerced or fraudulent, which violates a certain kind of moral intuition most people have about fairness.

10. For readers younger than fifty and those who find basketball references obscure, an explanation is useful. The difference between Wilt Chamberlain and his average competitor was perhaps the largest in the history of all professional sports. In a game against the Detroit Pistons on February 2, 1968, Chamberlain recorded a "double triple double," putting up twenty-two points, twenty-five rebounds, and twenty-one assists. A "double double" is a good single game; over the course of his long career, Chamberlain averaged a "double double double," with thirty points per game and twenty-three rebounds per game. He was not the best team player (Oscar Robertson was a better team player), but Chamberlain was utterly dominant for more than a decade. The only comparable sports figures are Babe Ruth in baseball in the 1920s and Tiger Woods in golf in the 2000s. One might protest that Michael Jordan was a better all-around player. Indeed. My claim for Chamberlain's dominance is based on the *difference* between his performance and that of his peers at the same time. Basketball had gotten a lot better by the time Jordan played. So although Jordan was better overall, Chamberlain was more individually dominant in his era.

11. Nozick, *Anarchy, State, and Utopia*, 163.

12. Radford, "The Economic Organisation of a P.O.W. Camp," 189–201.

13. See Munger (2011, 206–35).

14. Radford, "The Economic Organisation of a P.O.W. Camp," 191.

15. Munger, "Euvoluntary or Not, Exchange Is Just," 206–35.

16. In a private-property regime with small numbers, this assumption is easily met by Coasian bargaining (Coase 1960). If property is common and numbers are large, however, state action may be required. However, this is more a problem with the property-rights regime than with the exchange itself.

17. See Black (1916).

18. Thomas Hobbes argued that coercion must be relegated to government, not to private bargaining, because "covenants being but words, and breath, have no force to oblige, contain, constrain, or protect any man, but what it has from the public sword" ([1651] 1991, part 2, chap. 18).

19. As Mill famously put it, there is a distinction between production decisions and distribution decisions:

> The laws and conditions of the Production of wealth partake of the character of physical truths. There is nothing optional or arbitrary in them. Whatever mankind produce, must be produced in the modes, and under the conditions, imposed by the constitution of external things, and by the inherent properties of their own bodily and mental structure . . .

> II.1.2

> It is not so with the Distribution of wealth. That is a matter of human institution solely. *The things once there,* mankind, individually or collectively, can do with them as they like . . . Further, in the social state, in every state except total solitude, any disposal whatever of them can only take place by the consent of society, or rather of those who dispose of its active force. Even what a person has produced by his individual toil, unaided by any one, he cannot keep, unless by the permission of society. Not only can society take it from him, but individuals could and would take it from him, if society only remained passive; if it did not either interfere *en masse,* or employ and pay people for the purpose of preventing him from being disturbed in the possession." ([1848] 2004, 199, emphasis added).

20. Rawls, *A Theory of Justice,* 61.

21. Mill, *The Principles of Political Economy,* book II, chap. 1.

22. Mises, "Profit and Loss," sec. 5.

23. Mises, "Profit and Loss," sec. 5.

Chapter 5, Jackson and Palm

1. Arneson, "Luck Egalitarianism and Prioritarianism," 339–49.

2. Anderson, "Equality of Capabilities, or Equality of Outcomes," *Free Thoughts Podcast,* May 5, 2014. At https://www.libertarianism.org/media/free-thoughts-podcast/equality-capabilities-or-equality-outcomes.

3. See Kelley (1991) and (2009).

4. See Kelley (1991).

5. Anderson, "Equality of Capabilities, or Equality of Outcomes," *Free Thoughts Podcast,* May 5, 2014.

6. Mueller, "Bye-Bye Bismarck."

7. See Anderson (2014), Roosevelt (1944), and The Welfare State (2016).

8. Rawls, *A Theory of Justice.*

9. Wenar, "John Rawls," in *The Stanford Encyclopedia of Philosophy* (2012), edited by Edward N. Zalta. At https://plato.stanford.edu/entries/rawls/#BasStrSocIns.

10. David Kelley, "Altruism and Social Justice," *Forum for Classical Liberals,* podcast, 1991, University of Aix-en-Province. At https://www.libertarianism.org/media/video-collection/david-kelley-egalitarianism-welfare-rights-theory.

11. Hayek, *The Mirage of Social Justice,* 62, 75.

12. Kelley, "Altruism and Social Justice." *Forum for Classical Liberals,* podcast, University of Aix-en-Province.

13. Rawls, *A Theory of Justice,* 62.

14. Hayek, *The Mirage of Social Justice*, 80.

15. Rothbard, "Egalitarianism and the Elites," 39–57.

16. Anderson, "Equality of Capabilities, or Equality of Outcomes," *Free Thoughts Podcast,* May 5, 2014.

17. Rothbard, "Egalitarianism and the Elites," 39–57.

18. Rothbard, "Egalitarianism," 39–57.

19. Rothbard, "Egalitarianism," 53.

20. Sowell, *Black Rednecks and White Liberals*, 249–66

21. Sowell, *Black Rednecks and White Liberals*; Williams, *Race and Economics.*

22. Williams, *Race and Economics.*

23. Piketty, *Capital in the Twenty-First Century.*

24. Knack and Keefer, "Does Social Capital Have an Economic Payoff?" 1283.

25. See respectively Piketty (2014); Caron and Repetti (2013, 1255–89).

26. Hayek, *The Mirage of Social Justice*, 68.

27. Guvenen, Kuruscu, and Ozkan, "Taxation of Human Capital and Wage Inequality," 818–50.

28. Heckman, "Policies to Foster Human Capital," 3–56; Borghans, Duckworth, Heckman, and Weel, "The Economics and Psychology of Personality Traits," 972–1059.

29. Becker and Tomes, "Human Capital and the Rise and Fall of Families," 257–98.

30. Rawls, *A Theory of Justice*, 74; Rockwell, "The Menace of Egalitarianism," *Mises Circle, against P.C.* At https://mises.org/library/menace-egalitarianism.

31. North, *Institutions, Institutional Change, and Economic Performance.*

32. Putnam, "Bowling Alone: America's Declining Social Capital," 65–78; Putnam, *Bowling Alone: The Collapse and Revival of American Community.*

33. Chamlee-Wright, "The Structure of Social Capital," 45.

34. Knack and Keefer, "Does Social Capital Have an Economic Payoff?" 1251–88; Narayan and Pritchett, "Cents and Sociability," 871–97.

35. Boxman, De Graaf, and Flap, "The Impact of Social and Human Capital," 51–73.

36. Note that we are ignoring the potential ill effects from the dark side of human capital (Chamlee-Wright and Storr 2011).

37. See, for example, Alesina and La Ferrara (2000, 847–904); Portes (2014, 18407–8). To the contrary, it has been demonstrated that economic freedom is causally related to the most liberal of ideals, tolerance. See Berggren and Nilsson (2013) and (2016).

38. Jackson, Carden, and Compton (2015) uses a measure of social capital showing that there appears to be no causal link with economic freedom, and Jackson (2017) shows that the link may be in fact negative but due only to an imperfection in the social capital measure picking up on group associations of the type given in Olson (1982).

39. See, for example, Berggren and Jordahl (2006, 141–69); Jackson, Compton, and Maw (2016).

40. Easterlin, "Does Economic Growth Improve the Human Lot?" 89–125.

41. Bernanke, "The Economics of Happiness," speech given at the University of South Carolina commencement ceremony, Columbia, May 8, 2010. At http://www.federalreserve.gov/newsevents/speech/bernanke20100508a.htm.

42. Diener, "Subjective Well-Being," 34–43.

43. Goff, Helliwell, and Mayraz, *The Welfare Costs of Well-Being Inequality*.

44. Dolan, Peasgood, and White. "Do We Really Know What Makes Us Happy?" 94–122.

45. Diener and Oishi, "Money and Happiness," 185–218.

46. Blanchflower and Oswald, "Well-Being over Time in Britain and the USA," 1359–86.

47. Welsch, "Environment and Happiness," 801–13.

48. Kasser, *The High Price of Materialism*.

49. Kawachi, Kennedy, Lochner, and Prothrow-Stith, "Social Capital, Income Inequality, and Mortality," 1491–98.

50. Stutzer, "The Role of Income Aspirations in Individual Happiness," 89–109.

51. DeNeve and Cooper, "The Happy Personality," 197–229.

52. Helliwell and Putnam, "The Social Context of Well-Being," 1435–46.

53. Ryan and Deci, "Self-Determination Theory," 68–78; Verme, "Happiness, Freedom, and Control," 146–61.

54. Veenhoven, "Freedom and Happiness," 257–88; Gropper, Lawson, and Thorne, "Economic Freedom and Happiness," 237–55; Nikolaev, "Economic Freedom and Quality of Life," 61–96; Jackson, "Free to Be Happy," Currently available online only. doi:10.1007/s10902-016-9770-9.

55. Graham, "Adaptation amidst Prosperity and Adversity," 105–37.

56. Bartolini, Bilancini, and Sarracino, "Social Capital Predicts Happiness over Time," 175–98.

Chapter 6, Hill

1. Tibor Machan (1989), Robert Nozick (1974), and Douglas Rasmussen and Douglas Den Uyl (1997) are prominent natural-rights philosophers. In *Simple Rules for a Complex World* (1995), Richard Epstein uses rule utilitarianism to justify a set of rights that are remarkably similar to those espoused by the natural-rights advocates.

2. Aristotle, *Politics*, 1254a–55a.

3. Judaism allowed some forms of slavery but put far more restrictions on its practice than other religious or social groups.

4. Sowell, *Black Rednecks and White Liberals*, 127.

5. Joel Mokyr (2017) presents a summary of the varied influences on the process of cultural evolution.

6. Rodrik, "When Ideas Trump Interests," 191.

7. Ferry, *A Brief History of Thought*, 72.

8. Ferry, *A Brief History*, 76–77 (capitalization and italics in the original).

9. Siedentop, *Inventing the Individual*, 114.

10. English Standard Version.

11. Berman, *Created Equal*.

12. Deut. 29:10–15.

13. Berman, *Created Equal*, 29.

14. Siedentop, *Inventing the Individual*, 359.

15. Siedentop, *Inventing the Individual*, 65.

16. Galatians 3:28.

17. John 3:16, italics added.

18. Madigan, *Medieval Christianity*, 107.

19. Siedentop, *Inventing the Individual*, 95, 160.

20. Madigan, *Medieval Christianiy*, 22, 43.

21. Madigan, *Medieval Christianity*, 275.

22. Madigan, *Medieval Christianity*, 311.

23. Siedentop, *Inventing the Individual*, 206.

24. Siedentop, *Inventing the Individual*, 186.

25. Madigan, *Medieval Christianity*, 314.

26. Grynaviski, Jeffrey D., and Michael C. Munger. "Reconstructing Racism: Transforming Racial Hierarchy from 'Necessary Evil' into 'Positive Good.'" Social Philosophy and Policy 34, no. 1 (2017): 144–63.

27. Acemoglu and Robinson, *Why Nations Fail*, 9–19.

28. Quoted in Siedentop (2014), 117.

29. Siedentop, *Inventing the Individual*, 226.

30. Tierney, *The Idea of Natural Rights*, 69.

31. Forster, *The Contested Public Square*.

32. Witte, *God's Joust, God's Justice*, 5051.

33. Witte, *The Reformation of Rights*, 89.

34. Witte, *The Reformation of Rights*, 182.

35. Forster, *The Contested Public Square*, 153.

36. Witte, *The Reformation of Rights*, 213.

37. Witte, *The Reformation of Rights*, 12.

38. McCloskey, *Bourgeois Equality*. Although providing substantial evidence of the concept of human equality in seventeenth- and eighteenth-century England and the Netherlands, McCloskey sees such equality as springing up almost without any historical roots before that period. That view is in sharp contrast to the arguments given in this essay.

39. Hobbes, *Leviathan*.

40. Berkowitz, *Virtue and the Making of Modern Liberalism*, 36.

41. Locke, *Two Treatises of Government*.

42. Forster, *The Contested Public Square*, 161–65.

43. Forster, *The Contested Public Square*, 162.

44. Montesquieu, *The Spirit of the Laws*, 253.

45. Siedentop, *Inventing the Individual*, 338.

Chapter 7, Morgan

1. Herodotus, *Histories*, Book 5:92, 240–241.

2. Cf. Andrew and Rapp, *Autocracy and China's Rebel Founding Emperors*, 58 ff.

3. See also de Maistre (1797).

4. Lovejoy, *The Great Chain of Being*.

5. Hoppe, *Democracy: The God that Failed*.

6. Foucault, *Discipline and Punish*.

7. Foucault, Senellart, Ewald, and Fontana. *Security, Territory, Population.*

8. St. Thomas Aquinas makes virtually identical arguments. See Aquinas, *Summa Theologiæ*, Part II, 1, Question 2.

9. See Leigh (2014).

10. Cf. Voegelin, *The New Science of Politics.*

11. There is also, in the recent rise of "privilege" studies, a strong element of what Ayn Rand called "the sanction of the victim," or the moral failure that causes those who actually espouse values to apologize for doing so. See Wright (2016, 166).

12. Burnham, *The Managerial Revolution*; Francis, *Power and History*, 9; referring to Berle and Means, *The Modern Corporation and Private Property.*

13. Francis, *Power and History*, op. cit., 9–10.

14. As Ludwig von Mises points out in *Epistemological Problems of Economics*, much of this animus against business owners is likely born of envy and resentment. Or, as Thomas Sowell writes, "Envy plus rhetoric equals 'social justice'." Cf. also Mises, *Human Action*, 194 ff.

15. See also McInenerny, *Aquinas on Human Action.*

16. Mises, *Human Action*, 244–245.

17. Mises, *Human Action*, 245.

18. Mises, *Human Action*, 245.

19. Agamben, *State of Exception.* See also Schmitt (1922).

20. Mises, *Human Action*, 254.

21. Mises, *Human Action*, 290–291.

22. Mises, *Human Action*, 290.

Chapter 8, Harrigan and Yonk

1. Thomas Jefferson, "The Declaration of Independence."

2. Maier, *American Scripture.*

3. Rozin, "Comments on Yoram Shachar," 54–57; Shachar, "Jefferson Goes East," 589–618.

4. Minh, "Declaration of Independence."

5. Rudoren, "What's Hebrew for 'When in the Course of Human Events'?" *New York Times*, September 16, 2016. At http://www.nytimes.com/2016/09/16/world/what-in-the-world/israel-mordechai-beham-founding-document.html.

6. Thomas Jefferson, "The Declaration of Independence."

7. Paine, *Common Sense.*

8. Adams, Novangelus Letter: John Adams to the Inhabitants of the Colony of Massachusetts-Bay, February 1775. At https://www.masshist.org/publications/apde2/view?&id=PJA02dg5.

9. Mass. Const. art. I.

10. Mass. Const., preamble.

11. US Const. amend. I.

12. Hamilton, *Federalist* No. 23, 112.

13. Office of Personnel Management. n.d. Historical Federal Workforce Tables: Total Government Employment since 1962. Data, Analysis, & Documentation, Federal Employment Reports. At https://www.opm.gov/policy-data-oversight/data-analysis-documentation/federal-employment-reports/historical-tables/total-government-employment-since-1962/. Accessed December 16, 2016.

14. US Department of Agriculture. n.d. USDA–Farm Service Agency ARC/PLC Program Landing Page. At https://www.fsa.usda.gov/programs-and-services/arcplc_program/. Accessed December 16, 2016.

Chapter 9, Watkins Jr.

1. Hayek, *The Constitution of Liberty*, 148.
2. Optiz, *Religion*, 12.
3. Fletcher, "In God's Image," 1608.
4. Acts 10:34.
5. Hayek, *The Constitution of Liberty*, 167.
6. Hayek, *The Constitution of Liberty*, 170.
7. Hayek, *The Constitution of Liberty*, 173.
8. Jefferson, *The Complete Jefferson*, 132.
9. Obergefell v. Hodges, Slip Op. 14–556 (2015).
10. Robin West, "Is Progressive Constitutionalism Possible?" 3.
11. Strauss, "The Illusory Distinction between Equality of Opportunity and Equality of Result," 178.
12. Hayek, *The Constitution of Liberty*, 150.
13. US Const., amend. XIV, §1.
14. Holt, *Magna Carta*.
15. Black, *A Constitutional Faith*, 33.
16. Coke, *The Selected Writings of Sir Edward Coke*, 849.
17. Hamilton, *The Papers of Alexander Hamilton*, 35.
18. Lochner v. New York, 198 US 45 (1905).
19. Lochner v. New York, 198 US 45 (1905) at 57. For recent scholarship challenging that idea that the *Lochner* Court was activist in its use of substantive due process, see Mayer (2011).
20. Roe v. Wade, 410 US 113 (1973).
21. US Const., amend. XIV, §1.
22. Buck v. Bell, 274 US 200, 208 (1927).
23. Railway Express Agency, Inc. v. New York, 336 US 106 (1949).
24. Railway Express Agency, Inc. v. New York, 336 US 106 (1949) at 110.
25. Railway Express Agency, Inc. v. New York, 336 US 106 (1949) at 109.
26. Railway Express Agency, Inc. v. New York, 336 US 106 (1949) at 112.
27. United States v. Carolene Products Co., 304 US 144 (1938).
28. United States v. Carolene Products Co., 304 US 144 (1938) at 153.
29. Shapiro v. Thompson, 394 US 618 (1969).
30. Shapiro v. Thompson, 394 US 618 (1969) at 658.
31. Shapiro v. Thompson, 394 US 618 (1969) at 659.
32. Shapiro v. Thompson, 394 US 618 (1969) at 662.
33. Shapiro v. Thompson, 394 US 618 (1969) at 661.
34. Whole Woman's Health v. Hellerstedt, Slip Op. 16-274, 11 (2016).
35. Obergefell v. Hodges, Slip. Op. 14-556, 19 (2015).
36. Obergefell v. Hodges, Slip. Op. 14-556, 19 (2015) at 18.

37. Tucker, Blackstone, and Christian, *Blackstone's Commentaries.*

38. Tucker, Blackstone, and Christian, *Blackstone's Commentaries,* 104.

39. Tucker, Blackstone, and Christian, *Blackstone's Commentaries,* 100.

40. Tucker, Blackstone, and Christian, *Blackstone's Commentaries,* 101.

41. Tucker, Blackstone, and Christian, *Blackstone's Commentaries,* 92.

42. Tucker, Blackstone, and Christian, *Blackstone's Commentaries,* 94.

43. Tucker, Blackstone, and Christian, *Blackstone's Commentaries,* 101.

44. Tucker, Blackstone, and Christian, *Blackstone's Commentaries,* 105.

45. Tucker, Blackstone, and Christian, *Blackstone's Commentaries,* 103.

46. Kamper v. Hawkins, 1 Va. Cas. 20, 24 (1793).

47. Slaughterhouse Cases, 83 US 36, 71 (1872).

48. Slaughterhouse Cases, 83 US 36, 71 (1872) at 71.

49. Tucker, Blackstone, and Christian, *Blackstone's Commentaries,* 148.

50. Tucker, Blackstone, and Christian, *Blackstone's Commentaries,* 148.

51. See, for example, Rose (2010, 407) and Watson (n.d., 501).

52. Cox, "Foreword: Constitutional Adjudication and the Promotion of Human Rights," 91.

53. Dietze, "Hayek on the Rule of Law," 127.

Chapter 10, Shmanske

1. See Robbins (1932).

2. See Marshall (1890).

3. Hayek (1991) calls this "spontaneous order."

4. See Hayek (1945).

5. See Smith (1776).

6. See Pareto (1906).

7. See Debreu (1959).

8. Or in some cases, lack of stamina. For example, at Disneyland those in wheelchairs (and their whole parties) are often invited to the head of the queue.

9. See Shmanske (2015) for an extended discussion of all of these queuing issues with respect to rounds of golf at a popular, underpriced golf course in the New York State Park system.

10. One is reminded of Orwell's (1945) "All animals are equal, but some are more equal than others."

11. See O'Toole (2001).

Chapter 11, Wright

1. These terms are placed in scare quotations because they are problematic in several ways, though frequently resorted to as shorthand for African-Americans, Hispanics, and women on the one hand and males of Euroamerican ancestry on the other. The terms are problematic, in part, because women constitute a majority of the population, some groups of Asian-Americans have higher rates of mortgage acquisition than Euroamericans, and so forth. They are used here only as conventional shorthand.

2. See Avery, Beeson, and Sniderman (1992), (1993), and (1994).

3. See Liebowitz (2008, 292–97).

4. See Ensign, Overberg, and Andriotis (2016).

5. The two models of financial egalitarianism come directly from divisions in liberal thought more generally. For a recent overview, see Tomasi (2012).

6. See Wright (1997) and (2005).

7. See Wright (1997) and (2014); Rock (1984, 166–69).

8. See Yenawine (2010).

9. See Wright (2014); Beveridge (1985); Calder (1999, 66–68); Krooss and Blyn (1971, 122–24).

10. See Olegario (2016, 128–29); Black (1961, 167–68).

11. See Black (1961, 163–64) and Anderson (2008).

12. See Snowden (1987) and Frederiksen (1894).

13. See "A Reformed Stock Gambler" (1848, 8).

14. See Bubolz (1938); Moore (1905); Pierce (1958); Valgren (1924); Oviatt (1905); Wermiel (2000, 104–37); Rapone (1987); Wright and Sylla (2015); Pak (2013); Cropp (2014); Davis (1944); James (1947); Oates (1968, 18).

15. See Dawson (1905); Graham and Xie (2007); Lehrman (1994); Murphy (2010); Zanjani (2003).

16. See Hochfelder (2006).

17. See Caplan (2013, 31).

18. See Sparks (2006, 171).

19. See Caplan (2013, 87, 90).

20. See US Treasury (1978, 54).

21. See Caplan (2013, 120).

22. See Norman (1986).

23. See Caplan (2013, 135–43).

24. See Fisher (1990); Antilla (2003); Fisher (2012).

25. See Curry (1981, 196–215).

26. See Rose (1948, 110).

27. See Embree (1943, 131-32); Gunther (1947, 575); Rose (1948, 110).

28. See Hyman (2011, 184–85).

29. See Gunther (1947, 284).

30. See Pettigrew (1964, 42–43, 46).

31. See Abrams (1955, 176).

32. See Wright and Sylla (2015).

33. See Caplan (2013, 55–64).

34. See Wagmiller (2003).

35. See Hyman (2011, 283–85).

36. See Wright (2014).

37. The best survey of the massive literature on mortgage discrimination is still Ross and Yinger (2002).

38. See Hetzel (2012, 170–71).

39. See Spiegel, Gart and Gart (1996); Lajoux and Roberts (2014, 34, 48–49, 54); Wright and Sylla (2015).

40. See Norberg (2009, 26–28, 32–35).

41. See Barry (1951); Dahl (1965).

42. See Norberg (2009, 29–32).

43. See Jones (2013, 286).

44. See Hyman (2011, 270–75); Weller (2006, 2–3).

45. See Linden et al. (2007); Norberg (2009, 60).

46. See Snowden (1987).

47. See Norberg (2009, 38–41).

48. See Dickerson (2014).

49. See Norberg (2009, 36–37).

50. See Mihm (2008).

51. See Hetzel (2012, 22, 150–57, 296, 300, 309).

52. See Wright (2014).

53. See Baker and Smith (1998).

54. See Norberg (2009, 76).

55. See White (2009).

56. See Starr (2007, 34).

57. A reader of an early draft complained that this paper appears to promote segregation. Far from it, as consumers remain free to choose whatever service provider they wish and new service providers need not (and indeed should not) restrict their customer base to members of a particular group. The point here is that if discrimination is occurring, money is being left "on the table" by incumbents and members of the group being discriminated against should be able to profit from it, for reasons of both justice and efficiency, by entering the business.

58. See DeYoung and Hunter (2003).

59. See Mainelli and von Gunten (2014).

60. See Wright (2010).

Chapter 12, Carden, Estelle, and Bradley

1. Deaton, *The Great Escape*, 168.

2. Smith, *Wealth of Nations*, 23–24.

3. See McCloskey (2006), (2010), and (2016).

4. Pinkovskiy and Sala-i-Martin, "Parametric Estimations."

5. Plato, *Laws*, book XII.

6. Aristotle, *Politics*, VII.3.

7. Nicolini and Palencia, "Decomposing Income Inequality."

8. Cosgel and Ergene, "Inequality of Wealth."

9. Ryckbosch, "Economic Inequality and Growth," 17.

10. Di Matteo, "All Equal in the Sight of God."

11. Molitoris and Dribe, "Industrialization and Inequality Revisited," 193.

12. Smith, *Wealth of Nations*, 96.

13. Schumpeter, *Capitalism, Socialism and Democracy*, 67.

14. Deaton, *The Great Escape*, 83.

15. See McCloskey (2006), (2010), and (2016).

16. Gerencer, "10 Most Expensive Whiskies in the World," *MoneyNation*, March 16, 2016, http://moneynation.com/most-expensive-whiskey/.

17. See Nye (2002a) and (2002b).

18. Henderson, McNab, and Rozsas, "The Hidden Inequality in Socialism," 389–412.

19. Hayek, *The Constitution of Liberty*, 91.

20. Quoted and discussed in McCloskey (2016), 401.

21. Frankfurt, "The Moral Irrelevance of Equality," 100-103.

22. Frankfurt, "The Moral Irrelevance of Equality," 103.

23. See McCloskey (2016) for an exhaustive discussion.

Chapter 13, Wenzel

1. On problems with Piketty, see Mulligan (2015).

2. See Rawls [1971] (1999), Tomasi (2012), Lomasky (2005), or Wenzel (2016).

3. For a good example of such sophistry, see Stiglitz (2012), who rightly identifies interventionism as a root cause of much inequality, only to recommend more intervention as a cure; on sophisms generally, see Bastiat [1845] (1996).

4. Callahan, "Fantasy is Not an Adult Policy Option."

5. Mises, *Economic Policy*.

6. Caplan, "The Idea Trap," 183–203.

7. In more technical language, the MPC (marginal propensity to consume) varies with income levels—and with distribution of income (see Carroll, Slacalek, and Tukuoka 2014).

8. Hazlitt, *The Failure of the New Economics*.

9. See Hayek (1945), Hazlitt (1959), Read (1958).

10. Adapted from Tomasi, *Free-Market Fairness*, 235.

11. Mitchell (2005) goes into greater detail, listing the following costs of government intervention: the extraction cost, the displacement cost (as private-sector activity is crowded out), the negative multiplier cost (as regulations impose higher costs than just the enforcement of the regulations), the behavioral subsidy cost (as government creates perverse incentives), the behavioral penalty cost (as government discourages good behavior), the market distortion cost, the inefficiency cost, and the stagnation cost (as government thwarts innovation and growth). I have intentionally not gone into this level of detail.

12. https://www.cia.gov/library/publications/the-world-factbook/rankorder/2172rank .html

13. Hayek, "The Use of Knowledge in Society," 519–530.

14. For a delightful illustration, see Read, "I, Pencil."

15. See Buchanan and Tullock (1962), Bastiat [1850] (2012).

16. Horwitz, "Inequality, Mobility and Being Poor in America," 70–91.

17. Mises, *Economic Policy*.

18. This is an intentionally cursory overview, as such issues are elaborated in Hobbs and Wenzel (2016a).

19. Crews, "Ten Thousand Commandments 2016."

20. McGrath, "A Primer on Occupational Licensing," 9.

21. Gwartney et al., *Economics: Private and Public Choice*, 139.

22. See DeBow (1992) on the regressive nature of rent seeking.

23. This includes federal, state, and local spending. This does not include indirect welfare spending like education, Social Security, and Medicaid. See http://www.usgovernment spending.com/entitlement_spending.

24. Of course, one might argue the counter-factual, that poverty rates would have been higher than 15% today, there but for government involvement. But why assume a sudden reversal of the pre-1965 trends, especially considering that the economy has grown by a factor of almost four.

25. Hazlitt, *The Conquest of Poverty*, 49.

26. Hazlitt, *The Conquest of Poverty*, 147.

27. Sowell, *Wealth, Poverty and Politics*, 168.

28. See Hazlitt (1973), 56 and chapter 10.

29. See Schoenfeld, "The Mythical Link."

30. Sowell, *Wealth, Poverty and Politics*, 168.

31. Tanner and Hughes, "The Work v. Welfare Tradeoff."

32. See Tocqueville [1835] (2015, 23–25, 35); Hazlitt (1973, 71, 185–186); Sowell (2015).

33. Hazlitt, *The Conquest of Poverty*, 123.

34. Hazlitt, *The Conquest of Poverty*, 210.

35. Bastiat, "Luxury and Thrift."

36. In Hazlitt (1973, 214).

37. http://www.marketingcharts.com/online/smartphone-penetration-nears-80-of-the -us-mobile-market-65214/

38. See Hobbs and Wenzel (2016b).

39. Hayek (1960, 43–44). See also Mises [1929] (1985), I.5.

40. See Mises [1955] (2007).

41. Bauer, *Equality, the Third World and Economic Delusion*, 23.

42. Hazlitt, *The Conquest of Poverty*, 209.

43. Hazlitt, *The Conquest of Poverty*, 232.

44. Schumpeter, *Capitalism, Socialism and Democracy*, 67–68.

45. Posner, *Economic Analysis of Law.*

46. Mitchell, "The Impact of Government Spending."

47. See Baumol (1990), or Rosenberg (1960a and 1960b).

48. Bastiat, *What Is Seen and What Is Not Seen.*

49. See Beito (2000) on a century of voluntary, fraternal mutual aid efforts—efforts that were effectively killed by the rise of the welfare state.

50. Horowitz, "Inequality, Mobility and Being Poor in America."

51. Hazlitt, *The Conquest of Poverty*, 125.

Chapter 14, O'Neill

1. Rawls, *A Theory of Justice*, 100–108.

2. Marx, "Critique of the Gotha Program."

3. See McLellan (1977, 568–569); for a similar argument see Trotsky (1937), Chapter 3.

4. See Rand (1995) and Rothbard (2000). For other insightful critiques see Nozick (1974), Schoeck (1987), Narveson (1997), Kekes (2007).

5. See Walzer (1983).

6. Narveson, "Egalitarianism: Partial, Counterproductive and Baseless," 291.

7. See Baker (1974), Hare (1982), Nagel (1991).

8. Schmidtz, "Diminishing Marginal Utility and Egalitarian Redistribution," 263.

9. Le Grand, "Equity versus Efficiency."

10. More specifically, what I mean here is that wealth and other outcome variables in human affairs often follow statistical distributions which are roughly symmetrical when measured on a logarithmic scale (see e.g., Limpert, Stahel, and Abbt 2001). The lognormal statistical distribution is an example of this.

11. Kault, "The Shape of the Distribution of the Number of Sexual Partners."

12. Geisen, Zimmerman, and Suedekum, "The Size Distribution across All Cities."

13. See Bergson (1944), Pryor (1973), Wiles (1974), Abouchar (1977), Chapman (1979), Bergson (1984), and Millar (1987).

14. Bergson, *The Structure of Soviet Wages*, 1065.

15. Feldbrugge et al., *Encyclopedia of Soviet Law*, 538.

16. See Gastwirth (1972).

17. Warshawsky, "Earnings Inequality."

18. It is possible to construct a simple measurement of inequality in terms of utility using a specified mathematical form for an increasing concave utility function. Any concave utility function leads to diminishing inequality when aggregate wealth increases. That measure is not proposed in this paper (which instead uses a measure of compensating variation in time as the scale of measurement). However, a simple numerical example of this kind can be found in O'Neill (2015), 12–15.

19. See Stanton (2008) and O'Neill (2015).

20. Compensating variation is a standard welfare concept used in economics [e.g., Jehle and Reny (2001), 166–169]. In the present context, this compensating variation in time would work as follows: Consider what would happen if we could grant a person additional hours in each day, to allow them to do more things and acquire more goods. For each person, we ask ourselves how many additional hours we would need to give them in order for the person to get back to their original utility position if all their money and property were taken away. This number of hours (or other units of time) then gives us a measurement of the value of monetary wealth in the numéraire of time.

21. I recognize the possibility that such goods may be imparted to others indirectly through processes of teaching, learning, etc. Similarly, it is possible that some nonexchangeable goods may be created or dissolved by mutual action (e.g., friendship). These processes of change in possession of nonexchangeable goods are not treated as genuine "transfers" or "exchanges" akin to those that occur with exchangeable goods. In such cases the process involved generally creates a new good or destroys an existing good rather than transferring per se.

22. It is entirely likely that a society growing in wealth and productive capacity would also be attended by some aggregate growth in human capital which would render people able to acquire nonexchangeable goods at a lower time-price. Compared with their ancestors, people might plausibly grow to be more intelligent and hence able to acquire knowledge with less time and effort, grow more mature and sociable and hence be able to develop good friend-

ships and other relationships with less time and effort (and error), and so on. This entails growth in "nonexchangeable wealth" and a lowering of time-price, and this would derogate from the reduction in relative time-price for exchangeable goods. Nevertheless, all we need for the conclusion of a reducing relative time-price for exchangeable goods is the fact that growth in this class of goods would be *faster* than for nonexchangeable goods.

23. See Fogel (2000, Ch. 5.).

Chapter 15, Gaines

1. Arneson, "Egalitarianism."
2. See Hayek (1960, 103).
3. Quoted in Hayek (1994, 123).
4. Reagan, 1981 Inaugural Address.
5. See James Kluegel and Eliot Smith (1986).
6. Rawls, *A Theory of Justice.*
7. Frolich and Oppenheimer, *Choosing Justice,* 170.
8. See, inter alia, Kohut (2015), Newport (2015), Scheiber and Sussman (2015).
9. Barnes, "A Setback, Not a Catastrophe."
10. See White House (2012b).
11. See White House (2012a).
12. For details on the sampling technique, see Rivers (2006).
13. See "Americans Views on Taxes" (2003).
14. See Page and Jacobs (2009).
15. See "Tax System Seen as Unfair" (2011).
16. Hall and Rabushka, *The Flat Tax.*
17. All values taken from Hall and Rabushka's proposal from 1995.
18. I report elsewhere (Gaines n.d.) extensive statistical analysis of the heterogeneity in responses. Respondent wealth is a slightly significant predictor of higher "fair" rates, ceteris paribus, as is gender (women choose higher values than men). Both of those effects are much smaller than that of self-reported ideology, which behaves as expected: fair rates chosen by liberals are higher than those chosen by moderates, which are higher than those chosen by conservatives. Even those who describe themselves as "very liberal," however, do not, on average, endorse rates much higher than the status quo for very large incomes.
19. The survey was administered by YouGov in March 2015, with 1,000 respondents.
20. Buffet, "Stop Coddling the Super-Rich," *New York Times,* August 14, 2011.
21. See Page and Jacobs (2009).
22. Hayek, *The Constitution of Liberty,* 314–15.

Chapter 16, Stringham

1. Saez and Zucman, *Wealth Inequality in the United States since 1913,* 8.
2. Scheiber and Sussman, "Inequality Troubles Americans across Party Lines, Times/CBS Poll Finds," *New York Times,* June 3, 2015.
3. Rawls, *A Theory of Justice.*
4. These figures are derived from the data I compiled to create table 16.2.

5. Zillow estimates are not 100 percent accurate—one recently sold for $100 million, and another is on the market for $200 million—but you get the point.

6. See Zillow (2016), *Zestimate*. Seattle: Zillow Group.

7. The faculty directory for my college lists zero professors living in East Hartford and about fifty in the much more expensive and unequal West Hartford.

8. Lewis states, "I do not believe that God created an egalitarian world," but "if there is equality it is in His love, not in use" (1949, 33–34).

9. Hayek, *The Constitution of Liberty.*

10. Mises, *Socialism: An Economic and Sociological Analysis.*

11. Dolan, "Inside the 2016 Forbes 400," *Forbes,* October 4, 2016.

12. "Two Decades of Wealth," *Forbes,* September 13, 2002.

13. Zweynert, "World's Growing Inequality Is 'Ticking Time Bomb,'" *Reuters*, November 30, 2016.

14. Quoted in Kertscher, "Michael Moore Says 400 Americans Have More Wealth Than Half of All Americans Combined." *PolitiFact,* March 10, 2011.

15. See "Two Decades of Wealth" (2002) and Dolan (2016).

16. See World Bank (2016).

17. Cox and Alm, *Onward and Upward!*

18. See Aaberge and Mogstad (2015); Piketty (2015), 74.

19. Hayek, *The Constitution of Liberty*, 156.

20. Mises, *Socialism,* 66.

21. See "United to End Genocide" (2016).

22. Friedman, *The Other Victims.*

23. Leonard, *Illiberal Reformers.*

24. Piketty, "Putting Distribution Back at the Center of Economics."

Chapter 17, Geloso and Horwitz

1. See Ostry, Berg, and Tsangarides (2014).

2. See Winship (2013).

3. See Wilkinson and Pickett (2009).

4. Most notably Kahneman and Deaton (2010).

5. See Tomasi (2012).

6. See Welch (1999).

7. Rawls, *A Theory of Justice.*

8. Tomasi, *Free Market Fairness.*

9. See Galbraith (2012), Piketty (2014).

10. See Sala-i-Martin (2006).

11. Organization for Economic Cooperation and Development (OECD), *An Overview of Growing Income Inequalities in OECD Countries*, 24.

12. OECD, *An Overview,* 23.

13. See Aten and D'Souza (2008), 67.

14. Galbraith, *Inequality and Instability*, 144.

15. See Boskin (2005).

16. See Broda and Weinstein (2008a, 2008b); Broda, Leibtag, and Weinstein (2009).

17. See Broda and Weinstein (2008b), 45.

18. See Meyer and Sullivan (2013b).

19. See Piketty and Saez (2003).

20. See Burkhauser, Larrimore, and Simon (2012).

21. See Burkhauser, Larrimore, and Simon (2012).

22. See notably Jenkins and van Kerm (2009).

23. See Feldstein (2008).

24. See Burkhauser and Simon (2010); Burtless and Svaton (2010); Meyer and Sullivan (2010), (2011), and (2013a); Burkhauser, Larrimore, and Simon (2012); Bricker et al. (2015).

25. See Meyer and Sullivan (2010), (2011), (2013a), and (2013b).

26. See Pendakur (1998).

27. See Brzozowski et al. (2010).

28. See Eberstadt (2008), Horwitz (2015).

29. See Sarlo (2009).

30. See Attanasio and Pistaferri (2016).

31. See Moore and Pacey (2003).

32. See Card (2009).

33. See Peri (2012).

34. Lemieux, "Increasing Residual Wage Inequality," 461.

35. See Almås and Mogstad (2016).

36. See Nordhaus (2004), 33.

37. See Stevenson and Wolfers (2008).

38. See Stevenson and Wolfers (2013).

39. See Lemieux, MacLeod, and Parent (2009).

40. See Anderson, Cockburn, and Martin (2011).

41. See Niemietz (2012, 17).

42. See Hilber and Vermeulen (2016).

43. See Ganong and Shoag (2015).

44. See Chambers and Collins (2016).

45. See Carpenter (2015).

46. See Pettit (2012).

47. See Lott (1990), Lyons and Pettit (2011).

48. See Western and Pettit (2005).

49. See Western and Pettit (2005).

50. See Dumais (2012).

51. See Cardwell, Lawley, and Di (2015).

52. See Geloso and Moreau (2016).

Conclusion, Munger

1. Sumner, *The Forgotten Man and Other Essays.*

2. See Shlaes (2007).

3. Marina, "Egalitarianism and Empire," emphasis added.

4. See Higgs [1987] (2012).

5. Mill, *Principles of Political Economy*, Book II "Distribution" Chapter I "Of Property."

6. de Jasay, *The Indian Rope Trick*, 16–17, 43–49.

7. Mill, *Principles of Political Economy*, 43.

8. See Sen (1980).

9. See Sen (1980), 203.

10. See Sen (1980), 218.

11. Hume, *A Treatise of Human Nature*, Book III, 489.

12. See also Horwitz (2015).

13. See Schmidtz (2006), 31.

Bibliography

Introduction, Whaples

Gans, Herbert J. "The Positive Functions of Poverty." *American Journal of Sociology* 78, no. 2 (1972): 275–89.

Lewis, C. S. "Screwtape Proposes a Toast." *Saturday Evening Post,* December 19, 1959.

McIntosh, Peggy. "White Privilege: Unpacking the Invisible Knapsack." National SEED Project, 1989. At http://nationalseedproject.org/images/documents/Knapsack_plus_Notes-Peggy_McIntosh.pdf.

Rescher, Nicholas. *Fairness: Theory and Practice of Distributive Justice.* New Brunswick, NJ: Transaction Publishers, 2002.

Peltzman, Sam. "Mortality Inequality." *Journal of Economic Perspectives* 23, no. 4 (2009): 175–90.

Sacks, Jonathan. *The Dignity of Difference: How to Avoid the Clash of Civilizations.* Rev. ed. London: Bloomsbury, 2003.

Thomas Aquinas. *Summa Theologiae, First Part.* n.d. At http://www.newadvent.org/summa/1044.htm and http://www.newadvent.org/summa/1047.htm#article2.

Chapter 1, Martin

Blum, Lawrence. "Racism: What It Is and What It Isn't." *Studies in Philosophy and Education* 21 (2002): 203–18.

Bohman, James. "Critical Theory." In *The Stanford Encyclopedia of Philosophy,* edited by Edward N. Zalta. Stanford, CA: Stanford University Press, 2016. At https://plato.stanford.edu/archives/fall2016/entries/critical-theory/.

Bonilla-Silva, Eduardo. *Racism without Racists: Color-Blind Racism and the Persistence of Racial Inequality in America.* Lanham, MD: Rowman and Littlefield, 2013.

Elster, Jon. "Hard and Soft Obscurantism in the Humanities and Social Sciences." *Diogenes* 58 (2011): 159–70.

Franke, Katherine. "Making White Supremacy Respectable Again." *Los Angeles Review of Books* (blog), November 21, 2016. At http://blog.lareviewofbooks.org/essays /making-white-supremacy-respectable/.

Frankfurt, Harry G. *On Bullshit*. Princeton, NJ: Princeton University Press, 2005.

Greenberg, Jon. "Curriculum for White Americans to Educate Themselves on Race and Racism." n.d. At http://citizenshipandsocialjustice.com/curriculum-for -white-americans-to-educate-themselves-on-race-and-racism/. Accessed December 7, 2016.

Haslanger, Sally, Nancy Tuana, and Peg O'Connor. "Topics in Feminism." In *The Stanford Encyclopedia of Philosophy,* edited by Edward N. Zalta. Stanford, CA: Stanford University Press, 2015. At https://plato.stanford.edu/archives/fall2015 /entries/feminism-topics/.

Hayek, F. A. *The Fatal Conceit: The Errors of Socialism*. Chicago: University of Chicago Press, 1988.

———. *The Mirage of Social Justice*. Vol. 2 of *Law, Legislation, and Liberty*. Chicago: University of Chicago Press, 1976.

———. *The Road to Serfdom*. Chicago: University of Chicago Press, 1944.

———. "Scientism and the Study of Society." In *Studies on the Abuse and Decline of Reason,* edited by Bruce Caldwell, 75–166. Chicago: University of Chicago Press, [1942–44] 2010.

Holmes, Kim. *The Closing of the Liberal Mind*. New York: Encounter Books, 2016.

Lilla, Mark. "The End of Identity Liberalism." *New York Times,* November 18, 2016. At http://www.nytimes.com/2016/11/20/opinion/sunday/the-end-of-identity -liberalism.html.

Marcuse, Herbert. "Repressive Tolerance." In *A Critique of Pure Tolerance,* edited by Robert Paul Wolff, 81–123. Boston: Beacon Press, 1965.

McIntosh, Peggy. "White Privilege: Unpacking the Invisible Knapsack." National SEED Project, 1989. At http://nationalseedproject.org/images/documents /Knapsack_plus_Notes-Peggy_McIntosh.pdf.

Nowrasteh, Alex. "The Right Has Its Own Version of Political Correctness. It's Just as Stifling." *Washington Post,* December 7, 2016. At https://www.washingtonpost .com/posteverything/wp/2016/12/07/the-right-has-its-own-version-of-political -correctness-its-just-as-stifling/?utm_term=.7850d2c81292.

Rizzo, Mario J. "The Problem of Moral Dirigisme: A New Argument against Moralistic Legislation." *New York University Journal of Law and Liberty* 1, no. 2 (2005): 781–835.

Scruton, Roger. *Fools, Frauds, and Firebrands: Thinkers of the New Left*. London: Bloomsbury, 2015.

Spivak, Gayatri Chakravorty. "Can the Subaltern Speak?" In *Marxism and the Interpretation of Culture,* edited by Cary Nelson and Lawrence Grossberg, 271–313. Urbana: University of Illinois Press, 1988.

Willett, Cynthia, Ellie Anderson, and Diana Meyers. "Feminist Perspectives on the Self." In *The Stanford Encyclopedia of Philosophy,* edited by Edward N. Zalta. Stanford, CA: Stanford University Press, 2016. At https://plato.stanford.edu/archives/win2016/entries/feminism-self/.

Chapter 2, Otteson

Anderson, Elizabeth S. "What Is the Point of Equality?" *Ethics* 109, no. 2 (1999): 287–337.

Arneson, Richard. "Egalitarian Justice versus the Right to Privacy." *Social Philosophy and Policy* 17, no. 2 (2000): 91–119.

———. "Luck Egalitarianism Interpreted and Defended." *Philosophical Topics* 32, nos. 1–2 (2004): 1–20.

———. "Rethinking Luck Egalitarianism and Unacceptable Inequalities." *Philosophical Topics* 40, no. 1 (2012): 153–69.

Barry, Nicholas. "Defending Luck Egalitarianism." *Journal of Applied Philosophy* 23, no. 1 (2006): 89–107.

Buchanan, James, and Gordon Tullock. *The Calculus of Consent: Logical Foundations of Constitutional Democracy.* Ann Arbor: University of Michigan Press, 1962.

Cohen, G. A. *Why Not Socialism?* Princeton, NJ: Princeton University Press, 2009.

Dworkin, Ronald. "What Is Equality? Part 2: Equality of Resources." *Philosophy and Public Affairs* 10, no. 4 (1981): 283–345.

Fleurbaey, Marc. "Equal Opportunity or Equal Social Outcome?" *Economics and Philosophy* 11 (1995): 25–55.

Frankfurt, Harry. "Equality as a Moral Ideal." *Ethics* 98, no. 1 (1987): 21–43.

Hayek, F. A. "The Use of Knowledge in Society." *American Economic Review* 35, no. 4 (1945): 519–30.

Knight, Carl. "Luck Egalitarianism." *Philosophy Compass* 8, no. 10 (2013): 924–34.

Nagel, Thomas. *Equality and Partiality.* New York: Oxford University Press, 1995.

Nussbaum, Martha. *Creating Capabilities: The Human Development Approach.* Cambridge, MA: Belknap Press of Harvard University Press, 2011.

Otteson, James R. *Actual Ethics.* Cambridge: Cambridge University Press, 2006.

———. "Adam Smith and the Great Mind Fallacy." *Social Philosophy and Policy* 27, no. 1 (2010): 276–304.

———. *The End of Socialism.* Cambridge: Cambridge University Press, 2014.

Piketty, Thomas. *Capital in the Twenty-First Century*. Cambridge, MA: Belknap Press of Harvard University Press, 2014.

Rakowski, Eric. *Equal Justice*. New York: Oxford Clarendon Press, 1991.

Sen, Amartya. *Inequality Reexamined*. Cambridge, MA: Harvard University Press, 1992.

Smith, Adam. *The Theory of Moral Sentiments*. Edited by D. D. Raphael and A. L. Macfie. Indianapolis, IN: Liberty Fund, [1759] 1976.

Vallentyne, Peter. "Brute Luck, Option Luck, and Equality of Initial Opportunities." *Ethics* 112, no. 3 (2002): 529–57.

Van Parijs, Philippe. "Why Surfers Should Be Fed: The Liberal Case for an Unconditional Basic Income." *Philosophy and Public Affairs* 20 (1991): 101–31.

Voigt, Kristin. "The Harshness Objection: Is Luck Egalitarianism Too Harsh on the Victims of Option Luck?" *Ethical Theory and Moral Practice* 10, no. 4 (2007): 389–407.

Wilson, Kristin, and Stan Veuger. "Information Frictions in Uncertain Regulatory Environments: Evidence from U.S. Commercial Banks." *Oxford Bulletin of Economics and Statistics* 79, no. 2 (2016): 205–33.

Chapter 3, Munger

Black, Henry C. *A Treatise on the Rescission of Contracts and Cancellation of Written Instruments*. Kansas City: Vernon Law Book, 1916.

Caldwell, Bruce. *Hayek on Socialism and on the Welfare State*. History of Political Economy Working Paper no. 2010-02. Durham, NC: Duke University, 2010.

Coase, Ronald H. "The Problem of Social Cost." *Journal of Law and Economics* 3 (1960): 1–44.

Flew, Antony. *Equality in Liberty and Justice*. Piscataway, NJ: Transaction, 2001.

Hayek, F. A. *The Mirage of Social Justice*. Vol. 2 of *Law, Legislation, and Liberty*. Chicago: University of Chicago Press, 1976.

———. *The Road to Serfdom: Texts and Documents*. Edited by Bruce Caldwell. Vol. 2 of *The Collected Works of F. A. Hayek*. Chicago: University of Chicago Press, [1944] 2007.

Hobbes, Thomas. *Leviathan*. Cambridge: Cambridge University Press, [1651] 1991.

Mill, John Stuart. *The Principles of Political Economy*. Amherst, NY: Prometheus Books, [1848] 2004.

Mises, Ludwig von. "Profit and Loss." In *Planning for Freedom*. South Holland, IL: Libertarian Press, 1952. At https://mises.org/library/profit-and-loss.

Munger, Michael C. "Euvoluntary or Not, Exchange Is Just." *Social Philosophy and Policy* 28, no. 2 (2011): 206–35.

Nozick, Robert. *Anarchy, State, and Utopia*. New York: Basic Books, 1974.

Radford, R. A. "The Economic Organisation of a P.O.W. Camp." *Economica*, New Series, 12, no. 48 (1945): 189–201.

Rawls, John. "Constitutional Liberty and the Concept of Justice." In *Nomos, VI: Justice,* edited by Carl J. Friedrich and John W. Chapman, 98–125. Yearbook of the American Society for Political and Legal Philosophy. New York: Atherton Press, 1963.

———. *A Theory of Justice*. Cambridge, MA: Belknap Press of Harvard University Press. 1971.

Wilkinson, Will. "More on Hayek–Rawls 'Fusionism.'" *Fly Bottle,* November 16, 2004. At http://www.willwilkinson.net/flybottle/2004/11/16/more-on-hayekrawls-fusionism/.

Chapter 5, Jackson and Palm

Alesina, Alberto, and Eliana La Ferrara. "Participation in Heterogeneous Communities." *Quarterly Journal of Economics* 115, no. 3 (2000): 847–904.

Anderson, Elizabeth. "Equality of Capabilities, or Equality of Outcomes." *Free Thoughts Podcast,* episode 28. Libertarianism.org, May 5, 2014. At https://www.libertarianism.org/media/free-thoughts-podcast/equality-capabilities-or-equality-outcomes.

———. "What Is the Point of Equality?" *Ethics* 109, no. 2 (1999): 287–337.

Arneson, Richard. "Luck Egalitarianism and Prioritarianism." *Ethics* 110, no. 2 (2000): 339–49.

Bartolini, Stefano, Ennio Bilancini, and Francesco Sarracino. "Social Capital Predicts Happiness over Time." In *Policies for Happiness,* edited by Stefano Bartolini, Ennio Bilancini, Pier L. Porta, and Luigino Bruni, 175–98. Oxford: Oxford University Press, 2016.

Becker, Gary S., and Nigel Tomes. "Human Capital and the Rise and Fall of Families." In *Human Capital: A Theoretical and Empirical Analysis with Special Reference to Education,* 3rd ed., 257–98. Chicago: University of Chicago Press, 1994.

Berggren, Niclas, and Henrik Jordahl. "Free to Trust: Economic Freedom and Social Capital." *Kyklos* 59, no. 2 (2006): 141–69.

Berggren, Niclas, and Therese Nilsson. "Does Economic Freedom Foster Tolerance?" *Kyklos* 66, no. 2 (2013): 177–207.

———. "Tolerance in the United States: Does Economic Freedom Transform Racial, Religious, Political, and Sexual Attitudes?" *European Journal of Political Economy* 45, no. 3 (2016): 53–70.

Bernanke, Ben. "The Economics of Happiness." Speech given at the University of South Carolina commencement ceremony, Columbia, May 8, 2010. At http://www.federalreserve.gov/newsevents/speech/bernanke20100508a.htm.

Blanchflower, David G., and Andrew J. Oswald. "Well-Being over Time in Britain and the USA." *Journal of Public Economics* 88, no. 7 (2004): 1359–86.

Borghans, Lex, Augela L. Duckworth, James J. Heckman, and Bas Ter Weel. "The Economics and Psychology of Personality Traits." *Journal of Human Resources* 43, no. 4 (2008): 972–1059.

Boxman, Ed A., Paul M. De Graaf, and Hendrik D. Flap. "The Impact of Social and Human Capital on the Income Attainment of Dutch Managers." *Social Networks* 13, no. 1 (1991): 51–73.

Caron, Paul L., and James R. Repetti. "Occupy the Tax Code: Using the Estate Tax to Reduce Inequality and Spur Economic Growth." *Pepperdine Law Review* 40 (2013): 1255–89.

Chamlee-Wright, Emily. "The Structure of Social Capital: An Austrian Perspective on Its Nature and Development." *Review of Political Economy* 20, no. 1 (2008): 41–58.

Chamlee-Wright, Emily, and Virgil Henry Storr. "Social Capital, Lobbying, and Community-Based Interest Groups." *Public Choice* 149, nos. 1–2 (2011): 167–85.

DeNeve, Kristina M., and Harris Cooper. "The Happy Personality: A Meta-analysis of 137 Personality Traits and Subjective Well-Being." *Psychological Bulletin* 125 (1999): 197–229.

Diener, Ed. "Subjective Well-Being: The Science of Happiness and a Proposal for a National Index." *American Psychologist* 55, no. 1 (2000): 34–43.

Diener, Ed, and Shigehiro Oishi. "Money and Happiness: Income and Subjective Well-Being across Nations." In *Culture and Subjective Well-Being,* edited by Ed Diener and Eunkook M. Suh, 185–218. Cambridge, MA: MIT Press, 2000.

Dolan, Paul, Tessa Peasgood, and Mathew White. "Do We Really Know What Makes Us Happy? A Review of the Economic Literature on the Factors Associated with Subjective Well-Being." *Journal of Economic Psychology* 29, no. 1 (2008): 94–122.

Easterlin, Richard A. "Does Economic Growth Improve the Human Lot? Some Empirical Evidence." *Nations and Households in Economic Growth* 89 (1974): 89–125.

Goff, Leonard, John F. Helliwell, and Guy Mayraz. *The Welfare Costs of Well-Being Inequality.* National Bureau of Economic Research (NBER) Working Paper no. w21900. Cambridge, MA: NBER, 2016.

Graham, Carol. "Adaptation amidst Prosperity and Adversity: Insights from Happiness Studies from around the World." *World Bank Research Observer* 26, no. 1 (2010): 105–37.

Gropper, Dennis M., Robert A. Lawson, and Jere T. Thorne. "Economic Freedom and Happiness." *Cato Journal* 31, no. 2 (2011): 237–55.

Guvenen, Fatih, Burhanettin Kuruscu, and Serdar Ozkan. "Taxation of Human Capital and Wage Inequality: A Cross-Country Analysis." *Review of Economic Studies* 82, no. 2 (2013): 818–50.

Hayek, F. A. *The Mirage of Social Justice*. Vol. 2 of *Law, Legislation, and Liberty*. New York: Routledge, 1998.

Heckman, James J. "Policies to Foster Human Capital." *Research in Economics* 54, no. 1 (2000): 3–56.

Helliwell, John F., and Robert D. Putnam. "The Social Context of Well-Being." *Philosophical Transactions of the Royal Society of London, Series B, Biological Sciences* 359 (2004): 1435–46.

Jackson, Jeremy. "Economic Freedom and Social Capital: Pooled Mean Group Evidence." *Applied Economics Letters* 24, no. 6 (2017): 370–73.

———. "Free to Be Happy: Economic Freedom and Happiness in US States." *Journal of Happiness Studies*, 2016. Currently available online only. doi:10.1007/s10902-016-9770-9.

Jackson, Jeremy J., Art Carden, and Ryan A. Compton. "Economic Freedom and Social Capital." *Applied Economics* 47, no. 54 (2015): 5853–67.

Jackson, Jeremy J., Ryan A. Compton, and Aka Kyaw Min Maw. "Does Economic Freedom Create Social Capital in US States?" Unpublished manuscript, last modified 2016.

Kasser, Tim. *The High Price of Materialism*. Cambridge, MA: MIT Press, 2003.

Kawachi, Ichiro, Bruce P. Kennedy, Kimberly Lochner, and Deborah Prothrow-Stith. "Social Capital, Income Inequality, and Mortality." *American Journal of Public Health* 87, no. 9 (1997): 1491–98.

Kelley, David. "Altruism and Social Justice." *Forum for Classical Liberals* (podcast). University of Aix-en-Province, 1991. At https://www.libertarianism.org/media/video-collection/david-kelley-egalitarianism-welfare-rights-theory.

———. "The Fourth Revolution." *The Atlas Society* (blog), May 1, 2009. At http://atlassociety.org/commentary/capitalism-and-morality/capitalism-morality-blog/3774-the-fourth-revolution.

Knack, Stephen, and Philip Keefer. "Does Social Capital Have an Economic Payoff? A Cross-Country Investigation." *Quarterly Journal of Economics* 112, no. 4 (1997): 1251–88.

Mueller, Anthony P. "Bye-Bye Bismarck." *Mises Daily,* July 24, 2003. At https://mises.org/library/bye-bye-bismarck.

Narayan, Deepa, and Lant Pritchett. "Cents and Sociability: Household Income and Social Capital in Rural Tanzania." *Economic Development and Cultural Change* 47, no. 4 (1999): 871–97.

Nikolaev, Boris. "Economic Freedom and Quality of Life: Evidence from the OECD's Your Better Life Index." *Journal of Private Enterprise* 29, no. 3 (2014): 61–96.

North, Douglass C. *Institutions, Institutional Change, and Economic Performance.* Cambridge: Cambridge University Press, 1990.

Olson, Mancur. *The Rise and Decline of Nations: The Political Economy of Economic Growth, Stagflation, and Social Rigidities.* New Haven, CT: Yale University Press, 1982.

Piketty, Thomas. *Capital in the Twenty-First Century.* Cambridge, MA: Harvard University Press, 2014.

Portes, Alejandro. "Downsides of Social Capital." *Proceedings of the National Academy of Sciences* 111, no. 52 (2014): 18407–8.

Putnam, Robert D. "Bowling Alone: America's Declining Social Capital." *Journal of Democracy* 6, no. 1 (1995): 65–78.

———. *Bowling Alone: The Collapse and Revival of American Community.* New York: Simon and Schuster, 2001.

Rawls, John. *A Theory of Justice.* Cambridge, MA: Belknap Press of Harvard University Press, 1971.

Rockwell, Lew. "The Menace of Egalitarianism." Talk delivered at *Mises Circle, against P.C.,* Dallas–Fort Worth, Texas, October 3, 2015. At https://mises.org/library/menace-egalitarianism.

Roosevelt, Franklin D. State of the Union Message. American Presidency Project, University of California at Santa Barbara, January 11, 1944. At http://www.presidency.ucsb.edu/ws/?pid=16518.

Rothbard, Murray. "Egalitarianism and the Elites." *Review of Austrian Economics* 8, no. 2 (1995): 39–57.

Ryan, Richard M., and Edward L. Deci. "Self-Determination Theory and the Facilitation of Intrinsic Motivation, Social Development, and Well-Being." *American Psychologist* 55, no. 1 (2000): 68–78.

Sowell, Thomas. *Black Rednecks and White Liberals.* San Francisco: Encounter Books, 2005.

Stutzer, Alois. "The Role of Income Aspirations in Individual Happiness." *Journal of Economic Behavior and Organization* 54, no. 1 (2004): 89–109.

Veenhoven, Ruut. "Freedom and Happiness: A Comparative Study in Forty-Four Nations in the Early 1990s." In *Culture and Subjective Well-Being,* edited by Ed Diener and Eunkook M. Suh, 257–88. Cambridge, MA: MIT Press, 2000.

Verme, Paolo. "Happiness, Freedom, and Control." *Journal of Economic Behavior and Organization* 71, no. 2 (2009): 146–61.

The Welfare State. UK National Archives, document study with links to archived material. 2016. At http://www.nationalarchives.gov.uk/pathways/citizenship/brave_new_world/welfare.htm.

Welsch, Heinz. "Environment and Happiness: Valuation of Air Pollution Using Life Satisfaction Data." *Ecological Economics* 58, no. 4 (2006): 801–13.

Wenar, Leif. "John Rawls." In *The Stanford Encyclopedia of Philosophy,* edited by Edward N. Zalta. Stanford, CA: Stanford University Press, 2012. At https://plato.stanford.edu/entries/rawls/#BasStrSocIns.

Williams, Walter. *Race and Economics: How Much Can Be Blamed on Discrimination?* Stanford, CA: Hoover Institution Press, 2011.

Chapter 6, Hill

Acemoglu, Daron, and James A. Robinson. *Why Nations Fail: The Origins of Power, Prosperity, and Poverty.* New York: Crown, 2012.

Aristotle. *Politics.* Translated by Ernest Barker. Oxford: Oxford University Press, 1946.

Berkowitz, Peter. *Virtue and the Making of Modern Liberalism.* Princeton, NJ: Princeton University Press, 1999.

Berman, Joshua A. *Created Equal: How the Bible Broke with Ancient Political Thought.* Oxford: Oxford University Press, 2008.

Epstein, Richard. *Simple Rules for a Complex World.* Cambridge, MA: Harvard University Press, 1995.

Ferry, Luc. *A Brief History of Thought: A Philosophical Guide to Living.* New York: HarperCollins, 2011.

Forster, Greg. *The Contested Public Square: The Crisis of Christianity and Politics.* Downers Grove, IL: InterVarsity Press, 2008.

Grynaviski, Jeffrey D., and Michael C. Munger. "Reconstructing Racism: Transforming Racial Hierarchy from Necessary Evil into Positive Good." *Social Philosophy and Policy* 34, no. 1 (2017): 144–63.

Hobbes, Thomas. *Leviathan.* New York: Collier Books, [1651] 1962.

Locke, John. *Two Treatises of Government.* Cambridge: Cambridge University Press, [1689] 1960.

Machan, Tibor. *Individuals and Their Rights.* La Salle, IL: Open Court, 1989.

Madigan, Kevin. *Medieval Christianity: A New History.* New Haven, CT: Yale University Press, 2015.

McCloskey, Deirdre N. *Bourgeois Equality: How Ideas, Not Capital or Institutions, Enriched the World*. Chicago: University of Chicago Press, 2016.

Mokyr, Joel. *A Culture of Growth: The Origins of the Modern Economy*. Princeton, NJ: Princeton University Press, 2017.

Montesquieu. *The Spirit of the Laws*. Translated and edited by Anne M. Cohler, Basia Carolyn Miller, and Harold Samuel Stone. Cambridge: Cambridge University Press, [1748] 1989.

Nozick, Robert. *Anarchy, State, and Utopia*. New York: Basic Books, 1974.

Rasmussen, Douglas, and Douglas Den Uyl. *Liberalism Defended: The Challenge of Post-Modernity*. Northhampton, MA: Edward Elgar, 1997.

Rodrik, Dani. "When Ideas Trump Interests: Preferences, Worldviews, and Policy Innovations." *Journal of Economic Perspectives* 28, no. 1 (2014): 189–208.

Siedentop, Larry. *Inventing the Individual: The Origins of Western Liberalism*. London: Penguin, 2014.

Sowell, Thomas. *Black Rednecks and White Liberals*. San Francisco: Encounter Books, 2005.

Tierney, Brian. *The Idea of Natural Rights*. Grand Rapids, MI: Eerdmans, 1997.

Witte, John, Jr. *God's Joust, God's Justice: Law and Religion in the Western Tradition*. Grand Rapids, MI: Eerdmans, 2006.

———. *The Reformation of Rights*. Cambridge: Cambridge University Press, 2007.

Chapter 7, Morgan

Agamben, Giorgio. *State of Exception*. Chicago: University of Chicago Press, 2005.

Andrew, Anita M., and John A. Rapp. *Autocracy and China's Rebel Founding Emperors: Comparing Chairman Mao and Ming Taizu*. Edited by Anita M. Andrew and John A. Rapp. Lanham, MD: Rowan & Littlefield Publishers, 2000.

Aquinas, Thomas. *Summa Theologiæ*. 1485.

Berle, Adolf A., and Gardiner C. Means. *The Modern Corporation and Private Property*. New York: Macmillan, 1932.

Burnham, James. *The Managerial Revolution: What Is Happening in the World*. New York: John Day Company, 1941.

Foucault, Michel. *Discipline and Punish: The Birth of the Prison*. Translated by Alan Sheridan. New York: Pantheon Books, 1977.

Francis, Samuel T. *Power and History: The Political Thought of James Burnham*. Lanham, MD: University Press of America, 1984.

Herodotus. *The Histories*. Translated by Robin Waterfield. Oxford: Oxford University Press, 1998.

Hoppe, Hans-Hermann. *Democracy: The God That Failed*. Rutgers, NJ: Transaction Publishers, 2001.

Leigh, Catesby. "Natural Right and Art History." *Claremont Review of Books* 14, no. 3 (2014): 92–95.

Lovejoy, Arthur O. *The Great Chain of Being: A Study of the History of an Idea*. Cambridge, MA: Harvard University Press, 1933.

Maistre, Joseph Marie, comte de. *Considérations Sur La France*. 2nd ed. revue par l'auteur. Mars, Londres, 1797.

McInerny, Ralph. *Aquinas on Human Action: A Theory of Practice*. Washington, DC: Catholic University of America Press, 2012.

Mises, Ludwig von. *Epistemological Problems of Economics*. Translated by George Reisman. New York: D. Van Nostrand Company, 1960.

———. *Human Action: A Treatise on Economics*. New Haven, CT: Yale University Press, 1949.

Schmitt, Carl. *Political Theology: Four Chapters on the Concept of Sovereignty*. Translated by George D. Schwab. Chicago: University of Chicago Press, 2006.

Sowell, Thomas. *The Thomas Sowell Reader*. New York: Basic Books, 2011.

Voegelin, Eric. *The New Science of Politics: An Introduction*. Chicago: University of Chicago Press, 1952.

Wright, Darryl. "'A Human Society': Rand's Social Philosophy." In *A Companion to Ayn Rand*, edited by Allan Gotthelf and Gregory Salmieri. 1st ed. Hoboken, NJ: Wiley-Blackwell, 2016.

Chapter 8, Harrigan and Yonk

Adams, John. Novangelus Letter: John Adams to the Inhabitants of the Colony of Massachusetts-Bay. February 1775. At https://www.masshist.org/publications/apde2/view?&id=PJA02dg5.

Hamilton, Alexander. *Federalist* No. 23. In *The Federalist Papers*, edited by George W. Carey and James McClellan, 112. Indianapolis, IN: Liberty Fund, [1787] 2001.

Historical Debt Outstanding—Annual. 2015. TreasuryDirect. At https://www.treasurydirect.gov/govt/reports/pd/histdebt/histdebt.htm.

Ho Chi Minh. Declaration of Independence, Democratic Republic of Vietnam. September, 1945. At https://www.unc.edu/courses/2009fall/hist/140/006/Documents/VietnameseDocs.pdf.

Jefferson, Thomas. "The Declaration of Independence," *Historic American Documents*, Lit2Go Edition, (1776), accessed October 12, 2018, http://etc.usf.edu/lit2go/133/historic-american-documents/4957/the-declaration-of-independence/.

Johnston, Louis, and Samuel H. Williamson. "What Was the U.S. GDP Then?" MeasuringWorth, 2017. At https://www.measuringworth.com/datasets/usgdp/.

Maier, Pauline. *American Scripture: Making the Declaration of Independence*. New York: Knopf. Massachusetts Constitution, [1780] 1997. At http://press-pubs.uchicago.edu/founders/print_documents/v1ch1s6.html.

Office of Personnel Management. Historical Federal Workforce Tables: Total Government Employment since 1962. Data, Analysis, & Documentation, Federal Employment Reports. (n.d.) At https://www.opm.gov/policy-data-oversight/data-analysis-documentation/federal-employment-reports/historical-tables/total-government-employment-since-1962/. Accessed December 16, 2016.

Paine, Thomas. *Common Sense*. [1776] At https://www.gutenberg.org/files/147/147-h/147-h.htm. Accessed March 12, 2017.

Roosevelt, Franklin D. State of the Union Address. January 11, 1944. At http://www.fdrlibrary.marist.edu/archives/stateoftheunion.html.

Rozin, Orit. "Comments on Yoram Shachar, 'Jefferson Goes East: The American Origins of the Israeli Declaration of Independence.'" *Theoretical Inquiries in Law* 10, no. 2 (2009): 54–57.

Rudoren, Jodi. "What's Hebrew for 'When in the Course of Human Events'?" *New York Times,* September 16, 2016. At http://www.nytimes.com/2016/09/16/world/what-in-the-world/israel-mordechai-beham-founding-document.html.

Shachar, Yoram. "Jefferson Goes East: The American Origins of the Israeli Declaration of Independence." *Theoretical Inquiries in Law* 10, no. 2 (2009): 589–618.

US Bureau of the Census. *Historical Statistics of the United States, 1789–1945*. Washington, DC: US Department of Commerce, 1949. At http://www2.census.gov/prod2/statcomp/documents/HistoricalStatisticsoftheUnitedStates1789-1945.pdf.

US Department of Agriculture. USDA–Farm Service Agency ARC/PLC Program Landing Page. (n.d.) At https://www.fsa.usda.gov/programs-and-services/arcplc_program/. Accessed December 16, 2016.

US Office of Management and Budget. "Fiscal Year 2017." In *Historical Tables, Budget of the United States Government*. Washington, DC: US Government Publishing Office, February 9, 2016. At https://fraser.stlouisfed.org/scribd/?item_id=522154&filepath=/files/docs/publications/usbhist/BUDGET-2017-TAB.pdf.

Chapter 9, Watkins Jr.

Black, Hugo LaFayette. *A Constitutional Faith*. New York: Alfred A. Knopf, 1968.

Coke, Sir Edward. *The Selected Writings of Sir Edward Coke*. Edited by Steve Sheppard. Vol 2. Indianapolis, IN: Liberty Fund, [1642] 2003.

Cox, Archibald. "The Supreme Court, 1965 Term—Foreword: Constitutional Adjudication and the Promotion of Human Rights." *Harvard Law Review* 80 (1966): 91–121.

Dietze, Gottfried. "Hayek on the Rule of Law." In *Essays on Hayek*, edited by Fritz Machlup, 107–46. Hillsdale, MI: Hillsdale College Press, 1976.

Fletcher, George P. "In God's Image: The Religious Imperative of Equality under Law." *Columbia Law Review* 99 (1999): 1608–1629.

Hamilton, Alexander. *The Papers of Alexander Hamilton*. Edited by Harold C. Syrett & Jacob E. Cooke. Vol. 4. New York: Columbia University Press, [1787] 1962.

Hayek, F. A. *The Constitution of Liberty*. Chicago: University of Chicago Press, 1960.

Holt, J. C. *Magna Carta*. Cambridge: Cambridge University Press, [1215] 1992.

Jefferson, Thomas. *The Complete Jefferson*. Edited by Saul K. Padover. New York: Duell, Sloan and Pearce, Inc., 1943.

Mayer, David N. "Liberty of Contract: Rediscovering a Lost Constitutional Right." Washington, DC: The Cato Institute, 2011.

Optiz, Edmund A. *Religion: Foundation of the Free Society*. New York: The Foundation for Economic Education, Inc., 1944.

Rose, Henry. "The Poor as a Suspect Class under the Equal Protection Clause: An Open Constitutional Question." *Nova Law Review* 34 (2010): 407–421.

Strauss, David A. "The Illusory Distinction between Equality of Opportunity and Equality of Result." *William & Mary Law Review* 34 (1992): 171–188.

Tucker, St. George. *View of the Constitution of the United States: With Selected Writings*. Forward by Clyde N. Wilson. Indianapolis, IN: Liberty Fund, [1803] 1999.

Tucker, St. George, William Blackstone, and Edward Christian. *Blackstone's Commentaries: In Five Volumes: With Notes of Reference to the Constitution and Laws, of the Federal Government of the United States, and of the Commonwealth of Virginia: With an Appendix to Each Volume, Containing Short Tracts upon Such Subjects as Appeared Necessary to Form a Connected View of the Laws of Virginia as a Member of the Federal Union*. Union, NJ: Lawbook Exchange, [1803] 1999.

Watson, Jennifer E. "When No Place is Home: Why the Homeless Deserve Suspect Classification." *Iowa Law Review* 88 (n.d.): 501–537.

West, Robin. "Is Progressive Constitutionalism Possible?" *Widener Law Symposium. Journal* 4 (1999): 3–18.

Chapter 10, Shmanske

Debreu, Gerard. *Theory of Value: An Axiomatic Analysis of Economic Equilibrium*. New York: Wiley. Reprint. New Haven, CT: Yale University Press, [1959] 1971.

Hayek, F. A. *The Fatal Conceit: The Errors of Socialism*. Chicago: The University of Chicago Press, 1991.

———. "The Use of Knowledge in Society." *The American Economic Review* 35, no. 4. (Sep., 1945): 519–530.

Marshall, Alfred. *Principles of Economics*. 8th ed. London: Macmillan and Co. Ltd., [1890] 1920.

Orwell, George. *Animal Farm: A Fairy Story*. London: Secker and Warburg, 1945.

O'Toole, Randal. *The Vanishing Automobile and Other Urban Myths: How Smart Growth Will Harm American Cities*. Bandon, OR: The Thoreau Institute, 2001.

Pareto, Vilfredo. *Manual of Political Economy*. Edited by Aldo Montesano, Alberto Zanni, Luigino Bruni, John S. Chipman, and Michael McLure. London: Oxford University Press, [1906] 2014.

Robbins, Lionel. *An Essay on the Nature and Significance of Economic Science*. London: Macmillan, 1932.

Shmanske, Stephen. *Super Golfonomics*. Hackensack, NJ: World Scientific Publishing Co., 2015.

Smith, Adam. *An Inquiry into the Nature and Causes of the Wealth of Nations*. 2 vols. 5th ed. Edited by Edwin Cannan. London: Methuen, [1776] 1904.

Chapter 11, Wright

Abrams, Charles. *Forbidden Neighbors: A Study of Prejudice in Housing*. New York: Harper & Brothers, 1955.

Anderson, Elisabeth. "Experts, Ideas, and Policy Change: The Russell Sage Foundation and Small Loan Reform, 1909–1941." *Theory and Society* 37, no. 3 (June 2008): 271–89.

Antilla, Susan. *Tales from the Boom-Boom Room: The Landmark Legal Battles that Exposed Wall Street's Shocking Culture of Sexual Harassment*. New York: Harper-Business, 2003.

A Reformed Stock Gambler. *Stocks and Stock-Jobbing in Wall-Street, with Sketches of the Brokers, and Fancy Stocks*. New York: New York Publishing Company, 1848.

Avery, Robert B., Patricia E. Beeson, and Mark S. Sniderman. "Accounting for Racial Differences in Housing Credit Markets." Federal Reserve Bank of Cleveland Working Paper 9310, 1993.

———. "Cross-Lender Variation in Home Mortgage Lending." Federal Reserve Bank of Cleveland Working Paper 9219, 1992.

———. "Underserved Mortgage Markets: Evidence from HMDA Data." Federal Reserve Bank of Cleveland Working Paper 9421, 1994.

Baker, George and George D. Smith. *The New Financial Capitalists: Kohlberg Kravis Roberts and the Creation of Corporate Value.* New York: Cambridge University Press, 1998.

Barry, Arthur. Papers. Regular Board Meeting, September 12, 1951. Special Collections, Rush Rhees Library, University of Rochester, Rochester, NY.

Beveridge, Andrew. "Local Lending Practice: Borrowers in a Small Northeastern City, 1832–1915." *Journal of Economic History* 45, no. 2 (June 1985): 393–403.

Black, Hillel. *Buy Now, Pay Later.* New York: William Morrow and Company, 1961.

Bubolz, Gordon. *Farmers Mutual Windstorm Insurance Companies.* Washington, DC: Farm Credit Administration, Bulletin no. 21 (1938).

Calder, Lendol. *Financing the American Dream: A Cultural History of Consumer Credit.* Princeton, NJ: Princeton University Press, 1999.

Caplan, Sheri J. *Petticoats and Pinstripes: Portraits of Women in Wall Street's History.* Denver, CO: Praeger, 2013.

Cropp, Matthew. "The Origins of US Credit Unions." *Financial History* (Spring 2014): 24–27.

Curry, Leonard P. *The Free Black in Urban America, 1800–1850: The Shadow of the Dream.* Chicago: University of Chicago Press, 1981.

Dahl, A. E. *Banker Dahl of South Dakota: An Autobiography.* Rapid City, SD: Fenske Book Company, 1965.

Davis, Malvin. *Industrial Life Insurance in the United States.* New York: McGraw Hill, 1944.

Dawson, Miles. "Fraternal Life Insurance." *Annals of the American Academy of Political and Social Science* 26 (September 1905): 128–36.

DeYoung, Robert and William C. Hunter. "Deregulation, the Internet, and the Competitive Viability of Large Banks and Community Banks." In Benton Gup, ed. *The Future of Banking.* Westport, CT: Quorum Books, 2003.

Dickerson, Mechele. *Homeownership and America's Financial Underclass: Flawed Premises, Broken Promises, New Prescriptions.* New York: Cambridge University Press, 2014.

Embree, Edwin. *Brown Americans: The Story of a Tenth of the Nation.* New York: Viking Press, 1943.

Ensign, Rachel, Paul Overberg, and Annamaria Andriotis. "Jumbo Loans Benefit Few Blacks, Hispanics." *Wall Street Journal,* June 2, 2016, A1, A10.

Fisher, Anne B. *Wall Street Women.* New York: Alfred A. Knopf, 1990.

Fisher, Melissa S. *Wall Street Women.* Durham, NC: Duke University Press, 2012.

Frederiksen, D. M. "Mortgage Banking in America." *Journal of Political Economy* 2, no. 2 (March 1894): 203–34.

Graham, Loftin and Xiaoying Xie. "The United States Insurance Market: Characteristics and Trends." In J. David Cummins and Bertrand Venard, eds. *Handbook of International Insurance: Between Global Dynamics and Local Contingencies.* New York: Springer, 2007.

Gunther, John. *Inside U.S.A.* New York: Harper Brothers, 1947.

Hetzel, Robert. *The Great Recession: Market Failure or Policy Failure?* New York: Cambridge University Press, 2012.

Hochfelder, David. "'Where the Common People Could Speculate': The Ticker, Bucket Shops, and the Origin of Popular Participation in Financial Markets, 1880–1920." *Journal of American History* 93, no. 2 (September 2006): 335–58.

Hyman, Louis. *Debtor Nation: The History of America in Red Ink.* Princeton, NJ: Princeton University Press, 2011.

James, Marquis. *The Metropolitan Life: A Study in Business Growth.* New York: Viking, 1947.

Jones, Jacqueline. *A Dreadful Deceit: The Myth of Race from the Colonial Era to Obama's America.* New York: Basic Books, 2013.

Krooss, Herman E. and Martin R. Blyn. *A History of Financial Intermediaries.* New York: Random House, 1971.

Lajoux, Alexandra and Dennis J. Roberts. *The Art of Bank M&A: Buying, Selling, Merging, and Investing in Regulated Depository Institutions in the New Environment.* New York: McGraw Hill, 2014.

Lehrman, William. "Diversity in Decline: Institutional Environment and Organizational Failure in the American Life Insurance Industry." *Social Forces* 73, no. 2 (1994): 605–35.

Liebowitz, Stan J. "Anatomy of a Train Wreck: Causes of the Mortgage Meltdown." In Randall Holcombe and Benjamin Powell, eds. *Housing America: Building Out of a Crisis.* New Brunswick, NJ: Transaction Publishers for the Independent Institute, 2008.

Linden, Alexandre, Stefan Bund, John Schiavetta, Jill Zelter, and Rachel Hardee. "First Generation CDPO: Case Study on Performance and Ratings." Working Paper, 2007.

Mainelli, Michael and Chiara von Gunten. *Chain of a Lifetime: How Blockchain Technology Might Transform Personal Insurance.* Z/Yen Group, 2014.

Mihm, Stephen. "Dr. Doom." *New York Times Magazine,* August 15, 2008.

Moore, W. F. "Liability Insurance." *Annals of the American Academy of Political and Social Science* 26 (1905): 319–39.

Murphy, Sharon. *Investing in Life: Insurance in Antebellum America.* Baltimore: Johns Hopkins University Press, 2010.

Norberg, Johan. *Financial Fiasco: How America's Infatuation with Homeownership and Easy Money Created the Economic Crisis.* Washington, DC: Cato Institute, 2009.

Norman, Michael. "Wilma Porter Soss, 86, A Gadfly at Stock Meetings of Companies." *New York Times,* October 16, 1986.

Oates, James. *Business and Social Change: Life Insurance Looks to the Future.* New York: McGraw-Hill Book Company, 1968.

Olegario, Rowena. *The Engine of Enterprise: Credit in America.* Cambridge, MA: Harvard University Press, 2016.

Oviatt, F. C. "Historical Study of Fire Insurance in the United States." *Annals of the Academy of Political and Social Science* 26 (1905): 155–78.

Pak, Susie. *Gentlemen Bankers: The World of J. P. Morgan.* Cambridge, MA: Harvard University Press, 2013.

Pettigrew, Thomas. "White-Negro Confrontations." In Eli Ginzberg, ed. *The Negro Challenge to the Business Community.* New York: McGraw-Hill Book Company, 1964.

Pierce, John. *Development of Comprehensive Insurance for the Household.* Homewood, IL: Richard D. Irwin, 1958.

Rapone, Anita. *The Guardian Life Insurance Company of America, 1860–1920: A History of a German-American Enterprise.* New York: New York University Press, 1987.

Rock, Howard. *Artisans of the New Republic: The Tradesman of New York City in the Age of Jefferson.* New York: New York University Press, 1984.

Rose, Arnold. *The Negro in America: The Condensed Version of Gunnar Myrdal's 'An American Dilemma.'* New York: Harper & Row, 1948.

Ross, Stephen L. and John Yinger. *The Color of Credit: Mortgage Discrimination, Research Methodology, and Fair-Lending Enforcement.* Cambridge, MA: MIT Press, 2002.

Snowden, Kenneth. "Mortgage Rates and American Capital Market Development in the Late Nineteenth Century." *Journal of Economic History* 47, no. 3 (September 1987): 671–91.

Sparks, Edith. *Capital Intentions: Female Proprietors in San Francisco, 1850–1920.* Chapel Hill: University of North Carolina Press, 2006.

Spiegel, John, Alan Gart, and Steven Gart. *Banking Redefined: How Superregional Powerhouses Are Reshaping Financial Services.* Chicago: Irwin Professional Publishing, 1996.

Starr, Paul. "Why Liberalism Works." *American Prospect* (April 2007): 34–40.

Tomasi, John. *Free Market Fairness.* Princeton, NJ: Princeton University Press, 2012.

US Treasury Department Study Team. *Credit and Capital Formation: A Report to the President's Interagency Task Force on Women Business Owners.* Washington, DC: GPO, 1978.

Valgren, Victor. *Farmers' Mutual Fire Insurance in the United States.* Chicago: University of Chicago Press, 1924.

Wagmiller, Robert. *Debt and Assets Among Low-Income Families.* National Center for Children in Poverty, 2003.

Weller, Christian E. *Pushing the Limit: Credit Card Debt Burdens American Families.* Washington, DC: Center for American Progress, 2006.

Wermiel, Sara E. *The Fireproof Building: Technology and Public Safety in the Nineteenth-Century American City.* Baltimore: Johns Hopkins University Press, 2000.

White, Eugene. "Lessons from the Great American Real Estate Boom and Bust of the 1920s." National Bureau of Economic Research Working Paper 15573, 2009.

Wright, Robert E. "Banking and Politics in New York, 1784–1829." PhD. diss., SUNY Buffalo, New York, 1997.

———. *Corporation Nation.* Philadelphia: University of Pennsylvania Press, 2014.

———. *The First Wall Street: Chestnut Street, Philadelphia, and the Birth of American Finance.* Chicago: University of Chicago Press, 2005.

———. "Thinking Beyond the Public Company." *McKinsey Quarterly*, September 2010.

Wright, Robert E. and Richard Sylla. *Genealogy of American Finance.* New York: Columbia University Press, 2015.

Yenawine, Bruce. *Benjamin Franklin and the Invention of Microfinance.* New York: Routledge, 2010.

Zanjani, George. "The Rise and Fall of the Fraternal Life Insurer: Law and Finance in U.S. Life Insurance, 1870-1920." Working Paper, 2003.

Chapter 12, Carden, Estelle, and Bradley

Cosgel, Metin M., and Bogac A. Ergene. "Inequality of Wealth in the Ottoman Empire: War, Weather, and Long-Term Trends in Eighteenth-Century Kastamonu." *Journal of Economic History* 72, no. 2 (2012): 308–31.

Deaton, Angus. *The Great Escape: Health, Wealth, and the Origins of Inequality.* Princeton, NJ: Princeton University Press, 2013.

Di Matteo, Livio. "All Equal in the Sight of God: Economic Inequality and Religion in the Early Twentieth Century." *European Review of Economic History* 20, no. 1 (2016): 23–45.

Frankfurt, Harry. "The Moral Irrelevance of Equality." *Public Affairs Quarterly* 14, no. 2 (2000): 87–103.

Gerencer, Tom. "10 Most Expensive Whiskies in the World." *MoneyNation*, March 16, 2016. At http://moneynation.com/most-expensive-whiskey/.

Hayek, F. A. *The Constitution of Liberty*. Chicago: University of Chicago Press, 1960.

Henderson, David R., Robert M. McNab, and Tamas Rozsas. "The Hidden Inequality in Socialism." *The Independent Review* 9, no. 3 (Winter 2005): 389–412.

McCloskey, Deirdre N. *Bourgeois Dignity: Why Economics Can't Explain the Modern World*. Chicago: University of Chicago Press, 2010.

———. *Bourgeois Equality: How Ideas, Not Capital or Institutions, Changed the World*. Chicago: University of Chicago Press, 2016.

———. *The Bourgeois Virtues: Ethics for an Age of Commerce*. Chicago: University of Chicago Press, 2006.

Molitoris, Joseph, and Martin Dribe. "Industrialization and Inequality Revisited: Mortality Differentials and Vulnerability to Economic Stress in Stockholm, 1878–1926." *European Review of Economic History* 20, no. 2 (2016): 176–97.

Nicolini, Esteban A., and Fernando Ramos Palencia. "Decomposing Income Inequality in a Backward Pre-industrial Economy: Old Castile (Spain) in the Middle of the Eighteenth Century." *Economic History Review* 69, no. 3 (2016): 747–72.

Nye, John V. C. "Economic Growth. Part I. Economic Growth and True Inequality." *Library of Economics and Liberty*, January 28, 2002a. At http://www.econlib.org/library/Columns/Nyegrowth.html.

———. "Economic Growth. Part II. Irreducible Inequality," *Library of Economics and Liberty*, April 1, 2002b. At http://www.econlib.org/library/Columns/Nyepositional.html.

Pinkovskiy, Maxim, and Xavier Sala-i-Martin. "Parametric Estimations of the World Distribution of Income." *National Bureau of Economic Research* (NBER) Working Paper no. 15433. Cambridge, MA: NBER, 2009.

Ryckbosch, Wouter. "Economic Inequality and Growth before the Industrial Revolution: The Case of the Low Countries (Fourteenth to Nineteenth Centuries)." *European Review of Economic History* 20, no. 1 (2016): 1–22.

Schumpeter, Joseph. *Capitalism, Socialism, and Democracy*. Milton Park, UK: Taylor and Francis, [1942] 2003.

Smith, Adam. *An Inquiry into the Nature and Causes of the Wealth of Nations*. Indianapolis, IN: Liberty Fund, [1776] 1981.

Chapter 13, Wenzel

Bastiat, Frédéric. *Economic Sophisms*. Indianapolis, IN: Liberty Fund, [1845] 1996.

———. *The Law*. New York: Tribeca Books, [1850] 2012.

———. *What Is Seen and What Is Not Seen*. Indianapolis, IN: Liberty Fund, [1848a] 1995.

———. "Luxury and Thrift." In *What Is See and What Is Not Seen*. Indianapolis, IN: Liberty Fund, [1848b] 1995.

Bauer, Peter. *Equality, the Third World and Economic Delusion*. Cambridge, MA: Harvard University Press, 1981.

Baumol, William. "Entrepreneurship: Productive, Unproductive, and Destructive." *Journal of Political Economy* 98, no. 5 (1990): Part 1, 893–921.

Beito, David. *From Mutual Aid to the Welfare State: Fraternal Societies and Social Services, 1890–1967*. Chapel Hill: University of North Carolina Press, 2000.

Buchanan, James and Gordon Tullock. *The Calculus of Consent*. Ann Arbor: University of Michigan Press, 1962.

Callahan, Gene. "Fantasy is Not an Adult Policy Option." *The Freeman online*, February 24, 2010, at http://fee.org/freeman/fantasy-is-not-an-adult-policy-option.

Caplan, Bryan. "The Idea Trap: The Political Economy of Growth Divergence." *European Journal of Political Economy* 19 (2003): 183–203.

Carroll, Christopher, Jiri Slacalek and Kiichi Tukuoka. "The Distribution of Wealth and the MPC: Implications of New European Data." European Central Bank Working Paper Series no.1648, 2014.

Crews, Clyde Wayne. "Ten Thousand Commandments 2016: An Annual Snapshot of the Federal Regulatory State." Washington, DC: Competitive Enterprise Institute, 2016. At https://cei.org/10KC2016.

DeBow, Michael. "The Ethics of Rent-Seeking? A New Perspective on Corporate Social Responsibility." *Journal of Law and Commerce* 12, no. 1 (1992): 1–21.

Gwartney, James, Richard Stroup, Russell Sobel and David Macpherson. *Economics: Private and Public Choice*. 11th ed. Boston: Cengage Learning, 2005.

Hayek, F. A. *The Constitution of Liberty*. Chicago: University of Chicago Press, 1960.

———. *Law, Legislation and Liberty*. Volume 2, Chicago: University of Chicago Press, 1976.

———. "The Use of Knowledge in Society." *American Economic Review* 35, no. 4 (1945): 519–530.

Hazlitt, Henry. *The Conquest of Poverty*. New York: Foundation for Economic Education, Inc., 1973.

———. *The Failure of the New Economics: An Analysis of the Keynesian Fallacies*. New York: Foundation for Economic Education, Inc., 1959.

Hobbs, Brad and Nikolai Wenzel. "Poverty and Cronyism." Working Paper, 2016a.

———. "Cronyism and Financial Regulation." Working Paper, 2016b.

Horwitz, Steven. "Inequality, Mobility and Being Poor in America." *Social Philosophy and Policy* 31, no. 2 (2015): 70–91.

Lomasky, Loren. "Libertarianism at Twin Harvard." *Social Philosophy and Policy* 22, no. 1 (2005): 178–199.

McGrath, Lee. "A Primer on Occupational Licensing: With Professor Morris Kleiner." *Liberty & Law* (Institute for Justice), 2008. At http://ij.org/with-professor-morris -kleiner-2.

Mitchell, Daniel. "The Impact of Government Spending on Economic Growth." Backgrounder no. 1831, Washington, DC: The Heritage Foundation, 2005.

Mises, Ludwig von. *Economic Policy: Thoughts for Today and for Tomorrow*. Auburn, AL: Ludwig von Mises Institute, [1955] 2007.

———. *Liberalism: The Classical Tradition*. New York: Foundation for Economic Education, Inc., [1929] 1985.

———. *Planned Chaos*. Auburn, AL: Ludwig von Mises Institute, [1947] 2014.

Mulligan, Casey. "Review of *Capital in the Twenty-First Century*." *The Independent Review* 20, no. 1 (2015): 133–39.

Posner, Richard. *Economic Analysis of Law*. 3rd ed. New York: Aspen Publishers, 1986.

Rawls, John. *A Theory of Justice*. Cambridge, MA: Belknap Press, [1971] 1999.

Read, Leonard. "I, Pencil." NewYork: Foundation for Economic Education, Inc., 1958.

Rosenberg, Nathan. "Capital Formation in Underdeveloped Countries." *American Economic Review* 50, no. 4 (1960a): 706–15.

———. "Some Institutional Aspects of the Wealth of Nations." *Journal of Political Economy* 68, no. 6 (1960b): 557–570.

Schoenfeld, Matthew. "The Mythical Link between Income Inequality and Slow Growth." *Wall Street Journal*, October 12, 2015, http://www.wsj.com/articles /the-mythical-link-between-income-inequality-and-slow-growth-1434319942

Schumpeter, Joseph. *Capitalism, Socialism and Democracy*. New York: Harper Perennial Modern Classics, 1942.

Sowell, Thomas. *Wealth, Poverty and Politics: An International Perspective*. New York: Basic Books, 2015.

Stiglitz, Joseph. *The Price of Inequality: How Today's Society Endangers our Future*. New York: W. W. Norton, 2012.

Tanner, Michael and Charles Hughes. "The Work v. Welfare Tradeoff: 2013—An Analysis of the Total Welfare Benefits by State." Cato Institute, 2013.

Tocqueville, Alexis de. *Mémoire sur le Paupérisme*. CreateSpace Independent Publishing, [1835] 2015.

Tomasi, John. *Free-Market Fairness*. Princeton, NJ: Princeton University Press, 2012.

Wenzel, Nikolai. "Beyond Twin Harvard: A Rawlsian Must Be a Libertarian." Working Paper, 2016.

Chapter 14, O'Neill

Abouchar, Alan, ed. *The Soviet Price Mechanism*. Durham, NC: Duke University Press, 1977.

Baker, Edwin. "Utility and Rights: Two Justifications for State Action Increasing Equality." *Yale Law Journal* 84, no. 1 (1974): 39–59.

Bergson, Abram. "Income Inequality under Soviet Socialism." *Journal of Economic Literature* 22, no. 3 (1984): 1052–1099.

———. *The Structure of Soviet Wages*. Cambridge, MA: Harvard University Press, 1944.

Chapman, Janet G. "Are Earnings More Equal under Socialism?" In John R. Moroney, ed., *Income Inequality: Trends and International Comparisons*. Lanham, MD: Lexington Books, 1979.

Feldbrugge, Ferdinand J.M., Gerard P. Van Den Berg and William B. Simons, eds. *Encyclopedia of Soviet Law (Second Revised Edition)*. Dordrecht, Netherlands: Martinus Nijhoff Publishers, 1985.

Fogel, Robert. *The Fourth Great Awakening and the Future of Egalitarianism*. Chicago: University of Chicago Press, 2000.

Gastwirth, Joseph L. "The Estimation of the Lorenz Curve and Gini Index." *Review of Economics and Statistics* 54, no. 3 (1972): 306–316.

Geisen, Kristian, Arndt Zimmerman and Jens Suedekum. "The Size Distribution across All Cities—Double Pareto Lognormal Strikes." *Journal of Urban Economics* 68, no. 2 (2010): 129–137.

Hare, Richard M. "Ethical Theory and Utilitarianism." In Amarta Sen and Bernard Williams, eds., *Utilitarianism and Beyond*. Cambridge: Cambridge University Press, 1982.

Jehle, Geoffrey A. and Phillip J. Reny. *Advanced Microeconomic Theory (Second Edition)*. Boston: Addison-Wesley, 2001.

Kault, David A. "The Shape of the Distribution of the Number of Sexual Partners." *Statistics in Medicine* 15, no. 2 (1996): 221–230.

Kekes, John. *The Illusions of Egalitarianism*. Ithaca, NY: Cornell University Press, 2007.

Le Grand, Julian. "Equity versus Efficiency: The Elusive Trade-off." *Ethics* 100, no. 3 (1990): 554–568.

Limpert, Eckhard, Werner A. Stahel, and Markus Abbt. "Log-normal Distributions across the Sciences: Keys and Clues." *Bioscience* 51, no. 5 (2001): 341–352.

Marx, Karl. "Critique of the Gotha Program." In David McLellan, ed., *Karl Marx: Selected Writings*. Oxford: Oxford University Press, [1875] 1977.

Millar, James R, ed. *Politics, Work, and Daily Life in the USSR: A Survey of Former Soviet Citizens*. Cambridge: Cambridge University Press, 1987.

Nagel, Thomas. *Equality and Partiality*. Oxford: Oxford University Press, 1991.

Narveson, Jan. "Egalitarianism: Partial, Counterproductive and Baseless." *Ratio* 10, no. 3 (1997): 280–295.

Nozick, Robert. *Anarchy, State and Utopia*. New York: Basic Books, 1974.

O'Neill, Ben. 2015. "All Rich and Equal: The Long-run Effect of Expansion in Wealth." *Prices and Markets* 3, no. 3 (2015): 10–17.

Pryor, Frederic L. *Property and Industrial Organization in Communist and Capitalist Nations*. Bloomington: Indiana University Press, 1973.

Rand, Ayn. *The New Left: The Anti-Industrial Revolution*. New York: Signet, 1995.

Rawls, John. *A Theory of Justice*. Cambridge, MA: Harvard University Press, 1971.

Rothbard, Murray N. *Egalitarianism as a Revolt against Nature; and other Essays (Second Edition)*. Auburn, AL: Ludwig von Mises Institute, 2000.

Schmidtz, David. "Diminishing Marginal Utility and Egalitarian Redistribution." *Journal of Value Inquiry* 34, no. 2 (2000): 263–272.

Schoeck, Helmut. *Envy: A Theory of Social Behaviour*. Indianapolis, IN: Liberty Fund, 1987.

Stanton, Elizabeth. *Accounting for Inequality: A Proposed Revision of the Human Development Index*. Working Paper 119, Political Economy Research Institute, University of Massachusetts, 2006.

Trotsky, Leon. *The Revolution Betrayed*. New York: Pathfinder Press, 1937.

Walzer, Michael. *Spheres of Justice: A Defense of Pluralism and Equality*. New York: Basic Books, 1983.

Warshawsky, Mark J. "Earnings Inequality: The Implications of Rapidly Rising Cost of Employer-provided Health Insurance." *Mercatus Working Paper*, (June 2016). Mercatus Centre: George Mason University.

Wiles, Peter J. D. *The Distribution of Income East and West*. New York: Amsterdam, 1974.

Chapter 15, Gaines

"Americans Views on Taxes." An NPR, Kaiser Family Foundation, and Kennedy School of Government poll, April 2003. At http://www.npr.org/news/specials /polls/taxes2003/index.html.

Arneson, Richard. "Egalitarianism." In *The Stanford Encyclopedia of Philosophy, edited by* Edward N. Zalta. Stanford, CA: Stanford University Press, 2013. At https://plato.stanford.edu/archives/sum2013/entries/egalitarianism/.

Barnes, Fred. "A Setback, Not a Catastrophe." *Weekly Standard,* November 19, 2012.

Buffett, Warren E. "Stop Coddling the Super-Rich." *New York Times,* August 14, 2011.

Frolich, Norman, and Joe A. Oppenheimer. *Choosing Justice: An Experimental Approach to Ethical Theory.* Berkeley: University of California Press, 1992.

Gaines, Brian J. "Fair Taxes: A Public Opinion Approach." Manuscript in preparation (n.d.).

Hall, Robert E., and Alvin Rabushka. *The Flat Tax.* 2nd ed. Stanford, CA: Hoover Institution, 2007.

Hayek, F. A. *The Constitution of Liberty.* Chicago: University of Chicago Press, 1960.

———. *Hayek on Hayek: An Autobiographical Dialogue.* Edited by Stephen Kresge and Leif Wenar. Chicago: University of Chicago Press, 1994.

———. *The Road to Serfdom.* Chicago: University of Chicago Press, 1944.

Kluegel, James R., and Eliot R. Smith. *Beliefs about Inequality: Americans' Views of What Is and What Ought to Be.* New York: De Gruyter, 1986.

Kohut, Andrew. "Are Americans Ready for Obama's 'Middle Class' Populism?" Pew Research Center poll, February 19, 2015. At http://www.pewresearch.org/fact-tank/2015/02/19/are-americans-ready-for-obamas-middle-class-populism/.

Newport, Frank. "Americans Continue to Say U.S. Wealth Distribution Is Unfair." Gallup poll, 2015. At http://www.gallup.com/poll/182987/americans-continue-say-wealth-distribution-unfair.aspx.

Page, Benjamin I., and Lawrence R. Jacobs. *Class War? What Americans Really Think about Economic Inequality.* Chicago: University of Chicago Press, 2009.

Rawls, John. *A Theory of Justice.* Cambridge, MA: Harvard University Press, 1971.

Reagan, Ronald. Inaugural Address. January 20, 1981. At http://www.presidency.ucsb.edu/ws/?pid=43130.

Rivers, Douglas. *Sample Matching: Representative Sampling from Internet Panels.* Polimetrix White Paper, 2006. At http://www.websm.org/uploadi/editor/1368187057 Rivers_2006_Sample_matching_Representative_sampling_from_Internet_panels.pdf.

Scheiber, Noam, and Dalia Sussman. "Inequality Troubles Americans across Party Lines, Times/CBS Poll Finds." *New York Times,* June 3, 2015. At http://www.nytimes.com/2015/06/04/business/inequality-a-major-issue-for-americans-times-cb-poll-finds.html?_r=0.

"Tax System Seen as Unfair, in Need of Overhaul." Pew Research Center poll, December 20, 2011. At http://www.people-press.org/2011/12/20/tax-system-seen-as-unfair-in-need-of-overhaul/.

White House. Remarks by the President at the Associated Press Luncheon. April 3, 2012a. At http://www.whitehouse.gov/the-press-office/2012/04/03/remarks-president-associated-press-luncheon.

———. Remarks by the President at a Campaign Event—Hollywood, FL. April 10, 2012b. At http://www.whitehouse.gov/the-press-office/2012/04/10/remarks-president-campaign-event-hollywood-fl.

Chapter 16, Stringham

Aaberge, Rolf, and Magne Mogstad. "Inequality in Current and Lifetime Income." *Social Choice and Welfare* 44, no. 2 (2015): 217–30.

Barrientos, Miguel, and Claudia Soria. "Income Distribution." IndexMundi, data portal, 2016.

Cox, Michael, and Richard Alm. 2016. *Onward and Upward!* Dallas: Southern Methodist University O'Neil Center, 2016. At http://www.smu.edu/-/media/Site/Cox/CentersAndInstitutes/ONeilCenter/Research/AnnualReports/2016_annual_report_full.ashx?la=en.

Dolan, Kerry. "Inside the 2016 Forbes 400." *Forbes,* October 4, 2016.

Eyermann, Craig. "Visualizing Distribution of Income." *Political Calculations,* January 18, 2013.

Friedman, Ina. *The Other Victims: First Person Stories of Non-Jews Persecuted by the Nazis.* Boston: Houghton Mifflin, 1990.

Hayek, F. A. *The Constitution of Liberty.* Oxford: Routledge, [1960] 2011.

Kertscher, Tom. "Michael Moore Says 400 Americans Have More Wealth Than Half of All Americans Combined." *PolitiFact,* March 10, 2011.

Leonard, Thomas. *Illiberal Reformers: Race, Eugenics, and American Economics in the Progressive Era.* Princeton, NJ: Princeton University, 2016.

Lewis, C. S. *Transposition and Other Addresses.* Quebec: Samizdat University, 1949.

Mises, Ludwig von. *Socialism: An Economic and Sociological Analysis.* Indianapolis, IN: Liberty Classics, [1922] 1981.

Piketty, Thomas. "Putting Distribution Back at the Center of Economics." *Journal of Economic Perspectives* 29, no. 1 (2015): 67–88.

Rawls, John. *A Theory of Justice.* Cambridge, MA: Harvard University Press, 1971.

Saez, Emmanuel, and Gabriel Zucman. *Wealth Inequality in the United States since 1913.* National Bureau of Economic Research (NBER) Working Paper no. 20625. Cambridge, MA: NBER, 2014.

Scheiber, Noam, and Dalia Sussman. "Inequality Troubles Americans across Party Lines, Times/CBS Poll Finds." *New York Times,* June 3, 2015.

"Two Decades of Wealth." *Forbes,* September 13, 2002.

"United to End Genocide." *The Cambodian Genocide.* Washington, DC: United to End Genocide, 2016.

US Bureau of the Census. *Current Population Survey.* Washington, DC: US Department of Commerce, 2016.

US Federal Reserve. *Survey of Consumer Finances.* Washington, DC: US Government Publishing Office, 2013.

———. *Exploring the Racial Wealth Gap Using the Survey of Consumer Finances.* Finance and Economics Discussion Series 2015-076. Washington, DC: US Government Publishing Office, 2015.

World Bank. *DataBank.* Washington, DC: World Bank, 2016.

Zillow. *Zestimate.* Seattle: Zillow Group, 2016.

Zweynert, Astrid. "World's Growing Inequality Is 'Ticking Time Bomb'": Nobel Laureate Yunus. *Reuters,* November 30, 2016.

Chapter 17, Geloso and Horwitz

Almås, Ingvild, and Magne Mogstad. "Older or Wealthier? The Impact of Age Adjustments on the Wealth Inequality Rankings of Countries." Unpublished manuscript, 2016.

Anderson, Kym, John Cockburn, and Will Martin. "Would Freeing Up World Trade Reduce Poverty and Inequality? The Vexed Role of Agricultural Distortions." *World Economy* 34, no. 2 (2011): 487–515.

Aten, Bettina H., and Roger J. D'Souza. *Regional Price Parities: Comparing Level Differences across Geographic Areas.* Washington, DC: US Bureau of Economic Analysis, 2008.

Aten, Bettina H., Eric B. Figueroa, and Troy M. Martin. *Real Personal Income and Regional Price Parities for States and Metropolitan Areas, 2007–2011.* Washington, DC: US Bureau of Economic Analysis, 2013.

Attanasio, Orazio P., and Luigi Pistaferri. "Consumption Inequality." *Journal of Economic Perspectives* 30, no. 2 (2016): 1–27.

Boskin, Michael J. "Causes and Consequences of Bias in the Consumer Price Index as a Measure of the Cost of Living." *Atlantic Economic Journal* 33, no. 1 (2005): 1–13.

Bricker, Jesse, Alice Henriques, Jake Krimmel, and John Sabelhaus. *Measuring Income and Wealth at the Top Using Administrative and Survey Data.* Working Paper no. 2015-30. Boston: Federal Reserve Board of Boston, 2015.

Broda, Christian, Ephraim Leibtag, and David E. Weinstein. "The Role of Prices in Measuring the Poor's Living Standards." *Journal of Economic Perspectives* 23, no. 2 (2009): 77–97.

Broda, Christian, and David E. Weinstein. *Prices, Poverty, and Inequality: Why Americans Are Better Off Than You Think.* Washington, DC: American Enterprise Institute Press, 2008a.

———. *Understanding International Price Differences Using Barcode Data.* National Bureau of Economic Research (NBER) Working Paper no. w14017. Cambridge, MA: NBER, 2008b.

Brzozowski, Matthew, Martin Gervais, Paul Klein, and Michio Suzuki. "Consumption, Income, and Wealth Inequality in Canada." *Review of Economic Dynamics* 13, no. 1 (2010): 52–75.

Burkhauser, Richard V., Jeff Larrimore, and Kosali I. Simon. "A Second Opinion on the Economic Health of the American Middle Class." *National Tax Journal* 65, no. 1 (2012): 7–32.

Burkhauser, Richard V., and Kosali I. Simon. *Measuring the Impact of Health Insurance on Levels and Trends in Inequality.* National Bureau of Economic Research (NBER) Working Paper no. w15811. Cambridge, MA: NBER, 2010.

Burtless, Gary, and Pavel Svaton. "Health Care, Health Insurance, and the Distribution of American Incomes." *Forum for Health Economics and Policy* 13, no. 1 (2010): 1–41.

Card, David. *Immigration and Inequality.* National Bureau of Economic Research (NBER) Working Paper no. w14683. Cambridge, MA: NBER, 2009.

Cardwell, Ryan, Chad Lawley, and Di Xiang. "Milked and Feathered: The Regressive Welfare Effects of Canada's Supply Management Regime." *Canadian Public Policy* 41, no. 1 (2015): 1–14.

Carpenter, Dick M., Lisa Knepper, Angela Erickson, and John Ross. "Regulating Work: Measuring the Scope and Burden of Occupational Licensure among Low- and Moderate-Income Occupations in the United States." *Economic Affairs* 35, no. 1 (2015): 3–20.

Chambers, Dustin, and Courtney A. Collins. *How Do Federal Regulations Affect Consumer Prices? An Analysis of the Regressive Effects of Regulation.* Mercatus Working paper. Arlington, VA: Mercatus Center, George Mason University, February 2016.

Dumais, Mario. *The Negative Consequences of Agricultural Marketing Boards.* Montreal: Montreal Economic Institute, 2012.

Eberstadt, Nicholas. *The Poverty of the Poverty Rate: Measure and Mismeasure of Want in Modern America.* Washington, DC: American Enterprise Institute Press, 2008.

Feldstein, Martin. "Did Wages Reflect Growth in Productivity?" *Journal of Policy Modeling* 30, no. 4 (2008): 591–94.

Galbraith, James K. *Inequality and Instability: A Study of the World Economy Just before the Great Crisis.* Oxford: Oxford University Press, 2012.

Ganong, Peter, and Daniel Shoag. *Why Has Regional Income Convergence Declined?* Working Paper no. 21. Washington, DC: Hutchings Center, 2015.

Geloso, Vincent, and Alexandre Moreau. *Supply Management Makes the Poor Even Poorer.* Montreal: Montreal Economic Institute, 2016.

Hilber, Christian, and Wouter Vermeulen. "The Impact of Supply Constraints on House Prices in England." *Economic Journal* 126, no. 591 (2016): 358–405.

Horwitz, Steven. "Inequality, Mobility, and Being Poor in America." *Social Philosophy and Policy* 31, no. 2 (2015): 70–91.

Jenkins, Stephen, and Philippe van Kerm. "The Measurement of Economic Inequality." In *The Oxford Handbook of Economic Inequality,* edited by Wiemer Salverda, Brian Nolan, and Timothy Smeeding, 40–67. Oxford: Oxford University Press, 2009.

Kahneman, Daniel, and Angus Deaton. "High Income Improves Evaluation of Life but Not Emotional Well-Being." *Proceedings of the National Academy of Sciences* 107, no. 38 (2010): 16489–93.

Lemieux, Thomas. "Increasing Residual Wage Inequality: Composition Effects, Noisy Data, or Rising Demand for Skill?" *American Economic Review* 96, no. 3 (2006): 461–98.

Lemieux, Thomas, W. Bentley MacLeod, and Daniel Parent. "Performance Pay and Wage Inequality." *Quarterly Journal of Economics* 124, no. 1. (2009): 1–49.

Lott, John R., Jr. "The Effect of Conviction on the Legitimate Income of Criminals." *Economics Letters* 34, no. 4 (1990): 381–85.

Lyons, Christopher J., and Becky Pettit. "Compounded Disadvantage: Race, Incarceration, and Wage Growth." *Social Problems* 58, no. 2 (2011): 257–80.

Meyer, Bruce, and James X. Sullivan. *Consumption and Income of the Poor Elderly since 1960.* National Bureau of Economic Research (NBER) Working Paper no. NB10-08. Cambridge, MA: NBER, 2010.

———. "Consumption and Income Inequality and the Great Recession." *American Economic Review* 103, no. 3 (2013a): 178–83.

———. *The Material Well-Being of the Poor and the Middle Class since 1980.* American Enterprise Institute Working Paper no. 44. Washington, DC: American Enterprise Institute, 2011.

———. *Winning the War: Poverty from the Great Society to the Great Recession.* National Bureau of Economic Research (NBER) Working Paper no. w18718. Cambridge, MA: NBER, 2013b.

Moore, Eric G., and Michael A. Pacey. "Changing Income Inequality and Immigration in Canada, 1980–1995." *Canadian Public Policy/Analyse de Politiques* 29, no. 1 (2003): 33–51.

Niemietz, Kristian P. *Redefining the Poverty Debate—Why a War on Markets Is No Substitute for a War on Poverty.* London: Institute for Economic Affairs, 2012.

Nordhaus, William D. *Schumpeterian Profits in the American Economy: Theory and Measurement.* National Bureau of Economic Research (NBER) Working Paper no. w10433. Cambridge, MA: NBER, 2004.

Organization for Economic Cooperation and Development (OECD). *An Overview of Growing Income Inequalities in OECD Countries: Main Findings.* Paris: OECD, 2011.

Ostry, Jonathan, Andrew Berg, and Charalambos Tsangarides. *Redistribution, Inequality, and Growth.* Working Paper no. SDN/14/02. Washington, DC: International Monetary Fund, 2014.

Pendakur, Krishna. "Changes in Canadian Family Income and Family Consumption Inequality between 1978 and 1992." *Review of Income and Wealth* 44, no. 2 (1998): 259–82.

Peri, Giovanni. "The Effect of Immigration on Productivity: Evidence from U.S. States." *Review of Economics and Statistics* 94, no. 1 (2012): 348–58.

Pettit, Becky. *Invisible Men: Mass Incarceration and the Myth of Black Progress.* New York: Russell Sage Foundation, 2012.

Piketty, Thomas. *Capital in the Twenty-First Century.* Cambridge, MA: Harvard University Press, 2014.

Piketty, Thomas, and Emmanuel Saez. "Income Inequality in the United States, 1913–1998." *Quarterly Journal of Economics* 118, no. 1 (2003): 1–39.

Rawls, John. *A Theory of Justice.* Cambridge, MA: Harvard University Press, 1971.

Sala-i-Martin, Xavier. "The World Distribution of Income: Falling Poverty and . . . Convergence, Period." *Quarterly Journal of Economics* 121, no. 2 (2006): 351–97.

Sarlo, Christopher. *The Economic Well-Being of Canadians: Is There a Growing Gap?* Vancouver: Fraser Institute, 2009.

Stevenson, Betsey, and Justin Wolfers. *Happiness Inequality in the United States.* National Bureau of Economic Research (NBER) Working Paper no. w14220. Cambridge, MA: NBER, 2008.

———. *Subjective and Objective Indicators of Racial Progress.* National Bureau of Economic Research (NBER) Working Paper no. w18916. Cambridge, MA: NBER, 2013.

Tomasi, John. *Free Market Fairness.* Princeton, NJ: Princeton University Press, 2012.

Welch, Finis. "In Defense of Inequality." *American Economic Review* 89, no. 2 (1999): 1–17.

Western, Bruce, and Becky Pettit. "Black–White Wage Inequality, Employment Rates, and Incarceration." *American Journal of Sociology* 111, no. 2 (2005): 553–78.

Wilkinson, Richard G., and Kate Pickett. *The Spirit Level: Why Greater Equality Makes Societies Stronger*. London: Bloomsbury, 2009.

Winship, Scott. "Overstating the Costs of Inequality." *National Affairs* 15 (Spring 2013): 33–49.

Conclusion, Munger

de Jasay, Anthony. *The Indian Rope Trick*. Indianapolis, IN: Liberty Fund, 2014.

Higgs, Robert. *Crisis and Leviathan: Critical Episodes in the Growth of American Government, 25th Anniversary Edition*. Oakland, CA: Independent Institute, [1987] 2012.

Horwitz, Steven. "Inequality, Mobility and Being Poor in America," *Social Philosophy and Policy* 31, no. 2 (2015): 70–91.

Hume, David. *A Treatise of Human Nature by David Hume, reprinted from the Original Edition in three volumes and edited, with an analytical index*, by L.A. Selby-Bigge, M.A. Oxford: Clarendon Press, [1739] 1896. Accessed 4/18/2018. http://oll.libertyfund.org/titles/342.

Marina, William. "Egalitarianism and Empire." Oakland, CA: Independent Institute. Reprinted from *Studies in History and Philosophy*, no. 5 (1975). At http://www.independent.org/publications/article.asp?id=1410.

Mill, John Stuart. *Principles of Political Economy with some of their Applications to Social Philosophy*, Indianapolis, IN: Liberty Fund, [1848] 1990. http://www.econlib.org/library/Mill/mlP.html

Schmidtz, David. *The Elements of Justice*. New York: Cambridge University Press, 2006.

Sen, Amartya K. "Equality of What?" McMurrin S Tanner Lectures on Human Values, Delivered at Stanford University May 22, 1979. Volume 1. Cambridge: Cambridge University Press, 1980.

Shlaes, Amity. *The Forgotten Man: A New History of the Great Depression*. New York: Harper Collins Publishers, 2007.

Sumner, William G. *The Forgotten Man and Other Essays*. Edited by Albert Galloway Keller. New Haven, CT: Yale University Press, [1876] 1918. At http://oll.libertyfund.org/titles/2396.

Index

About the Editors and Contributors

About the Editors

Christopher J. Coyne is the F.A. Harper Professor of Economics at George Mason University, research fellow for the Independent Institute, coeditor and managing editor of *The Independent Review: A Journal of Political Economy*, North American Editor for the *Review of Austrian Economics,* and book review editor at *Public Choice.*

Michael C. Munger is director of the Philosophy, Politics, and Economics Program and professor in the Departments of Political Science and Economics at Duke University and coeditor and managing editor of *The Independent Review: A Journal of Political Economy.*

Robert Whaples is professor of economics at Wake Forest University, research fellow for the Independent Institute, and coeditor and managing editor of *The Independent Review: A Journal of Political Economy.*

About the Contributors

Anne R. Bradley is Academic Director at The Fund for American Studies.

Art Carden is an associate professor of economics at Samford University and a research fellow with the Independent Institute.

Richard A. Epstein is the Laurence A. Tisch Professor of Law at New York University School of Law, Peter and Kirsten Bedford Senior Fellow in the Hoover Institution at Stanford University, and the James Parker Hall Distinguished Service Professor Emeritus of Law at the University of Chicago Law School.

Sarah Estelle is associate professor of economics and Ruch Faculty Fellow at Hope College.

Brian J. Gaines is professor of political science in the Department of Political Science and the Institute of Government and Public Affairs at the University of Illinois.

Vincent Geloso is a postdoctoral fellow at the Free Market Institute at Texas Tech University and obtained his Ph.D. in economic history from the London School of Economics.

James R. Harrigan is senior fellow of the Institute of Political Economy at Utah State University and senior research fellow at Strata Policy in Logan, Utah.

Peter J. Hill is professor emeritus of economics at Wheaton College and senior fellow at the Property and Environment Research Center.

Steven Horwitz is the Schnatter Distinguished Professor of Free Enterprise at Ball State University.

Jeremy Jackson is director of the North Dakota Center for the Study of Public Choice and Private Enterprise and associate professor in the Department of Agribusiness and Applied Economics at North Dakota State University.

Adam Martin is assistant professor of agricultural and applied economics at Texas Tech University and political economy research fellow at the Free Market Institute.

Jason Morgan is a 2016 Ludwig von Mises Institute Fellow.

Ben O'Neill, Ph.D., is lecturer in Statistics at the University of New South Wales at ADFA in Canberra, Australia. He won first prize in the junior faculty division of the 2009 Sir John M. Templeton Fellowships Essay Contest.

James R. Otteson is Thomas W. Smith Presidential Chair in Business Ethics and professor of economics at Wake Forest University.

Jeffrey Palm is an undergraduate fellow at the North Dakota Center for the Study of Public Choice and Private Enterprise.

Stephen Shmanske is Professor Emeritus of Economics in the College of Business and Economics at California State University, East Bay.

Aeon J. Skoble is Senior Fellow at the Fraser Institute, a professor of philosophy, and chairman of the Philosophy Department at Bridgewater State University in Massachusetts.

Edward P. Stringham is the Davis Professor of Economic Innovation at Trinity College, Hartford, President and Director of Research and Education at the American Institute for Economic Research, and author of *Private Governance: Creating Order in Economic and Social Life* (2015).

William J. Watkins Jr. is a research fellow at the Independent Institute and author of the book *Crossroads for Liberty: Recovering the Anti-Federalist Values of America's First Constitution.*

Nikolai G. Wenzel is the L.V. Hackley Chair for the Study of Capitalism and Free Enterprise, and Distinguished Professor of Economics at Fayetteville State University (Fayetteville, NC).

Robert E. Wright is the Nef Family Chair of Political Economy at Augustana University in Sioux Falls, South Dakota, and the author or coauthor of eighteen books, including *The Poverty of Slavery: How Unfree Labor Pollutes the Economy* (2016).

Ryan M. Yonk is assistant research professor in the Department of Economics and Finance at Utah State University, one of the founders of Strata Policy, and a research fellow with the Independent Institute.

Credits

Independent Institute Studies in Political Economy

THE ACADEMY IN CRISIS | *edited by John W. Sommer*

AGAINST LEVIATHAN | *by Robert Higgs*

AMERICAN HEALTH CARE |
edited by Roger D. Feldman

AMERICAN SURVEILLANCE | *by Anthony Gregory*

ANARCHY AND THE LAW |
edited by Edward P. Stringham

ANTITRUST AND MONOPOLY | *by D. T. Armentano*

AQUANOMICS |
edited by B. Delworth Gardner & Randy T Simmons

ARMS, POLITICS, AND THE ECONOMY |
edited by Robert Higgs

A BETTER CHOICE | *by John C. Goodman*

BEYOND POLITICS | *by Randy T Simmons*

BOOM AND BUST BANKING |
edited by David Beckworth

CALIFORNIA DREAMING | *by Lawrence J. McQuillan*

CAN TEACHERS OWN THEIR OWN SCHOOLS? |
by Richard K. Vedder

THE CHALLENGE OF LIBERTY |
edited by Robert Higgs & Carl P. Close

THE CHE GUEVARA MYTH AND THE FUTURE
OF LIBERTY | *by Alvaro Vargas Llosa*

CHINA'S GREAT MIGRATION | *by Bradley M. Gardner*

CHOICE | *by Robert P. Murphy*

THE CIVILIAN AND THE MILITARY |
by Arthur A. Ekirch Jr.

CRISIS AND LEVIATHAN, 25TH ANNIVERSARY
EDITION | *by Robert Higgs*

CROSSROADS FOR LIBERTY |
by William J. Watkins, Jr.

CUTTING GREEN TAPE |
edited by Richard L. Stroup & Roger E. Meiners

THE DECLINE OF AMERICAN LIBERALISM |
by Arthur A. Ekirch Jr.

DELUSIONS OF POWER | *by Robert Higgs*

DEPRESSION, WAR, AND COLD WAR |
by Robert Higgs

THE DIVERSITY MYTH |
by David O. Sacks & Peter A. Thiel

DRUG WAR CRIMES | *by Jeffrey A. Miron*

ELECTRIC CHOICES | *edited by Andrew N. Kleit*

ELEVEN PRESIDENTS | *by Ivan Eland*

THE EMPIRE HAS NO CLOTHES | *by Ivan Eland*

THE ENTERPRISE OF LAW | *by Bruce L. Benson*

ENTREPRENEURIAL ECONOMICS |
edited by Alexander Tabarrok

FAILURE | *by Vicki E. Alger*

FINANCING FAILURE | *by Vern McKinley*

THE FOUNDERS' SECOND AMENDMENT |
by Stephen P. Halbrook

FUTURE | *edited by Robert M. Whaples, Christopher J.
Coyne, & Michael C. Munger*

GLOBAL CROSSINGS | *by Alvaro Vargas Llosa*

GOOD MONEY | *by George Selgin*

GUN CONTROL IN NAZI-OCCUPIED FRANCE |
by Stephen P. Halbrook

GUN CONTROL IN THE THIRD REICH |
by Stephen P. Halbrook

HAZARDOUS TO OUR HEALTH? |
edited by Robert Higgs

HOT TALK, COLD SCIENCE | *by S. Fred Singer*

HOUSING AMERICA |
edited by Randall G. Holcombe & Benjamin Powell

JUDGE AND JURY |
by Eric Helland & Alexander Tabarrok

LESSONS FROM THE POOR |
edited by Alvaro Vargas Llosa

LIBERTY FOR LATIN AMERICA | *by Alvaro Vargas Llosa*

LIBERTY FOR WOMEN | *edited by Wendy McElroy*

LIBERTY IN PERIL | *by Randall G. Holcombe*

LIVING ECONOMICS | *by Peter J. Boettke*

MAKING POOR NATIONS RICH |
edited by Benjamin Powell

MARKET FAILURE OR SUCCESS |
edited by Tyler Cowen & Eric Crampton

THE MIDAS PARADOX | *by Scott Sumner*

MONEY AND THE NATION STATE |
edited by Kevin Dowd & Richard H. Timberlake Jr.

Independent Institute Studies in Political Economy

INDEPENDENT
I N S T I T U T E

100 SWAN WAY, OAKLAND, CA 94621-1428

For further information:

510-632-1366 • orders@independent.org • http://www.independent.org/publications/books/